ENGLISH LANGUAGE TEACHING:

A SKILL-BASED APPORACH

ENGLISH LANGUAGE TEACHING:

A SKILL-BASED APPORACH

DR. PAYAL MITTAL

GenNext Publication

Published by

GenNext Publication
5, Ansari Road
Daryaganj, New Delhi-110002
Phone: 011-47034999, 9811692060
E-mail: gennextpublication@hotmail.com

Distribution Network
gyanbooks.com
India, USA, Canada, UK, Australia, France

ISBN: 978-93-5663-723-8 (PB)
First Published, 2025

Printed at: Gyan Press, Delhi.

ENGLISH LANGUAGE TEACHING:
A SKILL-BASED APPORACH

Author: DR. PAYAL MITTAL

ACKNOWLEDGEMENT

First and foremost, I'd express my gratitude to the Almighty God as without His mercy and support, this endeavour could not have been possible. He inspired me at every step with the right guidance and made the arrangements to meet the right persons who have provided their knowledge and expertise.

Then I am grateful to my supervisor, Dr Parvesh Lata for her mentorship. She had been there with me with all her never-ending guidance and support, especially in getting connected with the right teachers and research expertise. She also suggested me the best workshops and seminars that helped me to get the deep insight of research. She reviewed my progress constantly and gave outstanding feedback, many times late night, like a mentor and a friend.

I would like to highlight two truly exceptional people, my father, Mr Parmil Mittal and Dr Sansanwal for their unlimited support and unconditional guidance. Many times they helped when I was at the verge of quitting this project in between. Dr Sansanwal taught me many concepts of research in depth. His vast wisdom and wealth of experience have inspired me throughout my study.

A special Thanks to Mrs. Vijaya John Kohli, for her invaluable assistance and insightful discussion, without whom, this endeavour would not have been possible.

In addition, I would like to mention the few names of my Ph.D mates, Mrs Shayada, Mrs Monika Suri, my Ph.D coordinator, Dr. Rekha Kausal, and others as my brother, Pragun Mittal, Graphic Designer, Mr. Ramavtar Verma, Dr. John Vijaya Kohli, and many more, who helped me with their ideas and knowledge. The Principal of School of Open Learning, University of Delhi, Dr. Uma Shankar Pandey encouraged and appreciated this project. He welcomed me with open opportunities and facilities to conduct the experiment in the college premises.

The completion of this PhD would not have been possible without the immense love and emotional support of my mother, Mrs. Sneh Lata

Mittal. She would be the happiest person when I completed my Ph.D study. Last but not least, I appreciate the matchless believe of my husband, Mr Aman Walia, in me throughout the entire thesis process and every day. Furthermore, I value the love and encouragement of my family members.

– PAYAL MITTAL

TABLE OF CONTENTS

IV : DATA ANALYSIS

V: FINDINGS, EDUCATIONAL IMPLICATIONS, AND SUGGESTIONS FOR FURTHER STUDY

LIST OF TABLES

LIST OF FIGURES

LIST OF GRAPHS

LIST OF ABBREVIATIONS

CAPTIONS	DESCRIPTIONS
ACCESS	Automatization in Communicative Contexts of Essential Speech Segments
AICTE	All India Council for Technical Education
AISHE	All India Survey on Higher Education
B.COM (PROG.)	Bachelor of Commerce (Program)
BA (PROG.)	Bachelor of Arts (Program)
BPO	Business Process Outsourcing
CAI	Computer-Assisted Instruction
CALL	Computer-Assisted Language Learning
CBI	Content Based Instruction
CLT	Communicative Language Teaching
DE	Distance Education
DEC	Distance Education Council
DEIS	Distance Education Institutes
DHRD	Directorate of Human Resource Development
DU	University of Delhi
EFL	English as Foreign Language
EIL	English as International Language
ELT	English Language Teaching
ESL	English as Second Language
FFI	Form-Focused Instruction
HTML	Hyper-Text Markup Language
ICT	Information and Communication Technology
IGNOU	Indira Gandhi National Open University
L1	First Language
L2	Second Language
LMS	Learning Management System
LSRW	Listening, Speaking, Reading, Writing
MALL	Mobile-Assisted Language Learning
MHRD	Ministry of Human Resource Development

NCERT	National Council of Education & Research Training
NGO	Non-Governmental Organization
NOU	Nalanda Open University
ODL	Open and Distance Learning
PCP	Personal Contact Program
PPP	Presentation, Practice, Production
SCERT	State Council of Education & Research Training
SIM	Self-Instructional Material
SLA	Second Language Teaching
SLIM	Self-Learning Instructional Material
SLIML2	Self-Learning Instructional Material for Second Language
SLM	Self-Learning Material
SOL	School of Open Learning
TBI	Task Based Instruction
TBLT	Task-Based Language Teaching
TELL	Technology-Assisted Language Learning
UAC	University Academic Councils
UGC	University Grants Commission
VMOU	Vardhman Mahaveer Open University
WWW	World Wide Web
YCMOU	Yashwantrao Chavan Maharashtra Open University

CHAPTER - I

INTRODUCTION

1.1 BACKGROUND

English is an international language. It is called the link language as it provides the connectivity to major part of the world. Globalization and the World Wide Web make the whole world a condensed home, which in turn, increases the importance of learning English for young learner, especially in schools. With communicative skills in English, young learner can participate, identify themselves, and forge relationships in the world in their future. Nikmah & Azimah (2015) observe that English is the most common language used in international communication. No language is more broadly studied and applied as a Foreign Language than English. National Council of Educational Research and Training (2005) in the Position Paper of the National Focus Group on Teaching of English emphasizes the importance of learning English in schools as a means of providing full participation in national and international life. English language learning in school symbolizes people's desire to attain a quality education. The objective of teaching English language skills to children is to enable them to use this language effectively in their everyday tasks. This Position Paper also focuses on a curriculum that provides guidance and principles for teachers to organize or create an environment in which promotion of English language skills can be possible.

Any language's performance is dependent on the process by which it has been acquired. People have different language acquisition skills, which are the result of their different capacities for perceiving and comprehending a language and using words and sentences to communicate. This capacity depends on the linguistic richness of the environment or the exposure they get.

Good language acquisition improves a person's communication skills, which helps a person to maintain good relationships, whether personal or professional. Communication skills include good and attentive listening, reflecting, speaking, writing, and reading.

But in India, learning the English language remains focused on the teaching of a textbook and gets good scores in the examination. After learning the English language for 6 or 7 years, youngsters are still not able to use this language in their real life situations. Rahmatillah (2019) argues that even though students have been learning English since their elementary classes, but their proficiency in the language is very limited, which is why Universities have to teach English as a compulsory subject in colleges.

Vadivel (2018) asks why, even after twelve years of education (Grade 1 to Grade 12), college-level students struggle to communicate their thoughts in English. He claims that rather than teaching students to improvise their LSRW (Listening, Speaking, Reading, and Writing) abilities, the majority of schools teach English to pass the pre-planned exam. Teachers intentionally teach reading and writing skills since the questions are structured around them, leaving behind speaking and listening skills. And the result is that the majority of students struggle to form complete sentences and have weak reading and comprehension abilities.

Yarlagadda & Mantri (2016) also highlight that in India, communication in English is needed to reduce unemployability and enhance advancement in their current careers at both national and international levels. Individuals with good English communication skills have a better chance of employability, as recruiters consider effective speaking and writing skills in English important at the time of recruitment. Therefore, communication skills in English are one of the essential skills demanded by 21st century youth. So it is necessary, at the moment, especially in the Indian context, to make our English language classrooms a skill-based program where students can apply their knowledge of the language to their real life situations.

Also, Ananthi (2018) observes that although Universities have introduced English as a subject to develop students' communicative competence both in verbal and written aspects of the language, most students leave college with poor writing skills. Gomathy (2019) also stresses on bridging the gap between industry needs and talent supply. If the universities are able to minimize this gap, then the employability rate automatically gets high. One of the demands of the industry is that candidates should have good and effective English communication skills.

Bhakte (2019) emphasizes the importance of the English Language as a Comprehensive or World language, which helps people connect with other people globally and also has both communicative and educational value. From the words of Penny Ur (p. 6),

"English is a tool, like basic arithmetic, literacy, or computer skills: an ability they need to master in order to function effectively in today's world."

The same is the case with the students of the School of Open Learning (SOL). SOL, established in 1962, is the largest school for distance education affiliated with the University of Delhi (DU). This School provides opportunities for further education to students who could not get admission to the regular colleges of the University of Delhi or to any other university due to a variety of reasons. SOL students can only attend classes on weekends at their allotted study centers. After passing their graduation from SOL, there is not much difference in their degree as compared to those awarded from regular colleges- as the name of the college is not mentioned on the degree certificate. However, in general, it has been noted that graduate students from SOL lack English language skills. When they explore their world, many times they miss their goals only because of the lack of communication skills in English, which are, in great demand, at the present.

1.2 ENGLISH LANGUAGE IN GLOBAL CONTEXT

Mutairi (2020) aptly states, "English is now indispensable in all transnational aspects of life, including technology, commerce, telecommunications, medicine, and as a way of communication across

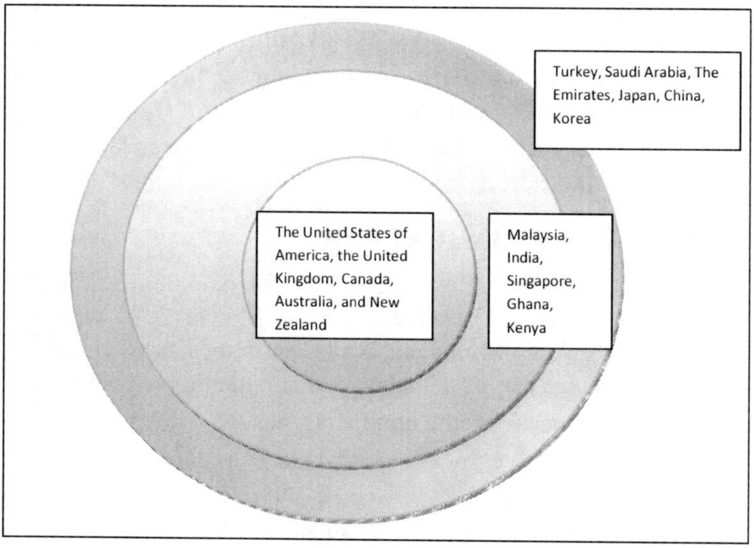

Fig. 1.1. The Three Circles in Kachru's Model of World English

cultures in many countries and regions. This resulted in the need to familiarize English Language Teaching with its new status."

First, it is important to understand the status of the English language throughout the world. For it, the best way is through Kachru's model of "World English". This model was introduced in 1985, and it helps to understand the status of the English language in a global context. Kachru (1985) describes the distribution of English in relation to three concentric circles: the Inner Circle, the Outer Circle, and the Expanding Circle (see Figure 1.1).

These circles signify "the type of spread, the pattern of acquisition, and the functional domains in which the English language is used across cultures and languages" (Kachru, 1985, p. 12).

- **The Inner Circle:** This is the area where English is the native language of the people living there. It is the smallest region, and people use English language in daily life and government institutions. For example, the United States of America, the United Kingdom, Canada, Australia, and New Zealand.
- **The Outer Circle:** It includes the regions where people use English as a second language (ESL). These countries or regions were British colonies in the past. Here, English is widely used in social life or in the government sector. For example, Malaysia, India, Singapore, Ghana, Kenya, and others.
- **The Expanding Circle:** In these countries and regions, English is used as a foreign language (EFL). They use the English language in education and primarily for the purpose of communicating in English with the Inner and Outer Circles. For example, Turkey, Saudi Arabia, The Emirates, Japan, China, Korea, and others.

1.3 ENGLISH AS A LINGUA FRANCA

Lingua Franca means languages used for communication among people speaking different first languages. Celce-Murcia (2016) writes about the significance of English language a lingua franca, which means that the English language acts as a language of communication between

- A native speaker and a non-native speaker
- Two non-native speakers who do not share a common L1 (First language)

So the teaching of the English language has been shifted. Now it is very important to consider English language teaching in the context in which a learner can communicate with a non-native speaker rather than only a native speaker. For this reason, English is also called an international language, as it acts as a tool of communication globally. Modiano (1999) presents his idea for the English language as an International language with centripetal circle model in which,

- Excellent communicators of English as an International Language (EIL) instead of native English speakers make up the inner circle. He excludes from the inner circle native speakers of English who have "excessive regional accents and dialects" and who are incapable of changing to EIL when the context needs it, as he feels that they are not competent communicators in an international context.
- The Middle Circle includes native and foreign language proficiency; they use the language locally. These native speakers of regional dialects enter the second circle with non-native Speakers, who speak internationally incomprehensible indigenized varieties.
- The Outer Circle has the people who are still in the process of acquiring the language and are called learners.
- There is the area beyond these circles which includes the people who do not know English.

As Modiano (1999, p. 25) said, "the proficient non-native speakers of EIL, rather than the native speakers who are not proficient in EIL, are better equipped to define and develop English as a tool in cross-cultural communication".

In India, people regard the English language as an International language through which they can communicate with native speakers as well as non-native speakers. So their aim is to achieve proficiency in the English language to become excellent communicators who can maintain their relationships with non-native speakers worldwide.

1.4 ENGLISH LANGUAGE TEACHING FOR ENGLISH AS SECOND LANGUAGE (L2)

Many scholars have been doing their best to discover the best approaches, methods, and techniques to teach English as a second language (L2). Many approaches and theories for teaching English as a second language have evolved up to this point. And In India, different approaches are being used to teach English as L2: the Grammar Translation method, Direct method, Audio-lingual method, Oral-Situational approach, PPP (Presentation, Practice, and Production), Communicative Language Teaching (CLT), and Task based Language Teaching.

Grammar Translation Method: This method was much popularized during the beginning of the nineteenth century. In this, a teacher explains the rules of the grammar of the target language and explains the text in the target language through translation into the students' mother tongue. It focuses on only the reading and writing skills, ignoring the listening and speaking skills. There is little use of the target language, as the focus is on translating sentences from the target language into the mother tongue.

Direct Method: By the end of the nineteenth century, the direct method had covered up the shortcomings of the Grammar Translation method as it largely focused on oral communication skills. In this method, only the use of the target language is allowed. It is a very popular method, and still in use by teachers as everything in the class is taught in the target language. Grammar is learned inductively, and the learning begins with dialogues and anecdotes.

During that time, many scholars like Henry Sweet, Paul Passy, and Wilhelm Vietor established the International Phonetic Association in Europe. They developed a system called the International Phonetic Alphabet, which represents the sound of any language. They also stressed the fact that speaking skills should be primarily taught to the learner based on International Phonetic Alphabet system.

Audio-Lingual Method: In the early twentieth century, the International Phonetic Alphabet and Skinner's behavioral theory led to the development of the audio-lingual method. This method is based on the theory that language is a set of habits. Students need to memorize the rules and have lots of drill practice with the language patterns. It is a teacher-centered approach. It is focused on listening and speaking skills.

Oral-Situational Approach: In this method, the most useful and new lexical and grammatical terms are introduced and practiced situationally. Teaching speaking skills is primarily done in the target language.

PPP (Presentation, Practice, and Production)**:** It means presentation, practice, and production. This 3P's method is the inheritance given by situational language teaching, or the oral approach. In this method, the teacher first presents the new set of language patterns in a context to which students can easily relate through text, audio, or any other visual. The second stage is practice, where students are provided many opportunities like drills, gap-filling activities, and cloze activities to practice the presented set of language patterns under the guidance of the teacher. The third stage is production, where students practice the learned language through dialogues and other activities without the help of a teacher.

The Communicative Language Teaching (CLT): This approach came up with solutions to the problems posed by situational language teaching. American linguist, Noam Chomsky criticized Situational Language Teaching (SLT) on the grounds that it was not able to make people efficient in making new sentences. He introduced the concepts of competence and performance based on linguistic theory. Dell Hymes criticized Chomsky's linguist view and coined the term "communicative competence" in 1966. He further explained that there is a need to move from teaching grammar and vocabulary to teaching skills for effective communication. For this, a person requires knowledge of the language as well as the skills to use that language. Hymes gave four components of communicative competence. Santos (2020) explained these four components as follows:

1. Language skill - knowledge about language symbols such as syntax, voice, word formation rules, vocabulary, etc.
2. Social language skill - excellent abilities to handle four skills in the daily life environment.
3. Textual competence - where speakers can handle both grammatical forms and context into a meaningful structure in both oral and written formats, and text unity can be completed by language convergence and semantic coherence.
4. Strategic competence - the skill to improve communication effectiveness or to avoid possible mistakes, both in verbal and nonverbal areas.

As a result, British and American linguists and academics introduced Communicative Language Teaching (CLT) around the 1970s to promote the communicative ability of second languages.

Some of the salient features of CLT mentioned by Celce-Murcia (2016) in *Teaching English in Foreign or Second Language* are:

- The main objective of teaching language is communicative proficiency rather than mastery of language structures.
- The content of the language course should include semantic notions and social functions.
- The teacher should use the target language fluently and appropriately and facilitate communication among learners primarily.
- The classroom is learner-centered and skills are integrated from the beginning.

- Learning is contextually based, which makes it meaningful for the students.
- It also helps to create healthy teaching-learning environment.

In other words, Communicative Language Teaching encourages students to use the language in unrehearsed contexts where learners negotiate meaning through interactions with others. Teachers encourage students to participate in activities that involve real communication and promote learning. This is the same way a child learns his mother tongue.

Bedadur (2018) rightly points out that Communicative Language Teaching is like natural language learning. It provides students with a learner-centered and rich language environment in which a teacher is a facilitator. She involves students in many communicative tasks and activities that reflect their lives and cultures. Dorneyi (2009) also explains that Communicative Language Teaching is all about creating meaningful interactive situations in L2 in which learners can participate to get those real life experiences.

1.5 ENGLISH LANGUAGE IN INDIAN CONTEXT

The situations in western countries led to the development of the pedagogy for English Language teaching, which was totally different from the Indian scenario. Many linguists and researchers in this field have worked to develop different strategies and ways to teach English to non native speakers. In the context of English Language Teaching (ELT) pedagogy, India was lagging far behind, as the English language received sufficient attention from policymakers, administrators, and teachers only around the year 1980. No formal teacher training was given to teachers who taught English in Indian schools, and for teachers and students, achievement in the examination was more prominent than performance.

In India, English is considered a second language as it is one of the national linguistic codes and holds a significant position in language policy. It is taught in schools to make students proficient enough to use it on a national and/or international level.

1.5.1 A Historical Sketch of ELT (English Language Teaching) in India

India got exposure to the English language for the first time when it became a British colony. As soon as the British began to rule India, they looked for Indians who could understand the English language to help them run the country. The Britishers hired a large number of high caste Indians, particularly Brahmanas, who were "Indians in blood and colour but English in taste, in opinions, morals, and intellect". The British policy was to establish a society of Indians who should think like the British.

Beginning in 1813, English-speaking Christian missionaries established primary schools in India for Indian students, where the local tongue served as the medium of instruction. Later, the missionaries constructed high schools where English served as the medium of instruction, obliging Indians who desired to pursue higher education to be proficient in the language. The British authorities began building their universities in India in 1857 on British models with an emphasis on English. The Indians studied at those British universities as well. The primary language of instruction in India is now English.

Indians with strong English skills were viewed as the country's new elite. English was used as the primary language of instruction in a large number of newly created schools. English remained India's primary language even after the country gained its independence. Today, English is considered the country's most important language, although it was granted the status of an assistant language and was expected to disappear after 15 years of Indian independence.

The development of the English language in India can be divided into three phases:

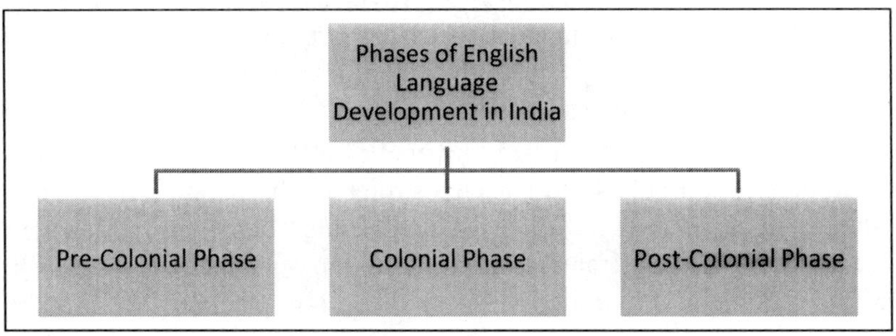

Fig. 1.2: Three Phases of Development of English Language in India

a) Pre-Colonial Period

The entry of the English language happened due to the arrival of the East India Company in the 18th century and the decline of the Mughal Empire. As the East India Company established its grip on India and made it a British colony, India's tryst with the English language began. During this period, English was the language of communication for the elite and not the lingua franca, which created one of the biggest social divisions in an already divided society – those who could speak English and those who could not.

b) Colonial Period

With the establishment of the East India Company in the 18th century, efforts began to teach Indians the English language. Initially, Britishers tried to learn Indian languages, but in vain, with the objective of getting employees who were Indian in blood and spoke English at work. This initiative was started in 1759 with the arrival of Christian Missionaries and the establishment of schools for teaching English. Another catalyst that worked on the concern of teaching English to non-Europeans was the book "The Tutor" by John Miller in 1797.

The year 1835 was a landmark year in the history of ELT in India, as in the same year, Lord Macaulay, in his "Minutes of Education," laid the foundation of English Language Teaching in India. He mentioned the importance and usefulness of the education that would be given to the natives through the medium of English. Through English medium education, he aimed to create a class of natives who were Indians in blood and colour, but English in taste, opinion, morals, and intellect bridge that gap, and become the interpreters between the rulers and the subjects, (Thirumalai, 2003). The East India Company took the responsibility of teaching English to Indians on its shoulders and released the Charter Act of 1813. To fulfill this objective, it needed the European institutions. This Lord Macaulay's Minute of Education provided the framework for formal English language teaching in India, which to a large extent is being followed even today. In the journey toward the aim of teaching English to Indians, many developments have taken place.

The British also established universities in India in 1857 that were based on British models and placed a strong emphasis on English. They established universities in Kolkata, Mumbai, and Chennai in 1857, where selective education and training in administration were imparted in English. In those universities, Indians also studied. The primary language of instruction in India is now English. The "modern" leaders of the era in India also provided assistance because they believed that it was the main factor in success. Indians with strong English skills were viewed as the country's new elite. English was used as the primary language of instruction in a large number of newly created schools. Indians who were ambitious tended to favour schools that placed a strong emphasis on English because, in accordance with British legislation, English was the language of instruction at the university level. Even now, English-focused schools in India are better. About one-third of Indian schools in the 1970s and 1980s had English as their primary language. Since English is the majority of these students' first language, they find it simpler to talk, read, and write in English than in any other Indian language, including their mother tongues.

Gradually, English became the language of government, higher education, advancement, and a symbol of imperial rule and self-improvement. With the mixed reactions of resistance and acceptance of Macaulay's policy, a three-language formula had emerged in the Indian context. However, the status of English in the three-language formula varied from state to state; in contrast, one thing was confirmed that English was introduced as a compulsory subject in almost all Indian schools at the secondary level, and all the students were supposed to complete their school education with five years of English learning.

It was confirmed that English was a prerequisite to seeking admission into any established university. However, the general populace's attitude toward the English language was quite pitiful, since nobody showed any interest in learning it. The adoption of the English language as the primary language of instruction for the fundamental sciences and mathematical sciences led to tremendous growth in secondary and higher education, particularly in metropolitan regions. Since India's independence, English has become increasingly important in the worlds of higher learning and research. In this context, the Kothari Commission, appointed by the Indian government's ministry of education, recommended the structural approach to teach English, which is now widely used in various regions of India. The study group also came up with a detailed syllabus for the study of the English language from grades V to XII. Today, in this nation of a billion plus people with a literate population of 74% in 2011, knowledge of English guarantees a job across the sectors.

In line with this, Olaizola (2021) evaluated that among the more than 600 languages that are spoken in India, English has surpassed them all and is now only second to Hindi in terms of usage. More Indians than people in the UK are thought to speak Standard Indian English, which is estimated to number around 130 million people. The East India Company's initial phase was conducted in a conventional capitalist manner, with the sole objective of conducting business with the locals. It is crucial to make clear that there were no governmental initiatives to force the language on the populace. Despite this, English became the official language of government at the beginning of the 18th century. English's exponential expansion led to its becoming the official language of the government, the social elite, and the national press.

c) Post-colonial period

With the emergence of the English language in India, the Indian masses divided into two groups: one who favored the vernacular or regional language as the medium of instruction in schools and another who wanted English as the medium of instruction.

In 1950, the constitution of India declared Hindi in Devanagri script the official language with the expectation that it would replace English and become the language of mass communication. However, it was not able to resolve the controversy over the status of languages in a diverse India. In 1965, Central Advisory Board of Education tried to resolve this controversy with the three formula language policy, in which there are the provisions for teaching

(i) The regional and the mother tongue when the latter is different from the regional language

(ii) Hindi or in Hindi speaking areas, another Indian language

(iii) English or any other modern European language

We cannot deny the fact that, despite putting so much effort into replacing the English language in the Indian scenario, English was still, after independence, not only the link language but also the language of administrators, policymakers, business, and the professional class.

Over time, the southerners grew increasingly opposed to the concept of making Hindi the official language in place of English because they believed Hindi to be a more foreign language. However, due to the slow development of Hindi, the parliament was forced to pass a law in 1963 designating English as an associate official language of India for all time. Even though English suffered greatly after Independence, it remains a significant language with a respected status in our society.

1.5.2 English Language in Indian Education System

Yesapogu (2016) emphasizes the special place of the English language in India's educational system. As the world's knowledge is expanding quickly, particularly in science and technology, India must not only maintain this progress but also significantly contribute to it. For this reason, the study of English should be reinforced. Today, one of the most common languages is English. English's elimination would be a major setback for India's educational cause. Therefore, it is important to keep the quality of English instruction as high as possible. More than 400 million people throughout the world speak English, which is the language of commerce and trade on a global scale.

In the modern environment of rapid communication, we cannot be satisfied with studying only in our mother tongue or regional languages. To foster global understanding, there is a need to learn the English language. Learning the English language can help us lead lives with better prospects by gaining scientific and technical information. It also serves as a means of communication for activities like trade, commerce, industry, and dealing with international politics. It may also be regarded as a cultural medium. Thus, English has a role to perform in contemporary Indian education that is interactive rather than literary.

According to the Secondary Education Commission (1952–53), "Our regional languages are not fully developed, and there is a dearth of books and efficient teachers in these languages. The official language at the center is English; hence, its study should be compulsory at the secondary stage". According to this viewpoint, the commission believed that no student should suffer from a language barrier that will ultimately influence his choice of career.

Given that India is a diverse country with many different cultures, secondary or higher education should attempt to prepare students not only for a university education but also for a variety of occupations and life in general. When reasonable English proficiency is attained, this is feasible.

Only the mother tongue or the regional language should be taught to the pupils studying from class I to class IV, according to the Kothari Education Commission (1964–1966). Then, from class VIII to class X, two languages, specifically a regional language and Hindi or English, should be taught. Thus, every child in our nation spends 10 years learning their mother tongue or regional language, 6 years learning a second language, and 3 years learning a third language. Nearly all educational levels in India now include English as a required subject. However, a wide range of social, political, and cultural factors have an impact on English's status in various boards, universities, and other institutions. Even the curriculum provided and the evaluation methods used vary greatly from state to state. The lack of consistency in the English model provided to students continues to pose a problem for policymakers and educators. While English is considered a second language in the majority of States, some treat it as a third language, with the national language and the regional languages taking precedence.

The debate above paints a picture of English under the new conditions. It no longer enjoys the status it did under the British government. It doesn't imply that English is any less significant. It will keep playing a crucial function as a window on the world, a link language for the advancement of national integration, and a language used in libraries. However, English needs to continue to be studied, according to the University Education Commission's 1948 recommendation. It is a language with a wealth of humanistic, scientific, and technical literature. We risk cutting ourselves off from the ongoing flow of knowledge if we give up English out of sentimental impulses. The only way to avoid becoming cut off from the outside world is to learn English. English is taught in secondary school but is not allowed in the early grades. Even in high school, English should be taught from a linguistic perspective rather than a literary one. The study of English as a second language is recommended.

An English language learner from India uses the English language to communicate with other Indians. It is astonishing to find that, despite our independence being declared sixty years ago, Hindi has not totally replaced English. The main contributing aspect is the growing perception that English belongs to everyone who speaks it as their first or second language, not only to the English people. English proficiency is seen as a successful employment passport. Practically, for every job in a government department, an English-speaking Indian is generally chosen over a non-English-speaking Indian. English is a world language in addition to being the native tongue of England. It may be referred to as the language of civilization because of how rich, elegant, beautiful, adaptable, and dignified it is.

All spheres of society and occupations now use English as a form of communication. English has established itself as the preferred language for cross-cultural communication, even inside the language-diverse nation of India. In terms of communication among speakers of various native languages, it has even surpassed Hindi, which is the nation's official language. In addition, the majority of the world communicates in English, therefore, if India has to be a part of the global scene, English could be a crucial link.

The twentieth century saw significant advances in science and technology, which made it possible for numerous new methods of exchanging information and conducting business. India's involvement in worldwide trade created a need for English proficiency on the global stage. English frequently serves as the connecting language between speakers of various dialects in India's linguistically diverse environments. Many educated Indians consider English to be their mother tongue. Thus, in the current environment, English is essential in bringing together speakers of various regional languages to foster greater interaction within India's social, educational, and administrative networks. It offers a language tool for a nation's administrative cohesion.

1.6 COMMUNICATIVE LANGUAGE TEACHING (CLT): A PARADIGM SHIFT IN ENGLISH LANGUAGE TEACHING (ELT) IN INDIA

All youngsters today need English as a new "basic skill" in order to properly engage in 21st-century civil society. It is to be understood that in India, English is a language of global necessity and not just a link language. Many significant numbers of commissions and committees have been constituted since India's independence and have recommended new policies and improved current education policy, including the ELT. Despite so many efforts, it is observed that the appropriate kind of education is required right now, in which language education or learning requires intricate and meticulous preparation with extreme regularity, continuity, coherence, and stability.

In a nation like India, coordination between primary, secondary, and higher education doesn't even seem to exist. These three educational levels are separate and constitute various groups, bodies, or institutions. It is distressing that the methods and approaches that have been implemented for ELT leave little room for adequate student screening in light of their age, ability, motivation, and other elements influencing the process of language learning or acquisition. All the attempts have been unsuccessful due to an unhealthy rivalry between languages on the one side and those who support literature on the other. The various educational boards—State Education and Research Training Councils (SCERT), University Academic Councils (UAC), University Grant Commission (UGC), Directorate of Human Resource Development (DHRD)—are all working to enhance and modernize study programmes across all disciplines. In the process of achieving all of these things, the ELT will also be improved, updated, and streamlined to the greatest extent possible.

India's three-language policy—Hindi, English, and the regional language—with inconsistent application leads to confusion in schools and colleges about the languages. The 2004 policy recommended the use of CLT techniques by teachers teaching English in India's public schools, yet minimal direction has been provided to teachers about what content should be taught or how to teach it (Christ & Makarani, 2009). Gupta (2005) discloses that in 1989, the Punjab University was the first to introduce a paper titled 'English Communicative' as a part of its three-year undergraduate course on the basis of the CLT approach. In India, teachers used to employ a teaching approach that was teacher-centered and exam-oriented. Teachers were supposed to change their methodology, but few were equipped adequately to teach students to practice CLT strategies in the classroom. Despite the implementation of the CLT approach, the result was the same; the classroom methodology remained the same as teachers used the same traditional grammar translation method for teaching. This was the situation with regard to CLT in 1989 and even up to the year 2000.

The CLT methodology was a failure at that time in India as there was no match between classroom activities and real-world activities; there was no similarity to Littlewood's definition of 'communicative Tasks' (1981). Then came the liberalization of the Indian economy in 1991 that allowed the entry of many international brands into India who were looking for proficient young personnel English speakers to work in the call centers, shopping malls, and trade fairs they started to set up, and there started the mushroom growth of institutes and academies offering courses to make Indian young people proficient English speakers.

The internet also played a major role in changing the context of Indian learners, which somehow led to one of the main factors for the success of the CLT methodology in India as it provides a resource-rich environment by giving a wide range of exposure to English. Becoming web-savvy has emerged as the need of the day, and this is possible only through English (Gupta 2004).

It is true that there are several obstacles in the way of CLT's adoption in India, but it still has a bright future. In India, the entire process of changing the curriculum is fraught with lengthy and time-consuming procedures, and although CLT has had some success, it has not yet been completely eliminated from the curriculum. In the long term, this was beneficial since, while teachers were able to become familiar with its methodology and approach, the context's shifting and changing environment also supported its current success.

Although the institutes in primary education are using the Communicative approach, the ripple effect is spreading slowly to the ELT classroom. This approach's sensitivity to learner requirements and responses has the biggest impact. The academic component of ELT in India has been deficient in this sensitivity. The entire academic procedure is so cumbersome that it fails to address the demands of the student; learner feedback is too frequently disregarded. Ironically, academicians refer to these learning centers as "shops" or "commercial institutes," despite the fact that they have had a significant impact on how the ELT paradigm has changed in India.

1.7 DISTANCE EDUCATION IN INDIA

For many students living in remote and distant areas for whom accessing colleges and universities on a regular basis is not feasible, distance education becomes the medium through which the students who are staying in these areas can obtain degrees. And due to this contribution, the literacy rate has been increasing. As per the All India Survey on Higher Education (AISHE) Report, 2017-18, 11% of all higher education enrollments are distance learners.

Table 1.1: Student Enrolment in Universities under Distance Mode (As per UGC Annual Report 2017-18):

Year	2014-15	2015-16	2016-17	2017-18	
No. of students enrolled in Distance Education	38,11,723	38,24,901	40,89,781	40,31,594	
Year	**2014-15**	**2015-16**	**2016-17**	**2017-18**	**2018-19**
No. of universities/ institutions recognized to offer programmes through distance mode	157	130	114	118	104

1.7.1 An Overview

'Open Learning' and 'Distance Education', generally, people use the two terms as synonyms. But in reality, they are not. Open learning is a philosophy that helps to democratize education; it means education should be accessible, affordable, and attainable to all, independent of their time, place, and income. Open Learning gives flexibility to the learner in regard to

- Entry and exit from a course
- Pace and place of study
- Method of study
- Choice and combination of courses
- Assessment

A sizable portion of society has the opportunity to access education that is not available through traditional colleges and universities-thanks to open learning. This larger section of society includes women, the physically disabled, professionals, and people living in remote areas where there are no colleges.

Distance Education is the means by which this philosophy becomes a reality. And then, to attain this aim, 'Open Learning' and 'Distance Education' are combined to make a broader term called 'Open and Distance Learning' (ODL).

Distance Education (DE) provides teaching and learning experiences in a setting in which the teacher and learner are separated by space and time. It is not a traditional classroom setting where students and teacher have face to face interactions, but in this setting, the teacher delivers instructions to learners in an asynchronous mode by means of different methods:

- Specially prepared materials called self-study learning materials are to be delivered to the learners' doorstep through various media such as print, television, radio, satellite, audio/video tapes, CD-ROMs, Internet, the World Wide Web, etc.
- The inter-personal communication between teacher and students is done through postal correspondence or electronic media such as telephone, mobile, teleconferencing, videoconferencing, chat sessions, email, website, etc.
- Personal Contact Programme which includes limited face to face contact sessions between teacher and students held at Study centers set up by the Distance Education institutions as close to the learners' homes as possible.

Distance education is different in the sense that educational technology plays a big part in the teaching and learning process. Educational technology, which includes audio- visual aids, the computer, the mass media, social media, etc., helps to make distance education dynamic and exciting.

There are various other names by which Distance Education is popularly known. These names are open learning, distance learning, correspondence courses, correspondence education, virtual education, extensive courses, etc.

India has one of the largest Distance Education systems in the world, second only to China. Earlier, there were six types of institutions that offered Distance Education:

- National Open University
- State Open Universities
- Distance Education Institutions (DEIs) at
  - Institutions of National Importance
  - Central Universities
  - State Universities
  - Deemed to be Universities
  - State Private Universities

- Distance Education at Stand alone Institutions
  - Professional Associations
  - Government Institutions
  - Private institutions

1.7.2 Historical Development of Distance Education

Being a very diverse country, India has the third largest higher education system in the world (Jayaram, 2007; cited by Panda & Garg, 2006). India accelerated the elementary and secondary education levels after gaining independence in 1947 and took over the British government's education system in their nation. As a result, the demand for higher education increased. Under the leadership of Daulat Singh Kothari (at that time, chairman of the University Grants Commission), the Kothari Commission (1964- 66) recommended Part-Time Education and Correspondence Courses.

"Part-time education and correspondence courses should be developed on a large scale at the university stage. Such facilities should also be developed for secondary school students, teachers, and agricultural, industrial, and other workers. Education through part-time and correspondence courses should be given the same status as full-time education."

At that time, UGC started a pilot project and opened the correspondence course only at one University, i.e., the University of Delhi. Then the University of Delhi's School of Correspondence Courses and Continuing Education was born in 1962.

In the 1970s, the opportunities of accessibility, affordability, and attainability promoted the growth of the Correspondence Education system in India. In the 1980s, the popularity of correspondence courses started a new era in Open and Distance learning with the establishment of Dr. B. R. Ambedkar Open University, Hyderabad, in 1982, followed by the establishment of Indira Gandhi National Open University at the national level by the Parliament of India in 1985.

After this, many more states came up with the idea of establishing more Open universities. As a result, many more open universities emerged, like Nalanda Open University (NOU), Patna, Bihar; Vardhman Mahaveer Open University (VMOU), Kota, Rajasthan; and Yashwantrao Chavan Maharashtra Open University (YCMOU), Nashik, Maharashtra.

The major point noted here is that UGC was not the coordination authority for Open and Distance learning; rather, this role was given to the Indira Gandhi National Open University (IGNOU). Thus, the IGNOU had two responsibilities on its shoulders:

- Works as an Open University and offers many courses and programmes in higher education through distance learning
- Acts as the promoter and coordinator of the Open and Distance Education system in India, determining and maintaining the standards of this system.

To attain these objectives, IGNOU set up the Distance Education Council (DEC) in 1991, in accordance with Section 16(7) and Section 5(2) of the IGNOU Act, 1985. As per the mandate of the DEC and the National Education Policy (NPE) 1986 (revised in 1992), the DEC developed guidelines for the establishment, regulation, and operation of Open and Distance Learning (ODL) institutions. After this, many State governments established Open Universities.

A Memorandum of Understanding (MoU) was signed in May 2007 by the UGC, AICTE, and DEC for a three-year period that ended in May 2010. In the form of the "Recognition of Open and Distance Learning (ODL) Institutions" Handbook 2009, the Joint Committee created guidelines. After that, in accordance with the Ministry of Education's directives, the Department of Higher Education of the Government of India issued an order dated December 29, 2012, giving the University Grants Commission regulatory authority over distance education programmes in higher education (excluding technical education), while the All India Council for Technical Education (AICTE) serves in that capacity for technical education through ODL.

In August 2010, the Ministry of Human Resource Development (MHRD) constituted a Committee to check the standard of distance education under the chairmanship of Prof. Madhava Menon. This committee gave two main recommendations: one is the creation of a new regulatory body for the ODL system, the Distance Education Council of India (DECI), and another is to transfer the DEC of IGNOU to UGC. Afterward, on December 29, 2012, the MHRD transferred the regulatory authority of distance education from IGNOU to UGC. Currently, UGC regulates, coordinates, and maintains open and distance learning. The Ministry of Education, on February 25, 2014, has directed UGC to act as a regulator for the higher education system in ODL mode, including for technical education in universities/affiliated colleges. For this, UGC established a bureau named DEB (Distance Education Bureau) in 2013, replacing the **Distance Education Council (DEC)**.

In India, open and distance learning systems have become crucial tools for educating all facets of society. Additionally, the ODL system's evolving dynamics over the past 60 years have been positive. The lines between the classroom and the campus are blurring up due to the expansion of ICT (Information and Communication Technology), and the country's amazing number of ODL institutions is evidence of this. In the 10th Plan period, there were 14 single-mode open universities, up from four in the 8th Plan period. There are already more than 200 dual-mode universities (DEIs) providing programmes using the distance learning format. This is because there are more potential students than there is infrastructure for face-to-face instruction, which means that it cannot keep up with the demand for education. Almost 25% of the nation's higher education students are currently enrolled in the ODL system. In the last six decades, the ODL system has registered phenomenal growth in the context of the expansion and diversification of higher education. From a single institution in 1962 (the University of Delhi), the number of ODL institutions has reached approximately 250, including Central, State, Deemed to be and Private Universities, along with many stand alone institutions.

From the academic session 2013 onward, the University Grants Commission started giving recognition to Universities and Institutions for providing programmes via distance learning. Following the transfer of regulatory responsibilities from the former DEC to the UGC, institutions and universities that had already received institutional recognition or program-specific recognition were granted continued status for one year, or 2014–15. In the absence of ODL Regulations, the Commission opted to maintain recognition of the institutions that had been approved to provide ODL programmes during 2014–15 for the duration of 2015–16.

For the first time, the UGC undertook a thorough exercise with the intention of taking into consideration the recognition of eligible

Table 1.2: Number of Universities Offering Distance learning programmes in the Year 2022-23

Central Open Universities	1
State Open Universities	15
Central Universities	10
State Universities	35
Private Universities	7
Deemed to be Universities	19

Source: University Grants Commission, Distance Education Bureau (retrieved on November 29, 2022).

universities and institutes. Based on the suggestions of the Expert Committees, recognition was given to the relevant universities and institutes. In the case of universities, recognition was given for the 2016–17 and 2017–18 academic years. However, in accordance with the UGC (ODL) First and Second Amendments, the Commission shall not grant any permission to the Open and Distance Learning programmes to Standalone Institutions beyond the academic year 2017–18.

For distance education, Panchabakesan's (2011) observation was acceptable that the old concept of distance education was exclusively associated with print materials, whereas the new concept of distance education includes supplementary material being used through non-print media such as radio, television, computers, laptops, recorded lectures in Mpeg and Avi formats on CDs and DVDs, and Self Learning Materials (SLM) through projectors, video conferencing, and interactive sessions between students and faculties via the internet.

1.7.3 Importance of Distance Education

Iqbal (2019) rightly comments that there is a need for an alternate educational system, namely distance education, in India because it is extremely difficult for the traditional mode of education to handle such an increasing number of students. As a result, distance learning expands educational options for groups of people who were previously unable to benefit from formal education at a lower cost than traditional learning. Researchers in the field of education discovered additional methods, such as distance learning, for demonstrating that it can satisfy needs. Distance learning is now offered in addition to the traditional educational system. The popularity of remote education has increased due to its ability to serve a vast number of students. Many developed nations, like the United Kingdom, Germany, Canada, Spain, and Japan, as well as emerging nations such as Sri Lanka, Thailand, India, and Pakistan, have accepted the idea of distance learning.

Distance education helps the citizens of the country in many ways.

- Working professionals can continue with their education, as distance education gives them the opportunity to study at flexible hours without any obstacles to their job or their studies. Along with their jobs, people can upgrade themselves and, hence, earn more.
- Distance education is also a boon for athletes, as they can continue their studies without dropping their sports career or practice.

- Distance education also plays very important role in building women's careers. It helps married women and other girls who dropped out of school due to some other reason to continue their education and fulfill their dreams.
- Students from diverse parts of the country can study at a specific university through distance education. Since it doesn't place a financial strain on the students or their parents, distance education is always economical. These assist the student in allocating their finances to other worthwhile endeavors that might in some way benefit the country.

One of the most recent educational trends is distance learning, which is assisting many aspirants in achieving their goals with the least amount of effort. Many candidates are finding life easier because of distance learning, which conveniently visits them at home. According to the Annual Report released by MHRD in 2016-17, there are 1 Central Open University, 13 State Open universities, 1 State open Private University, and 118 Dual mode Universities offering education through distance mode. Distance enrollment constitutes about 11.05% of total enrollment in higher education, of which 46.3% are female students.

The University Grants Commission established guidelines in 1974 that outlined the goals of correspondence and distance learning. The goal of correspondence education is to offer a different educational option so that many people with the appropriate ability can advance their knowledge and professional skills. Thus, correspondence courses are designed to serve the following groups of students:

(a) who had to stop their formal education due to financial or other reasons;

(b) who live in remote areas;

(c) who had to stop their education due to lack of aptitude or motivation but who may later become motivated

(d) who cannot find a seat or do not want to enroll in a regular college or university department despite having the required qualifications

(e) who view education as a lifetime activity and may want to brush up on their expertise in a current field or learn about a new one.

The University of Delhi's School of Correspondence Courses and Continuing Education introduced the first correspondence courses for the B.A. degree in 1962. It attracted a large number of students. In 1968, the Punjab University, Patiala, and the University of Rajasthan launched correspondence courses by opening the Institute of Correspondence and Continuing Education.

1.8 THE SCHOOL OF OPEN LEARNING (SOL), UNIVERSITY OF DELHI

The School of Open Learning (SOL), formerly known as The School of Correspondence Courses and Continuing Education, is a distance education institution established in 1962 at the University of Delhi. Previously, SOL was called the Directorate of Correspondence Courses. It was a pioneering institution in the field of Distance Education in India. In 1962, the SOL started with only 900 students, but now it has reached the level of taking admissions for 5 lakh students in the Academic Session 2019-20.

Initially, the Directorate of Correspondence Courses didn't have an official standing in the university; therefore, it wasn't considered a department or a university-maintained institution. However, in accordance with Ordinance XX of the Delhi University Calendar, it was designated as a university-maintained institution (college) in 1969, which means the institution will provide complete assistance to cover any shortfall.

SOL offers graduate and postgraduate courses to students in the subjects of Arts/Humanities and Commerce. The University of Delhi, like its other constituent colleges, handles the admissions process, the administration of exams, and the awarding of degrees to students.

SOL has its study center in the north at North Campus and in the south at Moti Bagh. Now, to cater to the needs of the growing number of students enrolled in SOL, it has been planned to open up new study centers in the National Capital Region of Delhi, especially in east and west Delhi, to reach out to more students. SOL has two primary teaching modes, or modes of interaction between students and teacher:

1. Well- prepared self-learning instructional material (hard copy as well as soft copy). A hard copy is given to students at the time of admission
2. A Personal Contact Program, conducted at the various study centres

A knowledgeable faculty member is always available to students for academic interaction at the main campus. The school provides learning via distance education as a feasible choice for students who need a flexible medium of instruction to gain higher education and occupational skills. The school also maintains a well-stocked library to allow for broad exposure to contemporary breakthroughs in the course streams being taught. Currently, to reduce postal and environmental costs, SOL has also begun quickly delivering the course's study materials in person at the time that admission and examination forms are submitted.

1.8.1 Personal Contact Programme (PCP)

Personal Contact Programs are crucial for distance learning. The majority of learning in distance education is self-directed. Students independently select their courses and pursue independent study of them. But guidance is required for this kind of self-directed learning, and SOL offers the learner guidance resources through PCP. A Personal Contact Program is also known as a brief lesson. PCP is carried out in regional study centres that have the necessary infrastructure and are well-equipped. Where distance learners from many locations get together to discuss and review with their teacher the courses they had previously learned through written or even audio-visual means, solving their problems in the process. The personal contact programmes are specifically designed to assist or support the learners and address any issues they may have with self-study. The Personal Contact Programme (PCP) offers the student the opportunity to communicate with their peer group and tutor.

a) Personal Contact Programme Classes (PCP Classes) in SOL Study Centers

The School has made efforts to advance flipped-classroom technology by emphasising virtual/audio-visual teaching-learning, followed by activity and skill-based experiential learning in various study centres, and by offering free access to all text-to-speech contents and study materials, audio lectures, and video lectures. The school has started using a Learning Management System (LMS) with an online dashboard that is user-friendly for students. For conducting PCP programmes, SOL has created more than 30 study centres in various institutions at the University of Delhi.

PCPs benefit the learner by encouraging, guiding, reinforcing, and providing feedback to the study, providing orientation to the students about the subject, imparting the knowledge of the subject in a condensed form, developing the understanding of the basic and challenging concepts of the subject, and helping learners to solve the learning problems. They also benefit the learner by preparing the students for responses and providing appropriate opportunities to discuss and seek coaching.

1.8.2 Self-Learning Instructional Material (SLIM)

In distance education, the mainstay of teaching is printed course material. The printed course material is still the most effective method of delivering instruction to numerous students remotely, even in developed nations where open universities are present and mass communication and information technology have brought about revolutionary changes in educational systems. Therefore, when creating the course materials, extra attention need to be paid to meeting academic standards. Anyone who works in or plans to work in the distance education system, as well as anyone interested in learning how to create SLM for distance learners and how to update those materials on a regular basis, should be aware of all key terms related to the ODL process. Tiarina et al. (2019) confirm that identifying and understanding students' needs is central to developing interactive learning material. Patel & Singh (2021) assert that Self-Instructional Materials (SIM) are designed to enable learners to study wholly by themselves, so called "Tutorial in Print". This self-instructional material opens the door for flexible learning and self-practices, which are most beneficial for independent learners as they are not teacher-centric. They take responsibility for their own learning.

Sultana (2016) defines self print material as material that is self learning, learner centered, and self-instructed and in which the teaching learning process, learning material, and learning experiences have objectives to meet only learners' needs. Learning material is divided into different units or lessons, and students have to make assignments after studying the self-learning instructional material. The students submit these assignments and get the teachers' feedback.

The study materials have a significant impact on the success and efficiency of distance education systems. Writing for self-learning instructional material in distance learning is more difficult and quite different than writing for face-to-face instruction, books, or journals. The creation of self-learning instructional materials is vital because it facilitates communication between teachers and students while meeting their needs. This is how a distant learner can participate in all aspects of independent study and learning. Distance learners rely largely on these particularly created SLMs and have less interaction with the institution or the professor. Every distance learning course must occasionally be updated to reflect changes in the subject in order to make the course more pertinent, learner-friendly, and intellectually rich in light of the feedback that it receives from students, tutors, counsellors, experts, and others.

1.8.3 Self-Learning Instructional Material (SLIM) for English Language Acquisition Skills

The English language is being taught in schools as a subject, not as a skill, which requires a lot of exposure to that language and opportunities to practice it. Naz (2016) highlights that English language acquisition is taught in schools to score marks rather than to make students skilled enough to use the language in innumerable real-life situations. The schools teach the format to the students, and the content is learned by rote learning. It is one of the biggest obstacles to English language acquisition. English language learning is a skill that can only be acquired through practice with a good amount of exposure to the language.

In line with this, Sreehari (2012) observes that in India, English has been considered another subject in schools and colleges. Teachers prefer accuracy in language over fluency and conversational skills, and to teach this, teachers employ the structural method to teach English, which is a very obsolete method. It is the need of the hour that English Language Teachers explore innovative methods of teaching language, as Indian English has the potential to give people a great chance of increasing their career prospects and communication skills.

This is one of the reasons why, despite getting training for 12 years in schools, students at the undergraduate level do not have enough proficiency and confidence to communicate in the English language. Katoky (2020) also argues that a large percentage of learners at the undergraduate level have low English proficiency despite being aware that good English communication skills are a pre requisite for a successful career.

Thakur (2021) observes while teaching the undergraduate students that, in spite of having good intelligence and good theoretical knowledge of grammar and sentence structure, the students still hesitate to use English in their real lives or in their speaking and writing as the medium of communication. Students are not able to put into practice their theoretical knowledge of sentences and grammar in their speaking and writing. They fail to express what they want to convey. She quotes Krashen's theory of second language learning and explains that effective second language acquisition requires not only the pursuit of LSRW activities in the target language but also the right approach through correct attitude and soft skills like focus, commitment, confidence, positivity of mind, patience, being a good listener, etc. In the same context, Ellis (Zhao 2015), emphasizes that acquisition of second language or acquisition of English language as L2 involves learning with subconscious mind, in which there is need to remove the boundary between class and outside world and Sengupta (2021) also studied that for ESL students from low socio-economic groups, the classroom is a primary source of comprehensible input. Students do not get a real life feel or a reason to genuinely interact, listen to, and speak meaningfully due to the lack of personalizing and authentic tasks. So to develop English language proficiency, they need numerous exposures through authentic material that is available in their surroundings and activities that can develop their communicative competence.

Meganathan, et al. (2020) quotes many research studies which demonstrate that the key elements for learning the English language are time spent by the learner actually using the language, learner-learner interaction, teacher-learner interaction, authentic materials and tasks, along with other variables of learner motivation and enabling conditions (resources for learning the language), etc. This calls for a change in teacher training to comprehend new language pedagogies and methods that support the language usage components. The present necessity and demand for English language as a skill for upward mobility are reflected in research on English language education at the university and for professional courses, which might be accomplished by employing efficient teaching techniques like task-based language teaching (TBLT) and communicative approaches. To achieve the above mentioned goal, a change from literature-based to language-focused courses is advised. It is essential to acknowledge the demand for significant English language proficiency for entry into higher education and employment, as well as the perception that these skills are essential for communication and negotiation. This calls for a change in the direction of curriculum development and material creation.

1.8.4 Preparation of Self-Learning Instructional Material (SLIM)

Self-learning instructional material is the main component of distance education. So it should be skillfully designed with the needs of the learners at the centre. "Creating Learning Material for Open and Distance Learning" explains Open and Distance Learning (ODL), which is characterized by two factors:

a. The philosophy of ODL, which aims at increasing educational access and educational choice,
b. The ODL systems' use of technology, such as printed workbooks, audio cassettes, radio, and the web, mediates learning.

1.9 INSTRUCTIONAL DESIGN MODEL

"Creating Learning Material for Open and Distance Learning" defines instructional design as

"The systematic development of instructional specifications using learning and instructional theory to ensure the quality of instruction. It is the entire process of analyzing learning needs and goals and developing a delivery system to meet those needs. It includes the development of instructional materials and activities and the tryout ODL situation."

Thus, instructional design is a process that employs a structured approach to translate learners' needs and objectives into effective learning.

There are some theories and approaches that guide the instructional designer in designing and creating instructional material. There are three theories or approaches available for instructional designs. They are:

- A Behavioural approach, which aims to create the instructional material based on the particular conditions needed for a particular type of learning.
- Cognitive approach, which emphasised on design based on the characteristics of individual learners.
- The constructivist approach, which is the most recent approach and stresses the learner's own activities as the mechanism for learning.

The researcher uses the cognitive approach to develop the self-learning instructional material, which provides many learning devices to be incorporated into the material, like:

- learning objectives stated
- the task is broken down into small steps
- learners are assessed against the stated learning objectives
- a wide variety of tasks, but within the scope of the stated objectives
- material is 'chunked' into small, meaningful pieces
- mnemonics are used to aid memory
- advance organisers are used to help learners see the structure of the topic
- simplification of real-world situations
- the learning package tends to prescribe what is to be learned.

1.9.1 Types of Instructional Design

There are several ways to classify instructional design. Rowntree (1994) provided an easy-to-use method in the following manner:

- tell-and-test
- tutorial
- reflective action guide

These align with behaviourist, cognitivist, and constructivist methodologies. The tutorial technique, is the one that ODL practitioners most frequently employ, which the researcher has also utilized. It is characterised by the writer providing some sort of input (for example, text, a diagram, or a case study) before putting an activity on it. The goal of the activity is to make sure the learner fully comprehends the subject matter. Multiple input-activity sequences make up a complete unit. This mirrors how teachers instruct their students in the classroom by providing some input before posing a question or assigning a job.

1.10 DIFFERENCE BETWEEN LANGUAGE ACQUISITION AND LANGUAGE LEARNING

Acquisition is the ability to pick up language, whereas learning is a conscious effort on the part of the learner. Krashen first defines the term acquisition and differentiates it from learning. According to Krashen (1982),

"Acquisition is a process through which children develop abilities in their first language. Language acquisition is a subconscious process; language acquirers are not usually aware of the fact that they are acquiring a language but are only aware of the fact that they are using the language for communication. Other ways of describing acquisition include implicit learning, informal learning, and natural learning. In non-technical term, acquisition is "picking-up" a language."

"Language learning refers to conscious knowledge of a second language, knowing the rules, being aware of them, and being able to talk about them. In non-technical terms, learning is "knowing about" a language, known to most people as "grammar", or "rules". Some synonyms include formal knowledge of a language, or explicit learning."

1.10.1 Explicit and Implicit Learning

Lightbown and Spada (2013), in their book "How Languages are Learned," explain why a second language learner takes more time to understand the text even though he is able to understand it fully.

When a second language learner uses the target language, he uses much more of his attention and time processing the meaning of individual words and their relationships among them. There is a lack of "automatic access" to the meaning of the words in the target language. In contrast, a proficient speaker automatically uses strings of words that usually occur together. While learning a second language, most learners pay more attention to the comprehension of the language than to how meaning is expressed through language. (p. 119)

The information-processing approach to second language learning suggests that the human mind processes learning in two ways: Declarative learning, which is also called explicit learning, and procedural knowledge, which is also called implicit learning.

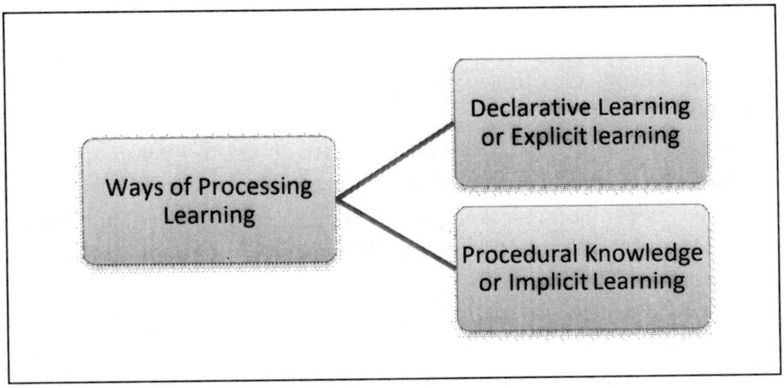

Fig. 1.3: Ways of Processing Learning

Declarative learning is self conscious or we know that we are learning, whereas procedural learning is learning from experience or the ability to use the declarative knowledge. It will get clearer with an example; Declarative learning is having the theoretical knowledge of driving a car by reading a book on it, and procedural learning is learning driving by driving a car yourself under guidance.

After continued practice, declarative learning gets converted into procedural learning, and communication skills in a second language get automated.

As cited by Lightbown and Spada in "How the language is Learned", Robert DeKeyser and others have explored that second language acquisition is skill learning, which includes automatization of Procedural knowledge tells how to perform an activity, and declarative knowledge tells what to do to perform an activity, which is related to the theoretical knowledge about that activity. As Declarative knowledge is easily communicable and evaluated, teachers use it mostly.

1.10.2 Turning Declarative Knowledge into Procedural Learning (Behaviour)

Declarative knowledge means consciously learning the grammar rules of language to produce sentences, which is also called explicit learning. Prodecural knowledge means subconsciously learning the grammar rules of language to produce sentences effortlessly, which is called implicit learning. For example, think about a car driver who is thinking and planning each move before actually making it. And with practice, he is able to drive the car effortlessly, skipping the thinking and planning mode and directly driving the car. Now his procedural knowledge is automated, and he forgets what he once learned explicitly.

Now the question is how to convert declarative knowledge into procedural knowledge through practice. In this context, Gatbonton & Segalowitz (2005) propose that students use language in genuine interactions. We present a specific approach to show not only how communicatively based automatization can work in principle but also how other means of promoting learning (e.g., explicit explanation of and practice of forms) can be integrated into a CLT framework without undermining its communicative character. Teachers believe in the strengths and outcomes of the CLT approach in English Language classrooms, but they are still very reluctant to use this approach in their classrooms. They mentioned the common reason for teachers not getting the right learning value from communicative activities. They explained that mostly teachers are not taking the real teaching with activities such as 'games', 'role play, and 'problem solving' and are still using the set pattern of teaching activities like teaching grammar rules, conducting drills, and teaching vocabulary lists. They also clarified that the main goal of CLT is to expose students to incomprehensible input so that they can use the language in genuine interactions.

The assumption used in many language instruction programs is that once the learners have learned the information, they will be able to use it through reading, writing, listening, and speaking. The disadvantage of this approach is that, having been trained to learn the language through "knowing" (competence), learners have difficulty actually "doing" (performance) something with the language.

In order to shift the focus of the learners more on the "doing" part of learning, which allows a more accurate measure of learners' language proficiency, a more communicative approach to teaching can be used. This type of approach concentrates on getting learners to do things with the language.

Sreehari (2012) discusses one retraining programme for English teachers teaching undergraduate students in colleges in Andhra Pradesh, India. This programme was conducted by the Directorate of Collegiate Education, AP, and the US State Department English Language Fellow Program, which aimed to upgrade teachers abilities to adapt the Communicative Language Teaching approach in their teaching, which further enhances the English language skills of students. He also emphasizes that due to the establishment of the Business Process Outsourcing industry (BPO) in India, the potentiality and importance of the English language have increased, especially for graduates because of the attractive salary they pay, which further increases their employability potential.

Sasstos (2020) cites Savignon's (1987) and his ideas of CLT (2002) and explains that the core principle of the CLT approach to learn the language to learn to use the language, but not the knowledge of the language. The main goal of the Communicative Language Approach is to make students proficient in the communication skills of the target language.

As the Structural method provides drill-based language activities, it is not apt for developing the communicative competence of the learners. Farooq (2015) rightly emphasized that in CLT, the focus on language teaching shifted from drill-based language activities to communicative-based activities to provide a natural growth of language ability.

Toro V. et al. (2019) confirmed that through CLT, students get a lot of opportunities or exposure to produce or use the language in real communicative contexts where they can exchange real information, which further motivates them to communicate verbally.

Sreehari (2012) suggested a variety of activities for integrating CLT in language classrooms, such as role plays, language games, interviews, information gap activities, discussions, problem solving tasks, language learning simulations, quizzes, and surveys. In these activities, focus is given to developing language skills in authentic contexts.

Abbas, Aslam & Yasmeen (2011) suggested a good way to integrate CLT with the local culture. Local culture must be appropriately integrated, and for this, teachers must be enabled or trained in the understanding of similarities and variations between the local and target cultures and handle the content or make tailor made or customized authentic material for their learners. If local culture is given appropriate importance, it can be an authentic aid rather than a hindrance to language learning. Chawla (2017) supported the same views by concluding that teachers should use "authentic material" such as wrappers, post cards, menu cards, metro time tables or maps, brochures related to health, or flyers of an event that the school is hosting to integrate the culture of learners into the classroom.

1.11 TASK BASED LANGUAGE TEACHING: SUBSET OF CLT

A method of instruction known as "Task-Based Language Teaching" (TBLT) emphasises the usage of the target language in real-world situations. TBLT, which is also known as task-based instruction (TBI), is regarded as a subset of communicative language teaching (CLT). The main idea in TBLT revolves around the task. Learning is evaluated on the basis of how well students complete tasks, not just how well they use the target language. For this reason, TBLT is seen as useful in helping students build their confidence and acquire fluency in the target language.

Nunan (1989) defines task as

"The communicative task is a piece of classroom work that involves learners comprehending, manipulating, producing, or interacting in the target language while their attention is principally focused on meaning rather than form. The task should also have a sense of completeness, being able to stand alone as a communicative act in its own right."

Richards & Rodgers (1986) underlined the assumptions in the TBLT method about the nature of language and the nature of learning:

Nature of language:

1. Language is primarily a means of making meaning.
2. Language is a means of achieving real-world goals.
3. Lexical units are central to language use and language learning.
4. Spoken interaction is the central focus of language and the keystone of language acquisition.
5. Language use involves integration of skills.

Nature of Learning in TBLT:

1. Language learning is determined by learner's internal rather than external factors. Learning is promoted by activating internal acquisition processes.
2. Language learning is an organic process.
3. A focus on form can facilitate language learning.
4. Negotiation of meaning provides learners with opportunities for provision of comprehensible input and modified output.
5. Tasks provide opportunities for learners to notice the gap.
6. Interaction and communication through tasks provide opportunities for scaffolding learning. Task activity and achievement are motivational.
7. Learning difficulties can be negotiated and fine-tuned for particular pedagogical purposes.

1.11.1 Designing of TBLT content

(a) Objectives

In TBLT, objectives are made according to the needs of the learners. For that, the teacher has to do a need analysis with the help of a questionnaire or interview. The need analysis helps to decide the learners' needs and the domains and situations on which the language course focuses. These objectives reflect the real-world needs of the learners. On the basis of the learners' needs, tasks are selected. The selection of tasks for a TBLT curriculum is based on how well they allow for meaningful discussion and engagement with topics and activities that are engaging and meaningful to the learners.

(b) The Syllabus

The assignments or tasks that the students are supposed to do are the main components of a TBLT syllabus, which are chosen on the basis of need analysis. Nunan (1989) contends that two different kinds of tasks can be used to create a task-based syllabus.

- **(i) Real-World Tasks**: These tasks are intended to practice or rehearse those tasks that are vital and useful in the real world and are discovered to be important in a need analysis. This would be the case with adult learners who have clearly defined needs.
- **(ii) Pedagogical Tasks:** These tasks are for learners who do not have defined needs, like young learners or children. These are the classroom activities, such as information gap activities or problem solving tasks, that develop the skills needed to do the tasks. The functions and language needed to perform the pedagogical tasks become the basis for designing the syllabus.

TBLT-based content can be developed using six principles, as mentioned by Nunan (2014, p. 459),

1. Make a list of the tasks that students will actually or potentially need to complete outside of the classroom. Then transform these into instructional tasks that require students to grasp, work with, produce, or interact in the target language in order to obtain a non-linguistic result.
2. Instead of learning and memorization, language users acquire the ability to speak a language by actually using it.
3. The learning process is heavily dependent on the individual experiences of the learners.
4. In addition to language content, learning processes and methods are emphasised.
5. Outside-of-classroom learning is systematically linked to classroom language learning
6. Students are exposed to authentic listening and reading texts.

(c) Types of Learning and Teaching Activities

Willis, in Richards & Rodgers (2001, p. 186) proposed that in TBLT, classroom activities provide opportunities to learn language by engaging adult learners with specific needs in task work that they will perform in their real world. They will learn about the language (both receptive and productive aspects) that they need to perform those communicative tasks. On the other hand, pedagogical tasks may be used for teaching young learners' with no identifiable needs. These pedagogical tasks can be of many types: Jigsaw tasks, information gap tasks, problem-solving tasks, decision-making tasks, opinion exchange tasks, etc.

(d) Learner's role

Learners are supposed to play some primary and active roles in TBLT to execute and complete the communicative tasks. The learners in TBLT are engaged in pair or small group activities instead of individual work. They have to monitor how language is used in communication. They need to not only complete the tasks but also pay attention to the form in which the messages are communicated. Many times, learners have to create and infer messages about which they have little idea. So in those cases, learners need to make guesses based on linguistic and contextual hints, clarify, and consult with other learners.

(e) Teacher's Role

Van den Branden, in Richards & Rodgers (2001, p. 187) defines some roles for teachers in TBLT. The teacher motivates the learners throughout the whole task activity. He/she organises the task activity efficiently by giving clear instructions, preparing learners for task performance through pre-task activities, helping learners recall or learn useful vocabulary for the completion of tasks, or using implicit or explicit cuing. The teacher's role is not merely limited to giving tasks to learners but also to observe and monitor their performance and intervene in between if required.

(f) The Role of Instructional Materials

Instructional material supplies the appropriate resources for the practice of authentic tasks to be used as classroom tasks and is hence very important in TBLT. There are two important key points about the instructional material that need to be taken care of in TBLT: authentic material as a resource for creating classroom tasks and the creativity and imagination of the teacher to use those authentic material to develop instructions in Task based language teaching. The media that can supply rich sources for such material are newspapers, television, the internet, and many more.

(g) Procedure

Different types of tasks are to be used in TBLT to make learners efficient in language usage in a particular method or procedure. Van Gorp and Bogaert (2006), cited in Richards & Rodgers (2019, p. 190) describe the chain of activities in task-based lessons. The lesson is divided into three phases and shown on Table 1.3 below:

Table 1.3: Three Phases of Task-Based Language Teaching

Phase 1: Introducing the task	Phase 2: Supporting task performance	Phase 3: The Post-Task Phase
•Teacher motivates learners to perform the task •Teacher discusses pre-supposed knowledge related to the task •Teacher gives clear instructions on the purpose of the task and how it will be carried out.	•teacher mediates between the task demands and the learner's current abilities •Clarifies meaning or guiding for the choice of language to the learners •incoporating meaning with form.	•Reflection on the task •Focus on form

Moreover, a variety of different lessons in TBLT format are available depending on the needs and environment of the learners.

1.11.2 TBLT - ACCESS Methodology

Gatbonton & Segalowitz (2005) added the important component of automization to TBLT Design. They proposed the methodology of ACCESS to design the task or activities in which automitization of fluency and accuracy of the English language and other means of learning like explicit learning and practice of forms can be incorporated into the CLT framework, i.e., the principle of communication, to attain the objectives of English Language Teaching. ACCESS stands for Automatization in Communicative Contexts of Essential Speech Segments. ACCESS guarantees that the essential speech segment, i.e., a targeted set of utterances, can be presented to students and practiced in a genuinely communicative context so that students can use them with greater accuracy and fluency.

Dao et al. (2016) rightly explained how the promotion of automatization takes place in ACEESS according to three main criteria:

1. Genuinely communicative need refers to the task in which information needs to be exchanged among the learners to continue the task and the learners are fully involved in a real communicative context. These language utterances produced and heard

by the learners can be recovered and used in different communicative contexts.

2. Inherent repetition means the inclusion of repetition of events or utterances to complete the task, which in turn, leads to the automaticity of language reception and production.
3. Formulaic function – It means the use of useful utterances learned in the task in different real-life communicative contexts.

These three phases ensure that many examples of the language will be presented, and students will use them repeatedly in a communicative context. So to develop the lesson plan for the English language classroom, a teacher can make use of this reformulated TBLT-ACCESS interaction based methodology, which ensures the automatization of accuracy as well as fluency, two important elements of language in learners.

Swain and Lapkin (2002, p. 119) in the book *How Languages are Learned* pointed out that from Swain's comprehensible output hypothesis and the idea that when learners are required to produce language, they must pay more attention to how meaning is expressed through language than they typically do for the comprehension of language. Swain also recommended the use of appropriate contextual learning in the English language, where language use and language learning can occur simultaneously. Nesa (2019) also supported the use of the ACCESS methodology for designing the English language acquisition activity in which students get authentically involved. She advocated more opportunities for learners to engage in verbal production.

CLT is considered an approach and not a method since it is compatible with many teaching methods. There is no specific teaching methodology available for CLT. The availability of a teaching methodology would be typical for a method (Richards & Rodgers 2007, p. 172). As the Structural method provides drill-based language activities, it is not apt for developing the communicative competence of the learners.

1.12 ANDRAGOGY

Andragogy is also popular, with names like "adult education" and "adult learning". Andragogy is an interdisciplinary field incorporating education and psychology that focuses on how adults learn. There is a difference between how children learn and how adults learn. The science of teaching children is called pedagogy, whereas teaching adults is called andragogy. With the aid of andragogy, educators can better understand adult learners' needs and how to create a stimulating learning environment for them. A number of authors have argued that adults have specific traits that influence how they approach and learn. The six traits that Knowles (1990) listed for adult learners are perhaps the most frequently referenced ones:

1. Adults must understand why they are learning. They are very clear about the objectives of their learning.
2. Adults view themselves as mature, self-reliant individuals. By giving adult learners the freedom to take the initiative and decide what they want to study, andragogy promotes independent learning. This gives students a sense of control over their learning process.
3. Adults bring a wealth of experience to post-secondary education.
4. When they are ready to learn, adults are likely to decide to do so. It means adult students study on their terms and at their own pace. Students don't simply rely on an instructor or other authority to guide them through their learning, as they are responsible for their learning outcomes.
5. Adult learners focus on solving problems.
6. Learning happens when internal factors motivate adult students. They learn because they require that knowledge or skill to excel in their real-life activities. Here, learning is not taking place because a teacher or curriculum is demanding it. It deals with the learner's life.

There are also other principles of adult learning, such as:

1. Learning is an active process, so good learning materials focus on learner activities rather than on exposition and explanation.
2. Learning tasks should always be meaningful to the learner.
3. Learning tasks should always match the assumed prior knowledge of the learners.
4. Learning requires feedback: Learners need to know whether they have learned something correctly and therefore need regular feedback on their progress.
5. Learning is enhanced by examples: learners can better understand and remember important points when presented with suitable examples.
6. Learners actively participate in the process of their learning as they are engaged with their surroundings. As a result, learning becomes fun and meaningful for the students.

In this study, the researcher has developed self-learning instructional material for English language acquisition skills for undergraduate adult learners who study through distance education by employing the principles of andragogy.

1.13 INTEGRATED SKILLS OF ENGLISH LANGUAGE

The term "integrated skills" refers to a teaching methodology that combines the four language skills of listening, speaking, reading, and writing in order to help students become more proficient communicators and better able to use English to access social, professional, educational, and/or occupational opportunities. As we can see in our daily lives, communication or interaction happens only when we use all four skills of language simultaneously. In classrooms, some teachers separate language skills and only emphasize one of them at a time. But even if it were possible to master one or two language skills early on without the other language skills, it does not guarantee genuine communication using the language, which requires the simultaneous use of both communicative and language skills. Consequently, despite knowing the rules and grammar of the target language, the students were unable to converse using it.

All four skills of the language—reading, listening, speaking, and writing—have to be dealt with inclusively to ensure effective language development. National Education Policy 2020 also emphasized the integration of these four skills of language to attain one of the skills of the 21st century. 21st century skills are classified into three categories: learning and innovation skills, literacy skills, and life skills. Pardede (2020) defines learning and innovation skills as the mental processes necessary to adjust to and enhance a modern work environment. The ability to distinguish between facts, publication sources, and the technology underlying them is referred to as literacy skills, sometimes known as IMT skills (information literacy, media literacy, and technology literacy). The intangible aspects of each person's daily life, such as their personal and professional qualities, are the focus of life skills.

In Communicative Language Teaching (CLT), unlike traditional teaching, which has a segregated language skills approach, all language skills are presented side by side in an integrated way so that learners can become fluent in the language they are studying as well as use it naturally in conversation.

Teachers can use task-based language instruction (TBLT) and content-based instruction (CBI) to support the integrated skills approach. In CBI, students engage in highly integrated communicative language practise while they study the subject matter and participate in activities that are focused on a particular subject, such as education, culture, literature, or science. In CBI, a subject matter issue or theme is used as a fundamental building block to assemble linguistic abilities. Language abilities are thus threaded across the common subject or issue being studied. Students participate in communicative tasks in the target language, which are tasks that call for understanding, generating, manipulating, or interacting in real language with a focus more on meaning than on form. Students are required to work in groups or pairs to perform tasks or produce products in order to improve their language abilities. Al-Mohammadi & Derbel (2015) also explained that the two advocates of the integrated-skill model are CBI and TBL, which strive to integrate all four language skills and have several benefits for both students and teachers. It allows the students to experience real language use, face the difficulties of conversing informally in the target language, and comprehend the difficulties of utilizing the English language for communication in an authentic setting.

1.13.1 Macro skills: Listening, Reading, Speaking, and Writing

Reading, listening, speaking, and writing are the basic skills of the English language and are called the macro skills. The following two factors, according to Aydogan (2014), connect these four fundamental skills to one another:

- The mode of communication - oral or written and
- The direction of communication - receptive and productive

1.13.1.1 Listening and Speaking Skills

In the oral mode of communication, listening is the receptive skill, and speaking is the productive skill. In listening, we hear what is being said and comprehend it. To communicate effectively, you must first listen. Messages are readily misconstrued if one lacks the skill to listen effectively. As a result, there is a breakdown in communication, and the message sender may become upset or dissatisfied. Instead of being passive spectators, learners who are actively listening are better able to assimilate the information and engage with the material.

Speaking is another useful skill. It is more difficult than it initially appears to be and entails more than just word pronunciation. Sengupta (2021) rightly argued that speaking should be the core of English language teaching classrooms, but, in reality, it is a neglected area of language development. It is imperative for teachers to incorporate as much oral activity as possible, and another important aspect is to align those oral activities with the content taught. Students need extensive exposure to authentic language and oral practice simultaneously to aid their speaking skills. In line with this, Abdelmageed & Omer (2020) conclude, "The communicative approach focuses on a balance between fluency and accuracy and is the most suitable for those students whose aim is to gain confidence in speaking and conversational abilities. Nevertheless, speaking in a foreign language has often been seen as the most difficult of the four skills."

Eddie & Aziz (2020), through the literature review they did, revealed many factors that inhibited the speaking interactions in the students like the fear of speaking in English, limited opportunities to speak in the language, discomfort in communicating with opposite gender, stress from families, learners' fear of being made fun of or feel insecure when speaking to more knowledgeable speakers, exam achievement anxiety (Tati, Paul and Golingi, 2016); the minimal use and familiarity of English language among young students (Cheng, Yunus & Mohamad, 2016); students receiving a harsh judgment did not view their speech mistakes as a regular part of the learning process but rather as a disruption to their reputation and a source of entertainment from the teacher or their peers (Ansari, 2015).

Speaking and listening are frequently linked. In line with this, the strong connection between listening and speaking is also emphasised by Temple and Gillet (1984, as cited in Aydoan, 2014) in the following way: It is impossible to separate oral communication's expressive components from listening. It is not possible to "teach listening" apart from speaking or to devote only a small fraction of the class period to listening education. In group debates, dramatic performances, or puppet shows, for example, listening is just as important as the dialogues and activities produced. Children's ability to listen with appreciation and receptivity grows along with their communication skills.

In this regard, Kerry (1982), as cited in *Five Components of Effective Oral Language Instruction*, Professional Development Service for Teachers, Dublin, recommended teachers ask open ended questions rather than focus on giving instructions, providing information, or correcting information, which only allows children to recall information.

1.13.1.2 Reading and Writing Skills

In the written mode of communication, reading is the receptive skill, and writing is the productive skill. The capacity to read, comprehend, and remember what you are reading is known as reading comprehension. You can absorb the main ideas from the author's material when you comprehend what you're reading. Knowing the language that is being used and being able to understand it - both necessary for reading comprehension. Reading can assist students in developing a vocabulary that is especially helpful for later levels of listening comprehension.

Writing often appears to be the most difficult of the skills, even for native speakers, because it entails not only the graphic representation of speech but also the development and structured presentation of thoughts. According to Ananthi (2018), "Writing skills are the skills of graphic representation of oral production. Writing involves a number of micro-skills like correct word order, using the right vocabulary, correct grammar, keeping writing cohesive and coherent, etc." Teachers are required to pay attention to developing these micro-skills so that students can convey their ideas clearly to a particular audience. He also observed that most of the graduate students have poor writing skills, and one of the reasons is that teachers do not pay enough attention to the students' writing skills. In the secondary classes, teachers are used to teach students to write as per the layout, spelling, and standard of correctness. Students are not taught to have their own voice and write about it in their writing at any level; rather, they follow only the pre-determined layout and standard and some particular phrases to write something down. Since, the students are not involved in their writings, they do not enjoy the writing task. They rather imitate the writing model presented before them. Students should learn to communicate, not only to write.

1.13.2 Microskills: Vocabulary and Grammar

All aspects of communication—listening, speaking, reading, and writing—benefit from a strong vocabulary. For the following reasons, vocabulary is essential to a child's success: Gaining vocabulary has a direct correlation with academic success. The capacity to learn to read is predicted by a child's kindergarten vocabulary.

Grammar is important because it provides information that helps the reader's comprehension. It is the structure that conveys precise meaning from the writer to the audience. Eliminate grammatical errors from your writing, and reward your readers with clear communication. The conclusions young students can draw from grammar studies teach them the valuable tool of deductive reasoning. In fact, it is through grammatical structure that people learn how to create strong arguments.

To be an effective language user, learners should study grammar because grammar skills will help them organize words and messages and make them meaningful. Knowing more about grammar will enable learners to build better sentences in their speaking and writing performances.

In an interview with Brian Tomlison (2021), he emphasized the importance of learning vocabulary as compared to grammar in the initial stages of learning. In the natural acquisition of a first language, learning grammar gets delayed for a long time, and learning vocabulary is emphasized. If you have a good vocabulary, you can communicate, and if you don't have a vocabulary and know grammar, you cannot communicate. When people learn naturally, listening is what they do initially. They spend a lot of time listening to the language before they can eventually produce it, but in L2, we always start by teaching them to speak the language directly.

1.14 EXPOSURE TO ENGLISH LANGUAGE: AUTHENTIC MATERIAL

Al-Zoubi (2018) defined exposure to language as the contact that the learners have with the target language. Inside the classroom, it's the role of the teacher to provide learners with sufficient exposure so that they can practice the target language in a variety of contexts. The teachers can give practical examples of language by using natural input from television, cassettes, video, web sites, books, and magazines. Mainly, language exposure in general, refers to contact outside the classroom. The forms of outside classroom language exposure can include: listening to English programme on the radio, watching English programme and movies on the television, traveling to English speaking countries, talking face to face with English native speakers (L2 interaction), using English language in real life situations, surfing the internet using English language as well as, reading English books, magazines, and newspapers.

Materials that are authentic were made for a purpose other than language study, and they are frequently, but not always, supplied by native speakers for native speakers. Or, in other words, anything written in English that was not intended for use in a classroom setting is considered authentic material. The English language learning process can be made even more interesting, creative, and motivational for pupils by using authentic material. Sreehari (2012) defined authentic materials as materials that give learners the feel of using real life language. Authentic materials serve as a tool for creating an authentic context to develop communicative skills. Authentic materials can include audio, audiovisual, and printed materials. Examples of these include TV news and programs, TV and radio commercials, music, movies, announcements at public places such as railway stations, airports, supermarkets, newspapers, magazines, photographs, paintings, drawings, stamps, currencies, restaurant menus, street signs, product labels, tourist information brochures, catalogs, telephone books, greeting cards, letters, memos, circulars, minutes of meetings, reports, billboards, notices, forms such as applications and tax forms, podcasting on the internet, and web based programs involving multimedia use. Authentic materials can be used both as a source of input for new languages and as the basis for their practical usage.

Septiyana (2019) proposed that teaching material plays a crucial and important role in the teaching and learning process, especially in distance education, as it has methods that create a conducive environment for the students to learn independently, and hence their learning improves.

Toro V. et al. (2019) clarified the importance of authentic materials, as they are naturally more interesting and motivating than materials that are not authentic. The use of authentic material as teaching learning material helps increase the chances of interaction among learners in the target language. For example, the use of TV and visual media can be considered not only tools for entertainment but also pedagogical technology.

Abbas, Aslam, & Yasmeen (2011) reveal a different and broad aspect of authentic material. They defined authentic materials as those resources that occur in the natural setting of the learners or are best obtained from the culture of the learners. For example, reading taken from real brochures, magazines, advertisements, and local newspapers, which consist of communication in real life situations from the learners' culture, Furthermore, learners should be given writing or speaking tasks about their own cultural issues like fashion, traffic problems, internet problems, education, friends, weddings, and dialogues between friends in the market. Reading materials can be taken from the local newspaper. For listening, learners can have their cultured English news, documentaries, recorded material from social contexts, and English movies depicting their local culture. For a deep understanding of this concept of integrated CLT with local culture or creating authentic material from learners' own culture, a good example has been given in the context of Indian schools, where learners' should be given the reading material - the usual subjects that we discuss in conversations with friends, on the street, and in interviews should also be used in spoken and written communication. Teachers might instruct their students to speak about local and cultural individuals, events, and objects. They could discuss Narendra Modi, for instance, more easily than Toni Morison.

Sengupta (2021) pointed out that by using authentic material in the classroom to develop English language skills, students are introduced to language used by real speakers rather than scripted, simplified, or unnatural material. This prepares them for the language they are likely to hear and use outside the classroom. Teachers are largely dependent on the prescribed textbook as a resource to develop the students' English language proficiency and give the students structured questions to practice given in the textbook. For ESL students in the School of Open Learning, self-learning instructional material is the only primary source of comprehensible input, so it should provide numerous exposures to learn new vocabulary in meaningful ways, for which authentic materials available in our immediate surroundings can be very helpful.

Richards & Rodgers (2006) consider four kinds of instructional materials apt for CLT: Text-based materials, task-based materials, Realia-based materials, and Technology- supported materials. They also asserted the incorporation of technology into ELT lessons because it gives students access to authentic language input that combines texts, images, audio, and video. Online tools that can promote real encounters include chat rooms, message boards, and teleconferences.

1.15 COMMUNICATIVE ACTIVITIES

"The development of effective communication skills means not only linguistic proficiency but also social and interpersonal skills to make contextual use of grammatically correct structures" (John, 2020). She discusses some Communicative Language Teaching (CLT) activities designed on the principles of Task Based Language Teaching (TBLT) that can be used to enhance the English language communicative ability of adult learners:

- conducting a mock interview or making an enquiry at an office;
- Opinion sharing activities: list out the qualities required to be a good teacher, manager, or professional HR Consultant.
- Task completion activities: Multimedia and technology can also be used to initiate the task; for example, video clippings shall be shown to the students without the audio, and the students have to come up with possible dialogues for the characters.
- Product Launch: Giving a presentation for launching a new product with two unique features
- Jigsaw activities: students collect the missing information from the other groups and complete the activity given to them.

Activities based on the communicative approach engage learners in real communication. It involves classroom activities that are focused on completing tasks, the negotiation of information, and information sharing that is mediated through language like in real-life situations. (Richards 2006, p. 96). Common CLT activities include jig-saw activities, task completion activities, information-gathering activities, opinion-sharing activities, information-transfer activities, reasoning gap activities, and role play.

1.16 DIGITAL TECHNOLOGY IN ENGLISH LANGUAGE TEACHING (ELT)

The revolution brought by computers and communication technology has been impacting the pedagogical nature of instruction, especially in English language teaching. ICT pervades all the disciplines of education as it is compatible with other media options, it helps teachers and learners record, store, analyze, and communicate words and figures with equal agility, and it absorbs text, sounds, still pictures, and meaningful images. These features of ICT have motivated educators to prepare self- learning instructional material using multimedia applications. Singh et al. (2011) define multimedia as "an exciting combination of computer hardware and software that allows you to integrate video, animation, audio, graphics, and test resources to develop effective presentations on an affordable desktop." They concluded from their study that the developed material, integrated with the World Wide Web, will provide a good interactive learning environment and bring improvement rather than being a substitute for traditional instruction material and methods. It will allow self-paced, independent learning and change the role of the instructor from 'Guide by the Side' to 'Guide behind the Screen'. In the era of Information Technology, it seems that the future belongs to computer based interactive multimedia modules.

Sokolik (2016) defines the term 'digital technology' as the technology that relies on computer chips, which ranges from an overhead projector to a desktop computer to a mobile device, from databases to software programs to the web pages that users access.

In the 1990s, with the advent of the Internet, stand-alone programs like *TestMaster* and *HyperCard*, video-based listening like *Real English Interactive, and* games like *Oregon Trail* were collectively called computer-assisted language learning (CALL). In 1994, there was the expansion of CALL with the World Wide Web (WWW), and as a result, CALL began to play an important role in innovative pedagogical practices. After that, many educators and students mastered HTML and started making their own webpages, consequently changing student-centered teaching to a more participatory platform. Now teachers can create their own materials on the web.

With the emergence of Web 2.0 in the 2000s, came the dramatic impact on teaching and learning practices through social media and social networking. Web 2.0 provides the users with autonomy in the creation of content with tools like blogs, wikis, video sites like YouTube, social networking sites like Facebook and Twitter, LinkedIn, ebooks, and many more. It facilitates communication between the users synchronously (at the same time) via text, voice, and video chats or indirectly asynchronously (at different times) via email, written comments.

Technology integration means the meaningful use of technology to achieve learning goals. Technology is necessary for holistic teaching and learning. Aykut (2008) emphasized the importance of technology in ELT and listed many advantages, like

- When listening and seeing are combined, as they are in the actual world, a more genuine learning environment is generated.
- The variety of media makes it easy to combine reading, writing, speaking, and listening in a single activity, which facilitates skill integration.
- Students have a significant deal of control over their education (autonomy), as they can not only go at their own pace but also follow their own unique path, moving forward and backward through the programme, focusing on some components while omitting others entirely.
- Technology enables a fundamental concentration on the content without sacrificing a secondary emphasis on language structure or study methods.

The use of ICT by teachers to make the learning process more engaging while maintaining the authenticity of the subject is known as ICT integration. Using technology to finish, complete, and aid the teaching-learning process is known as technology integration. According to Ahmadi (2018), due to its benefits for teachers and its ability to promote students' learning development, technology has become a crucial instrument in the English teaching-learning process in EFL classes. It led to the development of language skills in students and knowledge and self-efficacy in teachers. He added that as technology integration in the teaching-learning process is used, the class will become more engaging and appealing, and learners will be in charge of their own development, leading to meaningful learning. He went on to say that using technology allows students to learn independently in English, which is beneficial for their English language development.

Nesa (2019) notes the importance of the teacher's role and technology as a resource in English language acquisition. The main core is the task design, which actively engages the student rather than the resource. Computer technology serves as a tool for providing authentic language exposure, but the main part is the design of the applied language learning activity that motivates the learner to participate actively and promote genuine language use.

Vadivel (2018) emphasized the use and importance of already available mobile technologies and learning platforms on the Internet that can become the major resource for English language exposure, like Ted Talks, YouTube, watching English Movies with subtitles/ without subtitles, listening to native English conversation, English learning apps in the play store, Andy- auto responder robot app, Future Learning/ Coursera. He also suggested some language learning activities to be encouraged in the classroom by the teacher, like reading Short Stories, initiating thinking process in English, listening to others, preparing for Presentation in classrooms, role-play, mock Interview, etc.

Sokolok (2016), in her book *Teaching English as a Second or Foreign Language,* gives many ideas for the ELT classroom application of TELL (Technology-assisted Language learning) that can be implemented to enhance the

- Reading and writing skills via supplying authentic reading material, email, chat, blogs, wikis, and social networking sites;
- Listening skills via podcasts, talk radio broadcasts, interviews, and audio books;
- Speaking skills via Audacity, which is a free program that allows users to record their voice, insert comments, and edit the audio file;
- Presentation tools like PowerPoint Presentation;
- Grammar and vocabulary skills via grammar checker software, repetition exercises, online and electronic dictionaries, etc.

1.16.1 Role of Media in Self-Learning Instructional Material

Tiarina et al. (2019) assert that the use of technology and media gives ample opportunities for students to master the content, and moreover, it also increases their motivation to learn. The self-learning instructional material should promote verbal, visual, and kinesthetic learning for all types of learners, including slow and fast learners, therefore reflecting students' needs. To achieve this purpose, one should develop teaching material with interactive multimedia that includes variety of media like text, sound, voice, photos, graphs, maps, etc. Tiarina et al. (2019) stated that the use of media in the teaching and learning process is an innovation that aims to increase the learner's motivation towards learning.

Afsyah (2019) listed the benefits of the inclusion of media to facilitate the learning processes and outcomes for students as well as teachers in many ways:

- Simplify the presentation of messages and information
- Increase and direct the attention of the students
- Motivate students to learn
- Direct interaction between students and their environment
- Students learn independently
- Overcome sensory limitations, space and time

Mittal (2022) also argues that in distance education, ICT and its dynamic and innovative applications provide improved quality and sustainability in education and offer a vigorous learning experience. If the teacher uses these available educational technologies appropriately, it becomes easy to engage students actively, even in distance education.

The most recent media and technological advancement in distance learning is web- based learning, which replaced the print technology used in conventional correspondence education that was sent through text media. Commonly, the phrases "media" and "technology" cause confusion. These two terms are frequently regarded as synonyms. Santosh (2006) describes the distinction between the definitions of "media" and "technology."

- The word "media" refers to communication methods and knowledge representation. For instance, the five media—human contact, text, audio, video, and computing—all have distinctive organizational and presentational strategies that can be expressed in a range of ways or styles. These platforms enable conversations, transmit ideas, and promote self-education.
- Each of these media can be communicated using a variety of technologies, but they must also be transmitted using the right ones. Hardware and media message delivery systems are the main topics in technology. Print, audio and video cassettes, satellite, cable, broadcasting, video discs, video conferencing, and computers are a few examples of technologies that aid in the transmission of media messages. Other examples include other forms of communication such as print, cable, satellite, and broadcasting.

In this context, students who study English as a language in their first semester of BA (programme) and B.com (programme) in the School of Open Learning, 12 years of traditional schooling and taking one English class each year, are struggling to construct complete sentences in the

English language. With the habit of memorizing languages, students are even unable to understand English-language textbooks. In order to engage SOL students in language activities that encourage autonomous thought and authentic language use, self-learning instructional material for English language acquisition skills needs to be developed. In this research, the **Communicative Language Teaching (CLT)** approach will be used to improve the English language acquisition skills of students. In CLT, the English language is taught in a way that will help students use the target language in their everyday lives for communication, since communication is the only primary function of any language. Students are not supposed to memorize the rules and structure of grammar. Students have been learning and memorizing these grammar rules and lexical structures for 7-8 years of their lives in their schools, but they are still hesitant and afraid of communicating in English in their everyday lives. In CLT, the focus is not on using accurate rules of language but accurate communicative competence. CLT focuses more on the development of skills or talent to use the target language for communicating in real life situations than on a mastery of the structures of that language.

The design of self-learning instructional material for English language acquisition skills is based on Task Based Language Teaching (TBLT). The material is developed on a theme based approach; units are based on themes such as Travel, Entertainment, Food and Health, Working with Technology, and the workplace. Learners are engaged with authentic or naturalistic texts, and they are required to analyze the language into its component parts. This self-learning instructional material provides the students with their major source of contact with the language. In this, authentic materials are used over created materials, as authentic materials contain authentic language and reflect real-world use of language compared with the contrived content of much created material. The material is planned based on the need analysis, which provides the pathway to designing it in accordance with the real needs of the students. Another interesting component of this material is the use of accessible and free technology that enables the researcher to help students develop their language skills with ease and effectiveness. This material provides many different language practice exercises for all language skills. Mishra & Gaba (2001), citing IGNOU, defined activities as things that are asked the learners to do to let them engage in active learning, along with reading the self-learning instructional material or watching or listening to audio-video programmes. Activities include questions or tasks that help the learners apply the learning in real-life situations and think critically. They themselves regarded activities as an important element of the self-learning instructional material in distance education for complete learning. Distance education should include entertaining and motivating content that would increase students' interest in the process.

1.17 DEVELOPMENT OF SELF-LEARNING INSTRUCTIONAL MATERIAL FOR ENGLISH LANGUAGE ACQUISITION SKILLS

For distance education students, self-learning instructional material is the only tool to provide exposure or stimulus for learning. For English language acquisition skills, self- learning instructional material using the Communicative Language Teaching approach is student-centered and focuses on teaching skills of communication by integrating the four skills of the English language through the use of multimedia to provide authentic materials on different themes as exposure to the language, and then activities are provided for their rigorous practice. The sample lesson for the self-learning instructional material for English language acquisition skills of students of School of Open Learning is given as Appendix 9.

There is the process of developing the self-learning instructional material, which involves various phases and is shown in Fig. 1.4.

Fig. 1.4: Phases of Development of Self-Learning Instructional Material

The self-learning instructional material is developed through three phases: first of all, the need analysis for the English language acquisition skills of SOL students is to be done so that accurate needs can be addressed in the developed material; then, on the basis of students' needs, topics and content for English language acquisition skills are chosen; and finally, the self-learning instructional material is developed using the Communicative

Language Teaching approach, exploring the authentic material through different media. The last phase has different steps, which are shown in the figure 1.5 below and explained further.

Fig. 1.5. Steps of Development of Self-Learning Instructional Material

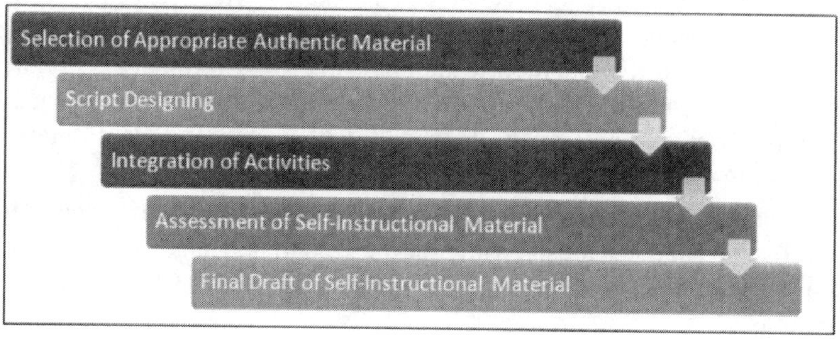

I. Selection of appropriate authentic material

In this step, the researcher chooses authentic material—communicative activities and content that the students use in their daily lives on a particular theme—from different sources like books, newspapers, cartoon magazines, TV, Podcast, radio, YouTube videos, etc. This material gives exposure to different macro and micro skills like reading, listening, speaking, and writing in an integrated manner.

II. Script design: After giving exposure through the selected authentic material, details of the concept or topic are explained through examples taken from the exposed material. Many more solved examples from different situations are also given to broaden the topic.

III. Integration of Activities

Many practice exercises are created to provide a full understanding of the topic and also opportunities through which the students can use the taught concept while having the conversation in English.

IV. Assessment of Self-Learning Instructional Material

After having a rough draft of the material, it was shown to the subject experts for the English and Education disciplines. Their valuable suggestions and recommendations were collected through the opinionnaire and the material was validated through this scale.

V. Final Draft of Self-Learning Instructional Material

After the validation, the final draft of the self-instructional material for English language acquisition skills is ready, incorporating the suggested changes.

1.18 RATIONALE OF THE STUDY

Chomsky (as cited in Newby, 2011), in his concept of linguistic competence and performance, concluded that there is a difference between knowing a language, which he named "competence" and using that known language in a real life situation, which he named "performance". In our English Classroom, teachers' approach must shift from the competence to the performance part of the language, which makes students more confident to use their language skills outside the classroom.

Most people think that the first language or native language is acquired naturally and subconsciously, while for the second language, you need to learn the grammar, syntax, vocabulary, and other parts of the language consciously.

Krashen (1982) differentiates between learning a language and acquiring a language, - and concludes that "Language acquisition occurs when it is used for what it was designed for- communication". Further, in his theory of second language acquisition, he tries to prove that the success of second language acquisition depends on the amount of comprehensible input that is supplied and then understood by the learner and their strength of affective filter level, which further helps them to acquire the second language.

Language should not be introduced to children as a set of rules but as the carrier of coherent textual meaning. Language is acquired well when it is taken as the combination of language form and the meaning of the messages. For this reason, NCERT (2006), in Position Paper of National Focus Group on the Teaching of English, suggests that "Input-rich communicational environments are a prerequisite for language learning".

As Prabhu (1988) also showed, the systematic learning of the rules and structures of language is not required for acquiring a second language. He developed a series of problem solving tasks that engaged learners in negotiated discourse, focusing on the message rather than the language codes.

In this research, effective self-learning instructional material was prepared on the basis of communicative language teaching so that students get rich exposure to comprehensible inputs or an input rich environment in the form of different task-based and problem solving activities that they actually use in their everyday lives. It provides them with opportunities to develop skills and the confidence to use the English language in their everyday lives.

Each language has four skills: reading, listening, speaking, and writing. Reading and listening are the receptive skills, and speaking and writing are the productive skills. Good reading and listening skills are the foundation of good speaking and writing skills. If a person is a good listener and reader, then he is likely to have better speaking and writing skills. So in this research, the focus is on providing students with effective instructional material that will enhance their speaking and writing skills in the English language because, through speaking and writing skills, anybody can effectively produce a message and interact with the world.

1.19 RESEARCH GAPS

With the review of related literature of many studies, the researcher come across with few research gaps in the area of implementation of Communicative Language Teaching in distance education for the development of English language acquisition skills at the undergraduate level. These few research gapes are listed below:

1. Importance of Skills of Communication in English: The skill of communication in English is not only important for the employability skills, not only restricted with the ability to make grammatically correct sentences but also important for the development of other skills like presentation skills, convincing and negotiation skills, and interpersonal skills which further helps in effective communication. Using English language for communication also helps in personal as well as global advancement and development.
2. Policy needs to be changed in Indian Context: With the review of related literature, the researcher has found the gap in the Indian education policy in the context of English Language Teaching. Though this gap has been already addressed in the National Education Policy 2020, which emphasizes that English Language Teaching (ELT) should provided experiential learning to the learners.
3. Communicative Language Teaching (CLT) and other theories of English Language Teaching (ELT): New theories and approaches related to ELT have been developed. The focus of ELT should be to provide experiential learning that uses the current methods for the current situations of 21st century. It can be possible only through the combining the 2-3 approaches of innovative English language teaching (called eclectic) in which Communicative Language Teaching (CLT) should be the one of the main approaches.

4. Implementation of CLT in Self-Learning Instructional Material for distance education learners: The researcher adopts CLT approach in developing SLIM for students of distance education for learning communicative English. The SLIM has been prepared for the students studying in the School of Open Learning (SOL), University of Delhi.
5. Incorporation of Information and Communication Technology (ICT) Tools: To provide the motivation and active participation for the students to enhance the English language skills in the integrated way, the researcher incorporated ICT tools especially listening and speaking skills.

So, the Present Study adopted Communicative Language Teaching and other approaches with the incorporation of ICT tools to teach all the four English Language skills in the integrated manner through the Self-Learning Instructional Material for undergraduate students of School of Open Learning, University of Delhi.

1.20 STATEMENT OF THE PROBLEM

It is observed that the English language acquisition skills of SOL students are not up to the mark that society demands. Students lack confidence in exploring themselves in the outside world due to less exposure to the environment needed to develop their English language acquisition skills, despite learning English in school for 6-7 years. So the present study will be carried out to develop self-learning instructional material for English language acquisition skills (SLIM) using the Communicative Language Teaching approach to provide the students with the exposure and learning environment that make them efficient at using English for communication in the outside world. The title of the study is

"Effect of Self-Learning Instructional Material on Achievement in English Language Acquisition Skills among the Students of School of Open Learning (SOL), University of Delhi"

1.21 OPERATIONAL DEFINITIONS OF KEY TERMS

1. **Development:** Development is the means by which a human being is enabled to bring out qualitative, positive, and long-term change or improvement in him for his better well-being. In this study, the researcher will develop the instructional material that will bring out the desirable improvements in English language acquisition skills of students.

2. **Effectiveness:** Effectiveness is the ability of a tool to generate the desired outcomes. The researcher evaluates the efficacy or capability of instructional material he created in this study.
3. **Instructional materials:** These are materials that are used to create effective teaching-learning environment for the attainment of the teaching objectives. Instructional material can be living or non-living in nature.
4. **Acquisition Skills:** Acquisition skills are the positive changes in a person's ability to use language to communicate in their everyday life. A person can communicate by using the language through four skills listening, reading, speaking, and writing.

1.22 RESEARCH QUESTIONS

1. What are the challenges faced by SOL students in acquisition of Listening, Speaking, Reading, and Writing (LSRW) skills?
2. What is the pedagogical support required for the acquisition of LSRW skills for students attending SOL classes and regular classes?
3. What is the efficacy of Communicative Language Teaching (CLT) approach in enhancing communication skills of students?

1.23 OBJECTIVES OF THE STUDY

1. To compare the adjusted mean scores of Achievement in English language acquisition skills of students taught through self-learning instructional learning material and lecture method (with existing study material) by considering their pre-achievement in English language acquisition skills as covariate,
2. To compare the adjusted mean scores of Achievement in English language acquisition skills of male and female students by considering their pre- achievement in English language acquisition skills as covariates.
3. To compare the adjusted mean scores of Achievement in English language acquisition skills of male and female students taught through self-learning instructional learning material and lecture method (with existing study material) by considering their pre-achievement in English language acquisition skills as covariate
4. To analyze the perception of students' towards the new developed self-learning instructional material

1.24 HYPOTHESES OF THE STUDY

1. There is no significant difference in the adjusted mean scores of Achievement in English language acquisition skills of students taught through self-learning instructional learning material and lecture method (with existing study material) by considering their pre-achievement in English language acquisition skills as covariate.
2. There is no significant difference in the achievement in English language acquisition skills of male and female students by considering their pre-achievement in English language acquisition skills as covariates.
3. There is no significant difference in the achievement in English language acquisition skills of male and female students taught through self-learning instructional learning material and lecture method (with existing study material) by considering their pre-achievement in English language acquisition skills as covariate.
4. Self-learning instructional strategy has significant effect on students' achievement in English language acquisition skills, therefore it is hypothesised that there is a positive attitude of the students towards the self-instructional learning material.

1.25 DELIMITATION OF THE STUDY

With the limited time frame and resources, some delimitations of the study are mentioned below:

1. The study was done on the students of first year, 1st semester of B.A. (Programme) students studying in SOL who have a compulsory English subject in their course.
2. It was not possible to design the self-learning instructional material for the students studying English at all three levels. So only self-learning instructional material was designed only for the students who took the paper 'English Fluency'
3. The study was conducted on the students only at the one centre of SOL.

1.26 CHAPTERIZATION SCHEME

There are five chapters in the present study. Chapter 1, 'Introduction', includes the study's Rationale, Objectives, Hypothesis, and Delimitation. The Review of Related Literature is covered in Chapter 2. The Research Methodology, Variables Involved, Sample, Tools, Procedure, and

Statistical Techniques have all been provided in Chapter 3. The analysis and interpretation of the collected data are presented in Chapter 4. The Results, Educational Implications of the Study, and Suggestions for Additional Research of the present study are all addressed in Chapter 5.

CHAPTER - II

REVIEW OF LITERATURE

2.1 INTRODUCTION

Any research work, which means finding new knowledge, needs to be linked with existing knowledge. For this purpose, we do a review of the literature. A thorough summary of earlier research on a topic is called a literature review. Scholarly books, journals, and other sources that are pertinent to a specific field of study are examined in the literature review. These earlier studies ought to be mentioned, summarized, objectively assessed, and clarified in the review. It must help the researcher define the study's scope and offer a theoretical foundation for the investigation. The literature review reassures the reader that your work has been carefully thought out by recognising the contributions of previous researchers. It is believed that the author has read, evaluated, and incorporated any references to earlier studies in the field into the current work.

A literature review covers information that has been published in a specific field of study within a specific time frame. Although a literature review might just be a list of the sources, it often follows an organisational structure and combines summary and synthesis. It could provide a fresh interpretation of fresh and outdated perspectives.

Randolph (2009) states the purpose of writing a literature review is to provide a framework for relating new findings to previous findings. Without establishing the state of the previous research, it is impossible to establish how the new research advances the previous research.

Rowley & Slack (2004) explain that a summary of the body of research in a discipline that enables the formulation of particular research questions is known as a literature review. A literature review must consult and assess a wide variety of sources, including books, articles from scholarly and professional journals, and web-based resources. Search engines can be used to browse through bibliographic databases and online resources. Conceptual frameworks can be a helpful tool for learning about a certain subject. The phases of preparing the literature review are: scanning, taking notes, structuring the review, writing the review, and creating a bibliography.

In the present study, the researcher studied the effects of two strategies of teaching on the achievement of English language acquisition skills of undergraduate students of the School of Open Learning (SOL), University of Delhi, i.e., Self-Learning Instructional Material in English language acquisition Skills and Traditional Method. Though a lot of work has been done on the development of self-learning instructional material for English language acquisition skills abroad, very few research studies have been taken up in India so far. So, the review for the present study has been done at both the national and International levels. A review of research studies that have been taken up in the recent past is listed on the following pages.

2.2 A REVIEW OF RESEARCH STUDIES

Jailakumari (2006) evaluated the effectiveness of Task-Based Communicative Activities in Learning English Grammar by the Teacher Trainee. She found out that this innovative method of teaching English grammar would develop the various skills of learning English Grammar among the experimental group of Secondary Grade Teacher Trainees. It further revealed that these communicative activities eliminate individual differences in various skills of English grammar among the Secondary Grade Teacher Trainees. She recommended that to develop various skills in learning English grammar through tasks-based communicative activities, at the secondary, higher secondary, and teacher training levels, teachers should be given Orientation courses for three or four weeks about the ways and means of developing tasks-based communicative activities to teach different categories of English grammar and various skills in learning English grammar.

Hiep (2007), in her research article on Communicative Language Teaching concluded that when CLT theory was put into practice in the Vietnam classroom context, teachers encountered lots of problems like traditional examinations, large class sizes, students' low motivation and unequal ability to take part in independent active learning practices, and teachers' limited expertise in creating communicative activities. She suggested that by giving training, support, and assistance to the teachers in the process of making communicative techniques and activities appropriate to their students' potential can solve this issue.

Vijila (2008) conducted an experimental study to assess the effectiveness of Task-Based Communicative Activities in Developing the

Writing Skills of the Teacher Trainee. The findings of the study assure that learners at all levels may start writing flawless English if they are taught through task-based communicative activities. Because when the teachers of English adopt new and innovative pedagogic practices based on TBLT rather than follow outmoded and stereotyped traditional instructional approaches, the mistakes committed by the trainees of the experimental group in the pre-test have been decreased throughout the experiment. The task-based communicative activities have motivated the teacher trainees through the group, pair, and individual activities adopted in the class.

Sung (2010) examined the level of effectiveness and suitability of three communicative language teaching-based projects in the teaching context of first-year Chinese language classroom at a university in Utah. By the findings, the researcher suggests that to design communicative language teaching-based projects, the first step is to learn about students' needs in a particular teaching context, which is key to ensuring project success. The researcher designed the communicative language teaching-based projects like Discussion on the participants' blogs, Story writing project, Video-making project. These projects were based on the CLT concept that once the students had relevant input from the interaction with authentic materials, they were expected to progressively become independent learners who were capable of producing authentic language.

Wang (2010) studied the use of communicative language games for teaching and learning English in Taiwanese elementary schools. According to the study's findings, communicative games increase students' motivation to learn English, and communicative game activities help teachers set up situations in which students must provide information, negotiate meaning, or express their own opinions so that they are actively engaged in the use of the language. As a result, students' spoken interactions are encouraged, which has long been neglected in Taiwan's traditional English education. It was also discovered that the teachers frequently used communicative language activities, which required less preparation, did not require the classroom to be moved, and were simpler to handle as contrast to activities like debate, miming, dramatization, and computer games. This is likely due to a lack of appropriate resources, time- consuming preparation, and inadequate facilities.

Abbas, Aslam & Yasmeen (2011) suggested a good way to integrate CLT with the local culture. Local culture must be appropriately integrated, and teachers must be enabled or trained to understand the similarities and variations of the local and target cultures and handle the content or make tailor-made or customized authentic material for their learners. If local culture is given appropriate importance, it can be an authentic aid rather than a hindrance to language learning. For example, in India, students should be asked about their own Indian leaders rather than Toni Morrison.

Chang (2011) found out from the experimental study that both the Communicative Approach and the Grammar Translation Method have significantly contributed to Taiwanese grammar instruction. The Grammar Translation Method and the Communicative Approach were both used to teach two different classes. The pre- test showed that there was no difference in the two classes' grammatical proficiency, and the post-test demonstrated the stark disparity in grammatical proficiency between the two classes. Students in the Experimental Class received higher grades than those in the Control Class. The outcome demonstrated that the Grammar Translation Method's framework for teaching grammar is superior to the Communicative Approach, as the Grammar Translation Method is focused on accuracy whereas the Communicative Approach promotes fluency. The goals of English learning are accuracy and fluency. The researcher concluded that the best way to change the situation is to teach English Grammar using both approaches.

Lu & Auman (2011) emphasized that English-language magazines and periodicals could be created for teaching English and instructional materials. They explained that the magazines and periodicals, with their updated student-centered, contextually based focus, were crucial supplementary teaching materials to acquire more practical knowledge of English. This is because students are able to connect global material in the magazines to their personal lives. So they will seek out more supplemental materials about their personal, and increasingly globalized, world when they are in a supportive learning environment.

Sreehari (2012) investigated a study on teaching of English teachers trained in implementing the CLT approach by the Andhra Pradesh English Lecturers' Retraining Program at undergraduate colleges in the state of Andhra Pradesh. A total of 1500 male and female respondents were selected randomly from 35 colleges in Andhra Pradesh, and the data was collected through a structured questionnaire and classroom observation for 3-5 months. The researcher found that the majority of the students had made improvements in their reading, writing, listening, and speaking skills when the CLT approach was implemented in the English classroom.

Irmawati (2012) conducted a study on 27 students studying in the 4th semester of the English Department, Faculty of Letters, Ahmad Dahlan University, Indonesia, aiming at the application of the CLT approach that focuses on all aspects of the English skills such as reading, listening, speaking, and writing as an alternative method to teach academic writing. The results showed that the application of the communicative approach effectively improved the students' ability, specifically in the aspects of reading, vocabulary, grammar, pronunciation, and communication in English. Their holistic development was also enhanced in terms of their ability to cooperate, collaborate, socialize, and share ideas, opinions, and suggestions.

Aromdee & Jansem (2012) studied the case study on the the effectiveness of using authentic material through Communicative Language Teaching for developing basic EFL literacy among factory workers at A.T.P. Co., Ltd., Bangkok. The sample used in this study was eight factory workers, and the data was collected through ten lesson plans, a performance assessment, and an open-ended questionnaire. The findings revealed after the analysis that the post-test scores were higher than the pre-test scores of all participants, and with the open-ended questionnaire, it was found out that all the participants had a positive attitude towards using authentic material based on CLT.

Gudepu (2013) conducted a study to determine the effectiveness of the communicative approach in improving the reading skills of 200 junior and senior intermediate students, at Kakatiya Institute of Technology and Science, Warangal, Andhra Pradesh. The researcher applied a communicative approach through group discussions, debates, and individual presentations based on the reading material to see the possibility of getting unconscious learning of grammar through this approach in reading classes. It was concluded that the communicative approach was successful in producing positive learning effects based on the opinion of the majority of the students, as they showed worthwhile performance, which supports the idea that the communicative approach helps students acquire knowledge of grammar and vocabulary in addition to comprehension reading classes.

Sanaa (2013) examined how the communicative approach to teaching language is used to help students increase their speaking abilities. At the Department of English at the University of Biskra, two questionnaires are given out to professors of oral expression and second-year students in order to determine and examine their perspectives on speaking ability and communicative approach. The results of this study's data collection indicate that teaching English through CLT to students is a highly effective strategy for enhancing their speaking abilities. Last but not least, this study tried to offer some ideas, tactics, and procedures that can aid teachers in imparting speaking ability by adopting Communicative language teaching approach.

Chipili (2013) investigated the viability of using literary texts as an alternative to ESL instruction in Zambia's senior English classes in this study. Instead of using a required course book, materials were created around a short narrative book and utilized to teach ESL communicatively in senior English classes in Zambia. When investigated and compared to the required course book, it was found that the objectives of the syllabus were attained satisfactorily, which proved the effectiveness of the teaching materials based on a literary text to teach ESL skills communicatively in senior secondary schools in Zambia.

Shawer (2013) examined and assessed two teachers' communicative and non- communicative teaching practices through case studies, interviews, and participant observations to find out the reason why the CLT failed to improve the student's performance in certain contexts. The finding showed that there are no inherent issues with CLT that impede instructors from understanding it in theory and putting it into practice in the classroom. It is confirmed that Communicative classroom practices help students develop their communicative competence and four skills; whereas non- communicative classroom practices hardly help students develop them. This study reinforces that CLT should support EFL/ESL curriculum, instruction, and teacher preparation in order to promote student learning and blames instructors for CLT failures.

Saico & Zhou (2013) conducted an experiment to find out whether the application of CLT activities helps to develop the students' oral expression in the target language among the 73 first-course students at Eloy Alfaro High School. After implementing CLT activities, the results revealed that these pupils had significantly improved in both their oral and listening production. This study also indicated that the CLT activities, such as role-play, information gaps, task completion, and jigsaw puzzles, had a significant impact on the students' speaking proficiency.

Dim (2013) explored that how TBLT works as the method to teach meaningful communication in the target language. In an academic environment in Chiang Mai, Thailand, this article investigates the effects of task-based language learning combined with language acquisition techniques. This research looked into how well the task-based strategies curriculum worked to improve students' communicative English proficiency. It also looked at self-directed learning practices. The results demonstrated a substantial improvement in the students' communicative English ability in the following contexts: achievement tests, presentations, debates, classroom activities, and teacher reflection. Learners are able to complete verbal tasks with confidence, adaptability, and independence using these skills and knowledge, which promotes autonomous learning.

Spada et al. (2014) compared the effects of two types of form-focused instruction (FFI) on L2 learning and their potential contributions to the development of different types of L2 knowledge. Two groups of adult learners of ESL received 12 hours of Integrated or Isolated FFI on the 'passive' construction. In Integrated FFI, attention to form was embedded within communicative practice; in Isolated FFI, it was separated from communicative practice. Learners' progress on a written grammar test and an oral communication task indicated no significant differences between the instructional groups over time. However, some advantages were observed for Integrated FFI on the oral production task and for Isolated FFI on the written grammar test. Both contribute positively to L2 learning given their combined focus on form and meaning.

Bellal & Nader (2014) conducted a study that deals with instructional design called "e-LATE" (e-Learning Activities for Technical English), in a university context. In this, the activities are designed as units of study for students in computer science in Algeria. "e-Shop" is designed using communicative language learning and collaborative learning approaches. The scenario is built on role-play as a learning situation. This project uses, firstly, the communicative approach to enable learners to get better language skills, then role-playing as a learning situation because it uses different communicative techniques and develops fluency in the language, promotes interaction in the classroom, and increases motivation and finally collaborative work so as to run those approaches among peers. This latter implies a cognitive conflict between/among peers that calls for a debate on a given subject and therefore lets students communicate and show/ express their opinions.

Brown (2014) did research to describe how higher education language instructors design mobile-assisted language learning (MALL) environments for communicative language teaching. The media richness and communication savvy of mobile devices offer authentic content and dialogue opportunities, and language instructors can take advantage of these devices to lead language learners to achieve proficiency. The data indicated that in order to accomplish those objectives, language teachers in higher education should identify them and then design authentic learning experiences through communicative modes. The results also indicated that teachers must hold strong beliefs in CLT and have theory alignments with situated learning and constructionism, as well as beliefs about mobility that influence how they create communicative MALL environments.

Siswita & Al-Hafizh (2014) experimented with teaching reading by using magazines, preparing pre-reading activities while reading, and post-reading activities. It was concluded that teaching reading using children's magazines can make the learning process interesting, make students understand the meaning of texts being read, and, as a result, enhance their reading skills. So children's magazines are very suitable for teaching reading skills because they are very familiar to students in their everyday lives, and they can be used as interesting teaching materials because they have many stories, quizzes, games, and pictures of well-known public figures. Children's magazines can supplement the course book for reading.

Kholis (2014) conducted research on the use of Communicative Language Teaching in teaching listening to eighth-grade students in a bilingual program at SMP N2 Ponorogo in the Academic year 2013-14. Students who participated were confused by listening activities and didn't focus on the lesson as they had low background knowledge and low intrinsic motivation. The researcher used the CLT approach to make the teaching-learning environment in listening activities enjoyable and meaningful, and as a result, students participated actively in the class. The researcher recommended that English teachers use CLT in teaching, especially in teaching listening.

Zhao (2015) presented a paper in a conference titled, "Implementation of Task- based Language Teaching in Classes of Second Language Acquisition". In this, he critically analyses the TBLT from the comparison with 3P approach. He concludes that Task-based Language Teaching confirms the principles of Second Language Teaching (SLA) in many ways. TBLT can construct real life contexts similar to students' life in which they can use the target language; hence students' efficiency of acquiring language is promoted.

Suwannoppharat & Kaewsa (2015) conducted research to investigate the effectiveness of the CBI (Content Based Instruction) approach in developing Thai EFL undergraduates' academic reading and writing skills at Mae Fah Luang University, Chiang Rai, Thailand. The study is entitled "Utilization of content-theme-based Instructions: An Overhaul of English Language Learning for non-native English Learners." They found out that the students, when taught with the CBI approach, got better results in their academic reading and writing skills at the tertiary level, and they were also satisfied and happy as they needed not to worry too much about grammar.

Farooq (2015) studied the teachers' perceptions of the implementation of Communicative Language Teaching (CLT) in their language classrooms and its impact on the students' communicative skills. He conducted an experimental study by collecting the quantitative data and the qualitative data. The results show that the EFL teachers, despite of being aware of the CLT implementation and its impact on the communicative skills of the students, are not optimistic about the complete adoption of CLT due to the problems and challenges they face in the classroom, like overcrowded classes, non-availability of AV aids, students' low level of proficiency, time constraints, etc. They believe that only by overcoming the difficulties and establishing more favourable conditions for the implementation of CLT can truly benefit from it in their classrooms.

Tikkakoski (2015) applied CLT approach to teach English pronunciation in the context of Finnish schools and the curriculum for grades 7.-9 in his research project. For this, the researcher developed three communicative pronunciation tasks (CPTs), which each include communicative features, to realise the principles of the theory of CLT. This research does not prove the functionality of the CPTs but rather aims to exemplify how to begin developing new language tasks rather than finish model examples of communicative pronunciation tasks.

Sector (2015) discussed a study in Cambodia, in which an EFL programme using CLT and TBLT was implemented at a Siem Reap government-accredited NGO language school, The Bayon English Academy (BEA), where children were living in extreme poverty in September 2010. He analyzes how these two methods were incorporated into each other and adapts the learning material according to the Cambodian context with the learner-centered approach. The findings revealed that the majority of the children preferred this integrated programme as evident from the students' comments. Children favoured communicative features like group work, learner-centered lessons, interesting lesson content, and the usefulness of the lessons.

Mehta (2015) conducted a study to examine the efficacy of a communicative approach in teaching English to students in a Middle School setting in an Indian context. He also investigated the challenges associated with the implementation of a successful communicative approach. There is a sample of 50 students, studying General English in the 8th class at the selected Government Middle School of Ujjain City. The researcher carried out experimental teaching for fifteen working days, comparing and analysing the outcomes with those from the pre-test. After testing the assumed hypothesis that the Communicative Approach helps learners use the English language more effectively in the specified social setting, the results demonstrated a significant level of proficiency in learning the English language through the application of the communicative approach.

Naz (2016) developed a sample study material for teaching the English language to the undergraduates of Aligarh Muslim University. This material follows a theme-based format in which activities, text, and examples have been woven around the theme, incorporating all four skills, sub-skills and enveloping skills like critical thinking. The SLM is well-illustrated, colourful, follows a cyclic gradation pattern, is highly interactive, and many more things.

Panambunan, Tulung & Maru (2016) conducted collaborative action research to improve the speaking ability of the 15 students in class X in the Megalia English course. Teachers use communicative language teaching to teach students to speak English, as it provides more opportunities for students to develop their speaking skills in English. CLT approach offers various CLT-based activities and games. It was concluded that there were improvements in the students' scores after implementing CLT in the class, and furthermore, students worked more cooperatively in the CLT class.

Ahmed & Bidin (2016) conducted a study to validate the effectiveness of Task-Based Language teaching in enhancing the writing skills of undergraduate learners at Malaysian universities in the private sector. The data was collected through mixed- methods research. They found through the learner's experiences reflected in their reflective journal that TBLT was a learner-centered approach, enabling learners to use their existing linguistic resources. There was an improvement in terms of L2 complexity, fluency, and accuracy in the L2 performance of the research participants from the experimental group as compared to participants from the control group.

West (2016) evaluated the advantages of CLT in an English textbook for students of language learning. The participants were taken from the National Institute of Development Administration (NIDA). The study was carried out during the second semester of B.E. 2558 and instructed two courses. The textbook used is *Academic Encounters: Life in Society, Level 3: Listening and Speaking* (Sanabria, 2nd edition, 2012), with supplementary reading material drawn from *Academic Encounters: Reading, Study Skills, and Writing* (Brown & Hood, 2009). It was assessed and concluded that the follow-up communicative activities that were specifically designed to work with the textbooks reinforced their content and resulted in increased understanding and knowledge of the content of the subjects covered by the textbook, therefore, the communicative teaching activities had been effective.

Ceper-Tangerang (2016), performed a quasi-experimental study to find out the empirical evidence for the effectiveness of using short stories towards students' reading comprehension of narrative text at the second-grade level of Mts. AT-TAQWA Batu Ceper Tangerang, Jakarta. There was a sample of 80 students divided into experimental and controlled groups. With the pre-test and post-test result analysis through statistical calculation, it was concluded that the use of a short story had better outcomes for the reading comprehension of narrative text than a short story without it.

Jain (2017) conducted research on the "Effectiveness of Programmed Learning and computer-assisted Instructions as self-learning Techniques in Teaching English Grammar at the Secondary Level.". She chose the grammar topic - Activity Verbs and Tenses, or class IX, and developed learning material using MS Word, MS Office XP, and executable records of the Adobe Flash Player variant. She divided the samples into 3 groups: (1) Experimental Group I (the programmed learning group), (2) Experimental Group II (the CALL Package group), and (3) Control Group (the traditional lecture method group). She interpreted the results of the experiment to mean that Programmed Learning and Computer Assisted Language Learning have positive effect on achievement scores. It was also concluded that the group who learned through Computer Assisted Language Learning scored higher than the scores of the group who learned through Programmed Instruction or the traditional lecture strategy. Also, Students who learned through Programmed Learning scored higher than those who studied through the traditional method.

Aalaei (2017) carried out quantitative research to measure the effect of the implementation of communicative language teaching on the speaking and listening skills of Iranian third-year secondary students. On the basis of the higher mean scores in the post-test of the experimental group, it was found that the CLT had a positive effect on the students' listening and speaking skills. The researcher also recommended that educational policy-makers in Iran should consider the applicability of the CA, in which a shift should be made from non-communicative to communicative ELT, and that EFL teachers should receive in-service training in applying CA principles.

Madhkhan & Mousavi (2017) investigated the impact of Task-Based Language Teaching (TBLT) on seventy Iranian EFL learners' reading comprehension performance in a study. Two groups - the experimental and control groups, were instructed with the same texts but different task types and activities during 20 sessions. Then, the learners' reading performance results were compared, and the analyzed data showed that TBLT had a significantly more positive effect on learners' reading performance as compared to traditional reading instruction. They also revealed that during reading, taking notes and discussing were found to be more effective in increasing learners' reading skills.

Ghofur et al. (2017) did a study to seek whether the learning methods (Communicative Language Teaching/CLT and Audio-Lingual Method/ ALM) and learning preferences (Visual, Auditory, and Kinesthetic) have an interactive effect on English-speaking ability. With a population of 383 students and 70 samples, the researchers utilised a quasi-experimental research design. The samples were divided into experimental and control groups. Three different instruments (a pretest, a posttest, and a questionnaire) were used to gather the data, which was then descriptively examined. The analysis of the pretest scores reveals that the English-speaking abilities of the two student groups using the two distinct approaches are identical. The analysis of the posttest results demonstrates that there was no interaction between the learning techniques and learning styles and English speaking ability. This suggests that students in CLT outperformed those in ALM in speaking English regardless of their preferred learning strategies.

Rana (2017) conducted an experimental design study with the purpose of determining whether the communicative language teaching approach is beneficial at Lahore's public sector colleges, in Pakistan, where English is considered a second language. The control group was taught through transmission models of instruction based on the grammar-translation method, and the experimental group was treated with interventions based on activities from communicative language teaching. The researcher monitored the development of intermediate-level low competent English language learners' writing and comprehension abilities. After the analysis of the pre-test and post- test results, it was found out that the subjects in the experimental group's learning process, understanding, and writing skills were significantly improved when compared to the control group. The investigation demonstrates the suitability of the communicative approach to teaching in an ESL setting. It demonstrates its efficacy in improving the writing and comprehension abilities of English language learners with little proficiency.

Parmar (2018) developed a material with computer-assisted instructions in English grammar for 9th-grade students studying at Gujarat Secondary and Higher Secondary Education Board and tested its effectiveness. He found out in his study that teachers, in schools, have to face many challenges, like lack of good English atmosphere, more emphasis on the mother tongue, poor prior knowledge of grammar, etc. After doing the experiment, he found that implementing CAI in English class was significantly more effective compared to the traditional way of teaching. He also interpreted overall students' positive feedback about the effectiveness of CAI for the learning of English grammar.

Ananthi (2018), in his article "Teaching Creative Writing in English among Undergraduate Students," analysed that the creative writing tasks help in developing the writing skills of the college students. Incorporating creative writing into teaching English gives students opportunities not only to develop their writing skills but also to practice grammar, acquire new vocabulary, develop creativity, and enhance their self- confidence and self-expression.

Al-Zoubi (2018) stressed in his study that insufficient exposure to the target language, the learner's anxiety and self-efficacy could be the causes of inefficiency in speaking and writing skills. He found a strong relationship between exposure to the English language and the development of the four language skills, i.e., English language acquisition, which can take different forms such as: listening to English programmes and songs on the radio; watching English programmes and movies on television; travelling to English speaking countries; talking face to face with English native speakers (L2 interaction); using the English language in real life situations; surfing the internet using the English language; using social media in the English language; as well as, reading English books, magazines, and newspapers. Multimedia (Internet, social media, television, radio, Video games), group work, and projects may assist learners in developing the target language appropriately. The studies cited in this study indicated that the significance of exposure in language learning means that the more the learner is exposed to the English language, the more he reads and speaks in the language - i.e. - the higher the exposure, the better the learner performs in the target language.

Rahmatuzzman (2018) did a study to know how the English language teachers in secondary schools in Bangladesh adopt the CLT approach in classroom practice. One of the key findings is that teachers have a positive attitude towards CLT for students' learning; this approach would be effective if some practical contextual constraints were removed. Teachers face many problems applying CLT principles in their classrooms, which is why many teachers are still practicing the traditional method. Some other problems mentioned are: teachers rely on reference books (the Model Question Book); the focus of stakeholders is on the grades achieved in large scale-tests; and the government cannot afford all the necessary logistical support due to the socio-economic condition of Bangladesh. Due to these problems in the way of applying CLT in the context of Bangladesh, it is advised to consider the contextual factors and accordingly modify the CLT approach.

Owen & Razali (2018) conducted a study with the purpose of determining whether integrating communicative activities, specifically information gaps and language games, in secondary schools in Libya has an impact on students' speaking abilities. In a private Libyan international school in Malaysia, a quasi-experimental, nonequivalent pre-test- post-test design was used with 42 first-year secondary school students. Eight different information gap and language game activities based on communicative language teaching (CLT) principles were used for eight sessions of 15-20 minutes each. A significant difference between the pre-test and post-test was found, moreover, with the implementation of the communicative exercises in the classroom, students' speaking abilities increased.

Varghese & Karki (2018), in their study, looked into how a sample of teachers and students from higher secondary schools in Bangalore, India, preferred to teach and learn the English language. This research involved 67 participants in total, including 30 students (m=14, f=16) and 37 teachers (m=16, f=21). The Situational Language Teaching (SLT) approach was found to be the least popular way for instructors to teach English, while the Communicative Language Teaching (CLT) approach was found to be the most popular. Similarly, it was discovered that students preferred learning a language through informal interaction over using written material such as books, newspapers, journals, etc. The students rated using audio resources as their least favourite way of learning English. Using independent sample t-tests, the gender gap in preferences was also examined. It was found that, compared to their female counterparts, male teachers and students significantly preferred the direct method and audio lingual method of instruction, respectively, while male students preferred the audio resources method of instruction. While the use of written content was chosen by both male and female students as the most preferable method for learning the English language, both male and female teachers favoured the CLT method of instruction.

Toro et al. (2019) conducted a study to determine which CLT strategies and resources are being used by English language teachers to improve the oral skills of students studying in elementary classes in schools in Ecuador and also their efficacy, which, further, helps in improving the English language teaching. The results not only showed that modeling, repetition, pair work, and group work are the main CLT strategies used by teachers to help students develop oral skills but also revealed that these strategies were not enough to promote active participation of students and that there is need to implement a variety of more strategies.

Septiyana (2019) conducted the research titled "Designing English Speaking Materials Using Task-Based Language Teaching (TBLT) for Islamic Economics Students". The researcher developed the English speaking material using Task-Based Language Teaching (TBLT) for the students of the Islamic Economics Department of IAIN Metro, Indonesia, and found that it was very useful for the students as it helped them to excel in their speaking skills.

Rahmatillah (2019) analyses through his study "Communicative Language Teaching through Role Play and Task based Instruction" many things, first whether Communicative Language Teaching (CLT) through Role Play and Task-Based Instruction is best implemented in the English learning process in STIE Madani Balikpapan. Second, it aims to prove whether this method can improve students' English skills based on the TOEFL score. Third, it aims to find out students' perceptions about the implementation of Communicative Language Teaching (CLT). The sample is 37 students from two classes that took English Practice/TOEFL subjects in the academic year of 2019-2020. The result stated that Communicative Language Teaching (CLT) is best implemented through role-play and task-based instruction. Since there is an increase between the pretest and the posttest, it means CLT helps students better achieve their TOEFL score. Through the use of this approach in class, students feel they have more interest in learning English and do not feel afraid to make mistakes again because they know they are still learning, which helps them better communicate.

Chen & Wang (2019), in their study, suggests a framework for a task-based teaching method and language assessment in an intensive reading class to investigate the positive effects on students' skills. This is done in the context of first-year English major students' oral presentations as well as written reports. The research technique includes semi-structured interviews and a questionnaire with 18 questions addressing various aspects of the learning and teaching processes. It aims to investigate the effects on students' competency in second language acquisition and at the cognitive level. All of the results of this empirical study show that TBLT used in Chinese English teaching classes is very advantageous and effective for the improvement of Chinese English learners. This article manifests that most students are in favor of TBLT because of its real-life authenticity and communicative interactions. It changed the passive, teacher-centered class into an active, student-centered class, which highly enhanced students' engagement in second language learning, especially in China.

Rohyani (2019), conducted a study whose objective was to determine how a communicative language teaching strategy using short films can enhance students' speaking practice and how the eleventh grade students of SMKN 2 Pacitan responded to the speaking practice using a communicative language teaching strategy. The 31 students in grade XI PM 1 at SMKN 2 Pacitan were the sample in this study, which was carried out in two rounds. The pupils' learning of English, particularly their speaking abilities, improved, and it was evident from the students' responses that they had a positive reaction. When speaking process was being taught, the students actively participated in communicative tasks. The interest of students in developing their speaking abilities through the use of short films in communicative language instruction is the second factor. In conclusion, using short films to teach communicative language skills could help students communicate more fluently.

Fithriani et al. (2019), did a study aimed at investigating whether Facebook, as the most popular social media in Indonesia, would be an effective learning tool for EFL university students taking an advanced writing class. Finally, it was concluded that Facebook, as a learning tool, helps the students boost their confidence in using English as a means of communication. That they are actively involved in almost all learning activities in the Facebook writing group. Another benet of Facebook use in EFL writing class, as perceived by the students, is the improvement of writing uency. The majority of the students admit that it is much easier for them to express themselves through written communication on Facebook after they experience various learning activities on the Facebook writing group.

Katoky (2013) conducted research on 450 undergraduate Assamese ESL learners from 3 colleges of Dibrigarh University and found that there is significantly strong relationship between Language Learning Strategies and reading and writing proficiency in English. He recommended that Language Learning strategies be incorporated into English Language teaching to increase Assamese ESL learner's English proficiency.

Pandya (2020), in his study "Teaching English Language Through Movies: An Experiment teaching English language through movies: An Experiment" found out that the use of movies in the classroom makes learning effective and entertaining. Teaching English through movies is effective way to teach listening and speaking skills and vocabulary, as English movies are able to motivate students to learn English well. Although Teaching English through movies is not effective in developing students' reading skills. It may be because of lack of exciting activities.

Anuradha (2020), in her study called "An Experimental Study on Teaching Language Through an Innovative Method," experimented to enhance English communication skills through a narrative approach with short stories and digital short stories. This syllabus focuses on vocabulary, comprehension, interpretation, report writing, and narration. The findings of this study showed that both the first year student of average competency and the final year student of above-average competency exhibited a positive attitude towards English language learning while performing the tasks. Both the students showed mastery of language in the creative process, and there was a tremendous improvement in narrating the incidents that were given as tasks. They also overcame the fear of narrating the incidents in front of others. The study suggests that this method may be implemented with students with special needs to teach English as a Second Language (ESL) and English as a Foreign Language (EFL) classrooms and also to improve their confidence as well as social and psychological skills. Storytelling is a powerful tool for inculcating a positive attitude towards narration and creating more engaging and exciting learning environments.

Ho (2020) investigated the influence of implementing Communicative Language Teaching (CLT) on cultivating 70 Taiwanese undergraduates' communicative competence in Tourism English in English as a Foreign Language (EFL) classroom. Findings indicated that students' significant progress towards better communicative competence in paper-based tests and oral-based tests and their perceptions of communicative competence were also in line with the results. It implies that Communicative Language Teaching (CLT) facilitates students' English learning, raises their confidence, and enhances their communicative competence in Tourism English.

Ravindran (2021) talks about an innovative method of creating a website by an English teacher in Telangana, India, to help college students in rural areas improve their proficiency in English. It includes many CLT activities, video lessons, PDFs, poems, comics, audio books, short news clippings, etc.

Shahid, Abbasi & Bhutto (2021) evaluated the implementation of CLT approach in the English language classrooms of undergraduate learners in Pakistan. They concluded that CLT is completely suitable and perfect strategy to be applied in classrooms when teaching second or foreign language. Due to certain factors like large class size, negative feedback from teacher's side, trial and error process, etc., make students feel demotivated and stop their attempts to speak the targeted language accurately and properly. Although it is great success in other countries, improvements are needed for it to work more efficiently in Pakistan.

Phoeun & Sengsri (2021) conducted a research study aimed at examining the effect of a flipped classroom with a Communicative Language Teaching (CLT) approach on aspects of the students' English speaking ability at the Royal University of Phnom Penh (RUPP), Cambodia. The results from the study indicated that students significantly improved their English speaking skills as they were exposed to authentic and communicative activities in the classroom and on the online platform. The students became active learners from passive learners who would just sit and listen to lectures to active ones. They recommended that teachers of English in Cambodia consider using the CLT approach and a flipped classroom concept in their classrooms if they face difficulty in teaching speaking skills and a time shortage to practice the language.

Manathunga (2021) investigated through research whether the Communicative Language Teaching approach used in the schools of Rathnapura district is effective in classroom teaching. The researcher took 240 students from grade 10 and six teachers from four schools teaching English to grade 10 students. After the analysis of collected data, it was proven that most of the schools use CLT approach instead of traditional approaches, but only one school has implemented the CLT approach to a satisfactory level. The study also concluded that using CLT approach enhances student engagement and their active participation in classroom activities. As a result, becomes a more effective way of teaching English, which enables the learners to communicate using the language rather than learning a set of grammar rules alone.

Kaushik (2022) found out with her qualitative study that commerce undergraduate students studying in different constituent colleges of the University of Delhi (DU) lack basic English language skills as well as communication skills. Six teachers for two focus group interviews recommended needs-analysis of stakeholders, revising the curriculum regularly, introducing interactive learning materials, and adopting innovative methods of teaching and evaluation.

Efendi (2022) carried out research aimed at designing supplementary speaking materials based on Communicative Language Teaching (CLT) for Indonesian students for the first semester of seventh-grade. The developed supplementary speaking material was based on the students' needs and engages them in the communicative activities in the classroom. The result showed the developed material was attractive for the students; hence, students are involved communicatively in the teaching and learning process, which helped them improve their speaking skills. The activities are: 'lead in the warm-up', 'enrich your knowledge', 'follow up activities', and 'reflection', which assist students in improving their speaking skills.

Hedia (2022) examined the efficiency of using communicative activities to improve Egyptian college students' English-speaking abilities.

The sample is a group of 40 students studying in first-year at a private university in Cairo (20 students in the experimental group and 20 students in the control group) in the academic year 2016–2017, which was tested using a control group in a quasi- experimental pretest-posttest approach. This study offers proof of the value of communicative activities in improving learners' speaking abilities. Activities in the pre-task and main-task phases are important in enhancing learners' lexical, phonological, and grammatical resources so they may successfully complete the speaking challenge at the end of the course.

Asrul & Dahlan (2022) did a study to ascertain whether the CLT technique enhances students' knowledge of English vocabulary both before and after studying it. It was tested on the students of SMP Negeri 50 Halmahera Selatan. It was determined from the findings that using the CLT approach improved the students' vocabulary. Additionally, there are some benefits to teaching English vocabulary using the CLT method, like the ability to speak English as the target language; SMPN 50 Halmahera Selatan students can expand their vocabulary and pronunciation.

Setiyorini, Yulia, & Robiasih (2022) examined through a study whether CLT enhances students' macro- and micro-reading comprehension skills throughout an intensive reading course. A case study was used as the research methodology, in which 21 first-semester students from an Indonesian private institution took part. The results demonstrated that after using CLT, students' macro- and micro- skills of reading comprehension in an intense reading course significantly improved. Additionally, students contend that CLT makes learning to read enjoyable, interesting, and understandable.

Yung (2023) undertook an action research project for the students in the senior secondary school in Hong Kong to promote communicative language teaching (CLT) with a process-oriented approach in the English language curriculum. He describes an innovation in teaching ESL through songs by 'packaging' it as exam practice to engage exam-oriented students in CLT. A series of activities derived from the song 'Seasons in the Sun' were implemented in the ESL classroom. It was found that the students were first motivated, at least instrumentally, by the relevance of the activities to the listening paper in the public exam when they saw the similarities between the classroom tasks and past exam questions. Once the students felt motivated, they were more easily engaged in a variety of CLT activities, which encouraged the use of English for authentic and meaningful communication.

2.3 CONCLUSION

After reviewing the related literature, it was found that most experimental studies stress the effective use of communicative language teaching approaches in the Indian context. The authentic material used in CLT with the integration of all four skills helps in delivering the educational material to students easily, and ICT integration for the authentic material plays a positive role in enhancing the general trend toward the use of computers in education. Moreover, it is a pupil- centered approach. Various researchers have found that CLT poses many challenges for teachers, but they cannot ignore the advantages of using the CLT approach for the acquisition of English language skills. Kumar, Philip & Kalaiselvi (2013) point out rightly that educator began to realize the goal of foreign language teaching is the communicative ability achieved by the learner. Communicative Language Teaching not only considers language in terms of grammatical structures and vocabulary but also in terms of the communicative function it performs. Knowledge of the rules of grammar alone is not sufficient. The ability to use these rules appropriately to communicate meaningfully is equally, if not more, important. "Communicative Competence", means the knowledge that speakers and listeners have when they communicate with an awareness of appropriateness in different social contexts. Communication in the classroom is achieved by creating real-life situations and making the learners role play them. Task-based activities are developed to ensure that communication takes place between the learners. Through these activities, the learner gets access to the social, cultural, and pragmatic aspects of the language. If learners achieve communicative competence, it means the success of CLT. The current study is an attempt to support the previous studies by using the experimental method to study variables. Perhaps this study is the first attempt to check the effectiveness of using a communicative language teaching approach for English language acquisition skills in distance education. Therefore, the investigator found it suitable to conduct a study to develop and evaluate the impact of Self-Learning Instructional Material on English language acquisition skills.

CHAPTER - III

RESEARCH METHODOLOGY

The methodology details the detailed procedure for gathering the data for the investigation. This chapter explains the research design, all the variables included, the population, the sample, the tools used for collecting data, all the statistical techniques used, and precautions.

3.1 DESIGN OF THE STUDY

The present study is experimental in nature. The objective of the present study is to see the effect of Self-Learning Instructional Material on the acquisition of the English language of the undergraduate students studying in the School of Open Learning, University of Delhi. In this study, the researcher uses the Pre-test and Post-test Control Group Design. Instructional treatment was studied at two levels: one was the control group, which was taught through the traditional lecture method using the existing material which they already had, and another was the experimental group, which was taught the English language through the developed self-learning instructional material. The design comprises three phases as shown in Table 3.1:

Table 3.1: Three phases of Experimental Design

	Experimental Group	Control Group
Pre-Test Phase	Achievement test for English language acquisition skill	Achievement test for English language acquisition skill
Treatment Phase	Teaching English through self-learning instructional material for 10 classes	Teaching through the traditional lecture method using the existing material for 10 classes
Post-Test Phase	Measurement of achievement in English language acquisition skill	Measurement of achievement in English language acquisition skill

1. Pre-Test phase

In this phase, the students in two groups—the control group and the experimental group were administered the achievement test in the English language developed by the researcher.

2. Treatment Phase

In this phase, the control group was taught 10 classes through the traditional lecture method using the existing material which they already had, and the experimental group was taught 10 classes of the English language through the developed self-learning instructional material. In the present study, the independent variable instructional treatment has two levels:

Fig. 3.1: Instructional treatment and its level

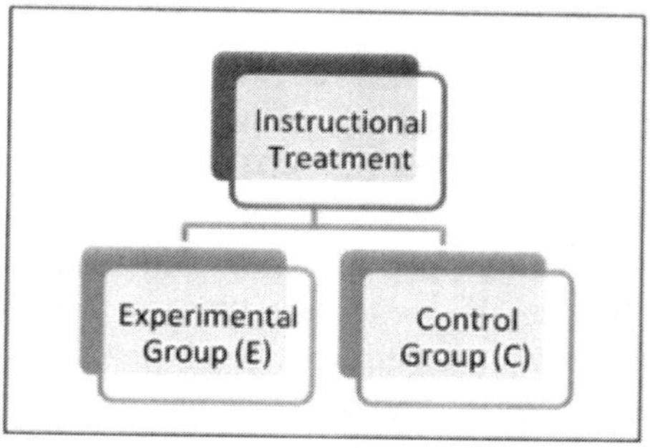

3. Post-Test Phase

In this phase, all the students in two groups were administered an achievement test in English to determine the effect of self-learning instructional material on their achievement in their English language acquisition.

3.2 VARIABLES INVOLVED

In experimental research, the effect of an independent variable on the dependent variable is studied. Dependent variables are the variables on which the effects of the Independent variable are felt.

3.2.1 Independent Variable

The developed self-learning instructional material and gender are the independent variables in this study whose effects on the dependent variable we are going to study.

3.2.2 Dependent Variable

In this study, the achievement test in English language acquisition skills is the dependent variable.

3.3 POPULATION

Commonly, a population is a distinct group of people who share a common citizenship, identity, or set of traits. In statistics, a population is a representative sample of a larger group of people (or even objects) that share one or more characteristics. In this study, the population is the BA (Prog) and B.com (Prog)1st-semester students studying in the School of Open Learning, University of Delhi, who have opted for the English language paper as a Generic paper.

3.4 SAMPLE

A sample is a representative group of a population chosen at random. It is a smaller group that was selected from the population and possesses all of the population's traits. In this study, the sample was selected through non-probability purposive sampling. A class of 150 students has given to researcher to teach English language paper at one of the SOL centre. From there, the researcher persuaded 60 students to participate in the research. So the 60 students who voluntarily participated in this study were the samples for this study. Now 60 students had to be divided into two groups: the Control Group and the Experimental group. For this, the researcher requested that 30 students be part of the experimental group, and the remaining 30 students became the Control Group. The detailed description of Sample is shown in Fig. 3.2.

Fig. 3.2 Detailed Description of Sample

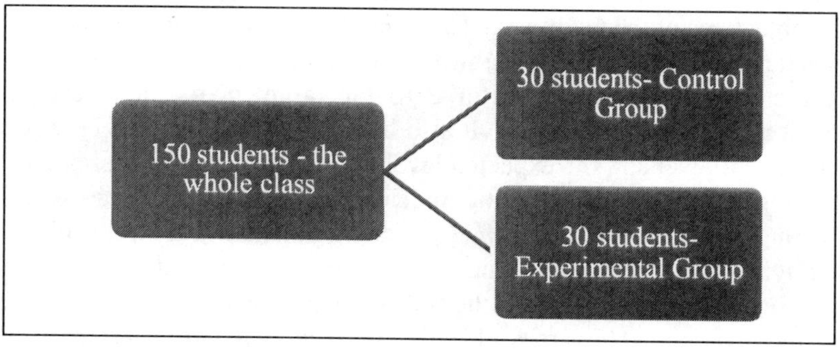

3.5 TOOLS USED

Some tools were used to collect the data related to the dependent variables in this study. All these tools are self-developed and are mentioned below:

1. A Need Analysis questionnaire for the students to find out the problem areas in their English language acquisition skills
2. A Need Analysis questionnaire for the interview to be carried out with a senior professors working in the Department of English, SOL.
3. An Opinionnaire for the subject experts and educators to give their opinions on the newly developed self-learning instructional material.
4. Achievement test for English Language Acquisition skills for the students is used to find out the existing proficiency level in English language acquisition skills of students. The same test is used to assess the effects of developed self- learning instructional material on English language acquisition skills of students.
5. Interaction scale to find out the interaction between students and the Self-learning instructional material.
6. Self-Learning Instructional Material for English Language Acquisition Skills (SLIM).

3.5.1 Need Analysis Questionnaire for the Students for English Language Acquisition Skills

Need analysis is a process that identifies the specific needs of students. A teacher, before planning and making any syllabus, curriculum, or teaching-learning material, should conduct need analysis of the students to make them proficient in the target language. According to Yana (2016), the objectives of the learning material should correspond to the students' actual needs. Need analysis is a strong technique that teachers may use to create materials that are tailored to the target goals and learning requirements of their students. It also helps to identify the gap between the current level and the expected level. Based upon this, the researcher developed a questionnaire for the students to identify the actual needs and existing learning gaps of 1st semester undergraduate BA (Prog.) students in English acquisition skills. The sample consists of 30 students studying the 'English Fluency' paper in the B.A. (Prog) 1st semester in the School of Open Learning, University of Delhi. Another telephonic interview was to be carried out with a senior professor working in the Department of English, SOL.

The questionnaire contains 10 multiple-choice questions and 2 open-ended questions related to students' actual needs in English communication skills. The population in the present study is composed of 1st-year undergraduate SOL students studying BA (Prog.). The population was divided into three streams: Language through Literature, English Fluency, and English Proficiency, offered to these students who have studied English up to classes XII, X, and VIII, respectively. The researcher decided to take a sample of 150 students, 50 from each group. Students were given a plethora of options to select from in order to obtain the most information.

As the Covid-19 was at its peak and everything was locked down, the tool was administered to the students online. So the Google Form was shared with the students through the link, and information related to their English language acquisition was elicited. The Need Analysis Questionnaire for students of School of Open Learning (SOL), University of Delhi, studying in B.A (Prog.) and B.COM (Prog.) is given as Appendix 1.

3.5.2 Need Analysis Questionnaire for the Senior Professors Working in the Department of English, SOL

To find out the learning gaps of the SOL students from the teacher's perspective, the researcher developed a pre-determined questionnaire in which five questions were asked to senior faculty members teaching in the School of Open Learning in a telephone interview. The Need Analysis Questionnaire for teaching faculties in the Department of English, School of Open Learning (SOL), University of Delhi is given as Appendix 2.

Data Analysis

To know the actual needs of the students, the responses or data from the questionnaire given by the students and interviewees were analysed and represented. Quantitative data from the questionnaire for the students was analyzed using percentages and presented using a pie chart. Qualitative data from the telephone interview is presented qualitatively.

3.5.3 An Opinionnaire for the Subject Experts and Educators to give their Opinions on the Newly- Developed Self-Learning Instructional Material

An Opinionnaire was developed by the researcher to assess the effectiveness of the self- learning instructional material for English Language acquisition Skills. The main aim of conducting this research effort is to assess the usability or effectiveness of the developed Self-Learning Instructional Material for English Language Learners. This effectiveness is measured by how easily and effectively a learner can use this material, given a particular exposure, and carry out fixed activities in a defined set of environments. This effectiveness testing is being done to identify problem areas, difficulties, weaknesses, and areas for improvement while using it. The Self-learning Instructional material should be enjoyable to use, interactive, motivational, diversified, and integrated for the learners. The Opionionnaire for Effectiveness of Self-Learning Instructional Material for English Language Learners is given as Appendix 3.

The researcher has developed self-learning instructional material for learning the English language for undergraduate students of SOL (School of Open Learning, University of Delhi)

The opinionnaire is divided into four categories: Authenticity of the Material which contains five statements; Presentation of Content; Utility for Students; and Activities for Assessment, which contains six statements each.

The method of assessment of each parameter above is based on a three-point scale, i.e.

A: Stands for Agree

B: Stands for Disagree

C: Stands for Undecided

3.5.3.1 Planning of Scale

The planning of the Scale is a crucial stage, as it is intended to cover all the areas of the self-learning instructional material in many statements with the objective of finding the opinions of the subject experts and educators through those statements. The planning stage aims at:

- Forming the objective of the Scale
- Defining the intended subject experts and educators' opinions
- Constructing the scale specifications
- Constructing the relevant statements

3.5.3.2 Preparation of the Scale and Pilot Testing (First Try-out)

In the preliminary draft of the Scale, 30 statements were constructed to extract the opinions of the subject experts and educators on a three-point rating scale. The Scale was given to the teachers from the Department of English and the Department of Education. The researcher showed the self-learning instructional material to all the teachers individually and requested that each one give their opinion on the statements made in the questionnaire based on the self-learning instructional material. The statements with 80% unanimity were selected. 23 statements were selected after the first try-out.

3.5.3.3 Validity

Seven subject and technical experts were given the scale, and they offered some changes that were implemented. The subject and technical experts largely accepted the scale, and their responses further supported its validity.

3.5.3.4 Administration

After the final draft of the Scale was finalized, it was given to and filled out by the five subject experts and five educators from various educational institutions across North India. The Scale provided the necessary information in several columns. They had to check the appropriate box in one of the three columns (agree/disagree/undecided) asking for their opinions. In order to understand the effectiveness of the Self-learning Instructional material for English Language acquisition Skills, it was requested that the teachers and educators give clear and to-the-point information.

3.5.3.5 Scoring

All the statements on the Scale are positive statements. Items were given a score of "1" for "Agree," "0" for "Disagree," and "None" for "Undecided," correspondingly. The total of these values reflects the effectiveness of the self-learning instructional material for English language Acquisition skills. The overall score, which ranges from 0 to 23, demonstrates the Self-learning Instructional material's efficacy from the least effective to the most effective. A column for remarks was given at the bottom of the scale for more suggestions.

3.5.4 Achievement Test for English Language Acquisition Skills of the Students

Elliott (2017) characterizes achievement tests as the tools used to assess how well individuals can demonstrate acquisition and apply the knowledge and skills taught and considered important for evaluating future learning or work. According to Gupta & Lata (2014), achievement refers to the level of success and proficiency attained in some specific area of academic work. To achieve the objective of the present study, the researcher developed an achievement test for assessing the English language acquisition skills of BA (Prog.) and B.Com (Prog.) 1st Semester undergraduate students of the School of Open Learning (SOL), University of Delhi. It was used to evaluate students' prior understanding of the subject and their final achievement after learning the material. The following list of steps was used in developing the test:

For the construction and standardization of achievement test for English language acquisition skills of undergraduate students in SOL, the researcher followed some steps:

3.5.4.1 Planning the test

3.5.4.2 Preparation of the test

3.5.4.3 Administration of the test (Pre tryout and final tryout)

3.5.4.4 Item analysis

3.5.4.5 Standardization of the test

3.5.4.1 Planning of the Test

Planning is the foremost and most crucial part of any process to make it successful and fruitful. The researcher planned out the achievement test by thinking about the needs analysis of the students that was done by the researcher, the content area, the objectives, the six skills to be tested, the type of questions, the themes, the availability of time, etc. The researcher did the planning on the basis of these four points:

(i) Objectives of the test

(ii) Content of the test

(iii) Size and the types of questions

(iv) Preparation of the blueprint

(i) Objectives of the test

In this achievement test, objectives are defined in the behavioral terms given in Bloom's Taxonomy, focusing only on knowledge, understanding, application, and skills. After that, the learning outcomes or objectives for observable terminal performance were constructed. The objectives and topics chosen to be taught throughout the experiment were outlined in the test specifications. The weightage for each objective in the achievement test is given below in the Table 3.2 and Fig. 3.3:

Table 3.2: Weightage for Each Objective in the Achievement Test (Pre tryout Stage)

Objective	Weight age
Knowledge	27
Understanding	32
Application	31
Skill	10
Total	**100**

Fig. 3.3. Objective-wise weightage in Achievement test in English Language Acquisition Skills (Pre - tryout Stage)

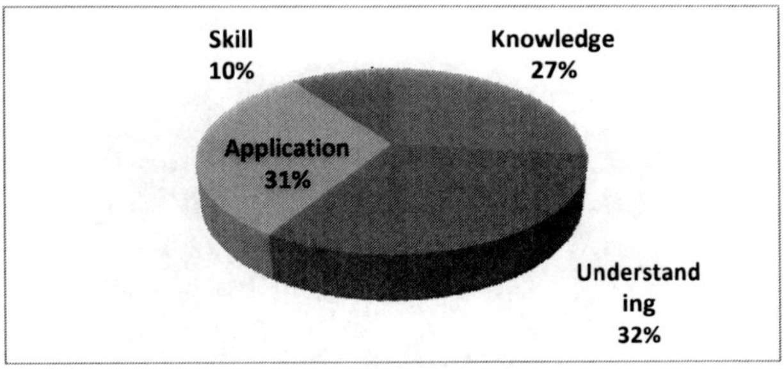

(ii) Content of the Test

The content of the achievement test is very important. The researcher focused on the measurement of the six skills of the English language: reading, listening, speaking, writing, grammar, and vocabulary. Many tests used are not so comprehensive in terms of measuring skills as they only measure reading, writing, grammar, and a little bit of vocabulary, leaving behind the other two important skills of language: listening and speaking. That's why the researcher felt the need to construct the achievement test and standardize it. From the need analysis done by the researcher, the content was selected from the areas where the students were lacking, and they could get lots of opportunities to have exposure to all the English language skills in an integrated way.

Table 3.3: Content-wise Weightage in Achievement Test

Skill	Weightage
Reading	15
Listening	15
Writing	16
Speaking	9
Grammar	30
Vocabulary	15
Total	**100**

Fig. 3.4: Content-wise weightage in achievement test in English Language Acquisition Skills (Pre-Tryout Stage)

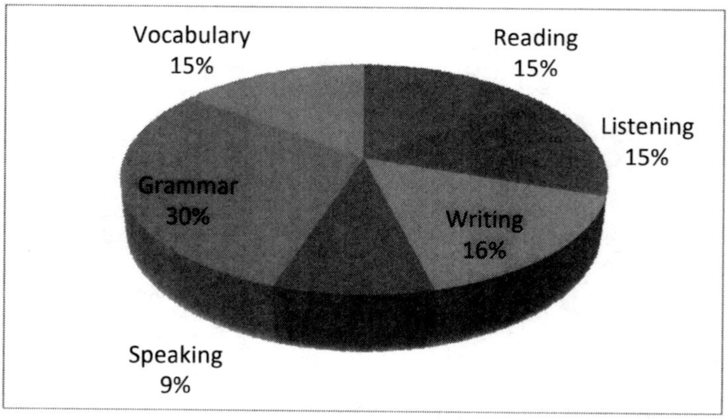

(iii) Size and Types of Questions

The size of the test means the number of items in the achievement test, and the types mean what types of questions are there. The researcher consulted expert teachers in the English language from colleges and schools for the types and number of items to be included in the achievement test. In the first draft of the achievement test, there are a total of 66 questions. As this achievement test measures all the skills of the English language, it has different types of questions: Multiple choice questions, Fill in the blanks, and Long questions. Question-wise weightage of the achievement test is given in Table 3.4.

Table 3.4: Question-wise Weightage of the Achievement Test

Types of Questions	Weightage
Multiple Choice Questions	56
Fill in the Blanks	7
Long Answers Questions	3
Total	**66**

(iv) Preparation of the Blueprint

A blueprint is the model or plan that acts as a guide for the preliminary draft of the achievement test. In the blueprint, the researcher plans the number of questions and assigns marks to those questions according to the time given. The researcher presents its final decision in the form of the blueprint given below in the Table 3.5:

Table 3.5: Blueprint for Pre-Tryout Achievement Test

Objectives	Knowledge			Understanding			Application			Skills			Total
Forms ofQuestion	MCQ	FB	LA	MCQ	FB	LA	MCQ	FB	LA	MCQ	FB	LA	
Topic													
Reading	6(6)			6(6)			3(3)						15(15)
Writing	3(3)			4(1)				4(1)				5(1)	16(6)
Vocabulary	4(4)			5(5)				6(1)					15(10)
Listening	4(4)			8(8)				2(2)		1(1)			15(15)
Speaking					3(1)			2(1)				4(1)	9(3)
Grammar	2(1)	8(1)		6(6)			8(8)		6(1)				30(17)
Total	19(18)	8(1)		29(26)	3(1)		11(11)	14(5)	6(1)	1(1)		9(2)	**100(66)**

MCQ: Multiple Choice Questions
FB: Fill in the Blanks
LA: Long Answer Question
The numbers in brackets are the number of questions.
The numbers outside the brackets are the marks assigned to these questions

3.5.4.2 Preparation of the Test

The preliminary draft of the achievement test was constructed under the guidance of some teacher experts and was also shown to them when it was completed for their suggestions and editing. The achievement test contains a total of 66 questions of three types: multiple choice, fill-in-the-blank, and long questions. These questions were constructed corresponding to the 5 units based on different themes and cover the exposure of many concepts related to the six skills of the English language: reading, listening, writing, speaking, grammar, and vocabulary for undergraduate students of SOL. In multiple-choice questions, the respondents are given four choices for their answer s, and they have to tick the correct answer. In fill in the blanks, the respondents have to provide a word or phrase to complete the sentence. In long questions, they have to speak or write a paragraph with connected sentences. After being evaluated by the experts, some questions were reframed under their guidance and finalized.

- Preparation of directions for test items: The proper test item instructions were prepared. The instructions were straightforward and easy for the students to understand. There are fill-in-the-blank, objective-type questions, and long questions in the test. Detailed instructions for each section are given at the beginning of the test.
- Preparation of directions for administration: The instructions for administering the test were given in a clear and precise manner.
- Preparation of directions for scoring: Scoring keys were prepared to make the scoring process easier.

The English Language Acquisition Achievement Test for students of School of Open Learning (SOL) studying English Fluency (English B) in B.A. (Prog.) or B.COM (Prog.) for Pre-Tryout is given in Appendix 4.

3.5.4.3 Administration of the Test

After finalizing the achievement test with 66 questions and a scoring key, the achievement test was administered in two phases: a preliminary tryout and a final tryout.

(i) Preliminary Tryout

The preliminary draft of the achievement test was first administered to 30 students to find out the errors or mistakes in the achievement test and its administration. The preliminary tryout was done to find out whether

- there is any ambiguity in the language
- the directions to the items were followed by students.
- the time allowed was enough
- If there is any difficulty students face during administration,

All the problems and errors were noted, and further, the 10 questions were reframed for the ease of the students.

(ii) Final Tryout

In the final tryout, the achievement test was tried out on 90 students studying in BA (Prog.) and B.com (Prog.) 2nd Semester who had studied 'English Language' as Modern Indian Language in their 1st semester. The initial target was to take 180 students, but the researcher was able to convince only 90 students as the test was a little long and the students did not have much spare time with them. It was very difficult for the researcher to convince students to participate in the pilot testing of this experimental research. As students are studying through distance learning, it is difficult for them to find out the spare time to participate and fill out the achievement test. All the students were given the test, and they were supposed to mark or write the answers in the achievement test as the space was already provided for the answer. Two hours were given to complete the test, and the students were supposed to tick the right answer in the multiple choice questions and write one word or phrase in fill in the blanks, and in the long questions, they were supposed to write a paragraph with connected lines and also speak some lines related to the question asked of them.

(iii) Scoring

After that, the answer sheets were collected from the students and scored according to the scoring key that had already been made beforehand. The Scoring Key for Valid Achievement Test is attached as Appendix 6.

In multiple choice and fill-in-the-blanks, correct answer was awarded one mark, and incorrect or not attempted answers were given zero. In long questions, marks were given on the basis of the rubric.

3.5.4.4 Item analysis

In order to evaluate the effectiveness of the test as a whole and of individual test items (questions), item analysis was done. In item analysis, the researcher looks at student responses to specific test items (questions). Item analysis can be used to remove unclear or misleading items from a single test administration and identify particular areas of course content that require further emphasis or clarification. In other words, item analysis is the statistical technique used for selecting and rejecting the items of the test on the basis of their difficulty value and discrimination index. The researcher did the item analysis in Microsoft Excel, which makes the calculation and analysis easier. The following steps were taken to do the item analysis:

(i) First, the average score of each respondent was calculated, and the respondents were arranged in descending order on the basis of the average marks they got.

(ii) Then the "upper group" and the "lower group" were calculated by using the formula – 27% of total respondents. So

The total number of respondents = 45, 27% of 45 =12.1, and

We have already arranged the average scores in descending order. So for each item or question, we take the total score of the first 12 respondents as the upper group and name it UG, and the last 12 respondents as the lower group and mark it LG. The middle 46% of the answer sheets were kept aside.

(iii) Calculate the Difficulty Value: After having an "upper group' and a 'lower group', the marks of each respondent were marked and tabulated. The larger the total number, the easier the item. By calculating the percentage of students who properly answered the question, the item difficulty was calculated. According to J. P. Guilford, "the difficulty value of an item is defined as the proportion or percentage of the examinees who have answered the items correctly." The percentage was converted into proportions. The estimated difficulty value for each item was assumed to be the average of the proportions of right answers on each item in the two end groups.

The formula for computing the difficulty value 'dv' of each item was: dv = PU + PL /2,

where dv is the difficulty value of the items.

PU = proportions of correct responses to the items from the upper group. PL = proportions of correct responses to the items from the lower group.

(iv) Internal Consistency Discrimination Index (rb):

The internal consistency discrimination index (rb) of an item refers to the relationship between the overall test scores and item scores. Examining the bi- serial coefficient of correlation between the item and overall score in J.C. Flanagan's abac led to this discovery. When the sample has been limited to the top and lowest 27% of the distribution of total scores and the middle 46% of the examinees of the total score have been eliminated, Flanagan's abac should be used. The ordinate showed the percentage of test takers who passed the item in the upper criterion group, and the abscissa showed the same percentage for the lower criterion group. At the intersection of the perpendiculars at these values, the coefficient rb's value was determined. Items for the final draft were chosen once each item's difficulty levels and internal consistency discrimination indices had been computed, as mentioned below:

DV = (UG + LG)/(NH + NL)

Whereas, UG = Average score of that item

LG = Average score of that item

NH = Number of respondents in highest group

NL = Number of respondents in lower group

Item Selection for Final Draft

The difficulty value and discrimination index of each item were taken into consideration during the final selection of the items. Karadag & Sahin (2016) asserted that the percentage of students who correctly responded to an item is called item difficulty, and it ranges from 0.0 to 1.0. An item becomes increasingly difficult as its difficulty value gets closer to zero, and this ability to distinguish between students with high and low scores is represented by an item's discrimination index. The item is good when its value is closer to 1, and it can differentiate between students who receive high scores and those who receive low scores. The difficulty and discrimination indices of each item are analysed to provide feedback on what the learners have learned and to help teachers identify and fix the problematic items. In other words, by indicating whether or not the items are functioning properly, it helps to increase the validity and reliability of the tests.

The distribution of the items finally selected according to the 'dv' and 'rb' which have been given in the Appendix 9.

To analysis the test items in this achievement test, Ebel's (1979) criteria and guidelines for categorizing discriminating indices are used.

Table 3.6: Ebel's Guidelines (Discriminating Powers)

Discriminating powers	Description
.40 and above	The item is functioning quite satisfactorily
Between 0.30-0.39	Little or no revision is required
Between 0.20-0.29	The item is marginal and needs revision
<.19	The item should be eliminated or completely revised

Based on Ebel's guidelines mentioned in the above Table 3.6, the 66 test items were categorized in the Table 3.7 and 3.8 given below:

Table 3.7: Distribution of Discrimination Powers of all the Items of Achievement Test

Discriminating Power	Frequency	Item Numbers	Remarks
.40 and above	29	1, 3, 8, 9, 12, 14, 20, 21, 23, 31, 32, 38, 41, 42, 44, 47, 48, 49, 52, 53, 55, 56, 58, 59, 60, 63, 64, 65, 66	Very Good Items
.30-.39	06	28, 33, 34, 35, 39, 43	Reasonably Good
.20-.29	11	6, 7, 10, 15, 19, 25, 26, 29, 37, 51, 62	Needs Improvement
<.19	20	2, 4, 5, 11, 13, 16, 17, 18, 22, 24, 27, 30, 36, 40, 45, 46, 50, 54, 57, 61	Very Poor Item
Total	66		

Table 3.8: Bi-Variate Scatter Diagram for Achievement Test in English Language Acquisition Skills between Difficulty Value (dv) and Discrimination Index (rb)

Rbdv	.00-.09	.10-.19	.20-.29	.30-.39	.40-.49	.50-.59	.60-.69	.70-.79	.80-.89	.90-.99
.00-.09	13,45,57	11,27,46,54	2,4,30,61		5,24,40	16,17,36				
.10-.19			50	22	18					
.20-.29		62	25	6,10,15,19,51	7,26,29,37					41
.30-.39		34		35,39	28,33.43					
.40-.49		1,60	55	14,20	8					
.50-.59			52,53	12,21,32,47,49,56	38					
.60-.69			3,44	23						
.70-.79										
.80-.89				9						
.90-.99		58		66			48,63		31,42, 59, 64, 65	

It is revealed from Table 3.7 and 3.8 that 29 items have discriminating powers of .40 or above; hence, these were selected in the final draft, and 17 items have discriminating powers ranging from .20 to .39. These were revised in terms of language clarity, content complexity, and item difficulty level. The language was clarified and made easier to grasp. Items that were vague were clarified. Clearer instructions were provided for attempting the items, and finally, these items were included in the final draft. The remaining 20 items have discriminating power below .19 and were rejected.

3.5.4.5 Reliability of the Achievement Test

To calculate the reliability, the researcher employed the split-half methodology. The items in a test have been split into two tests that are equivalent in content and difficulty by splitting the test items into odd and even-numbered items. The researcher found 0.833 as the calculated value of the Reliability coefficient, which means 83.3% of the variance of test scores is true-score variance and only 16.7% is error variance. So, we can say that the achievement test is fairly reliable as per the general guidelines for interpreting test reliability given below in Table 3.9 and Table 3.10.

Table 3.9: Reliability Test for Achievement Test

Reliability Statistics

Reliability Statistics			
Cronbach's Alpha	Part 1	Value	.772
		N of Items	23[a]
	Part 2	Value	.855
		N of Items	23[b]
	Total N of Items		46
Correlation Between Forms			.714
Spearman-Brown Coefficient	Equal Length		.833
	Unequal Length		.833
Guttman Split-Half Coefficient			.694
a. The items are: Q_1, Q_2, Q_3, Q_4, Q_5, Q_6, Q_7, Q_8, Q_9, Q_10, Q_11, Q_12, Q_13, Q_14, Q_15, Q_16, Q_17, Q_18, Q_19, Q_20, Q_21, Q_22, Q_23.			
b. The items are: Q_24, Q_25, Q_26, Q_27, Q_28, Q_29, Q_30, Q_31, Q_32, Q_33,Q_34, Q_35, Q_36, Q_37, Q_38, Q_39, Q_40, Q_41, Q_42, Q_43, Q_44, Q_45, Q_46.			

Table 3.10: General Guidelines for Interpreting Reliability Coefficients

S.No	Reliability coefficient value	Interpretation
1.	0.90 and above	Excellent
2.	0.80 – 0.89	Good
3.	0.70 – 0.79	Adequate
4.	Below 0.70	May have limited applicability

3.5.4.6 Validity of the Achievement Test

The purpose of the current investigation and the nature of the test items limited the use of exhaustive statistical methods for test validation. Validity was obtained through the Content Validity criterion. Content Validity is concerned with the adequacy of sampling a specified universe of content. The panel, which consisted of five subject matter experts and three test item experts, was provided the test items and a list of outcomes in order to establish the validity of the content. The panel was asked to determine which test item related to which learning outcome. The experts agreed with the researcher on the assignment of test items to objectives 95% of the time. The percentage was taken as evidence of Content Validity.

3.5.4.7 Final Draft of the Achievement Test

The test items in the achievement test were finalized and rearranged accordingly. Instructions for how to attempt the test were printed on the cover page. The scoring key was also prepared according to the final draft of the test and has been given along with the achievement test. The final test contains 31 test items, and the time limit was restricted to two hours. The blueprint for the final achievement test is given in Table 3.11, in which the test items for each skill were arranged and presented according to the different cognitive levels.

Table 3.11: Blueprint for the final Achievement Test

Objectives	Knowledge			Understanding			Application			Skills			Total
Forms of Question	QB	FB	LQ	QB	FB	LQ	QB	FB	LQ	QB	FB	LQ	
Topic													
Reading	2(2)			3(3)			2(2)						7(7)
Writing	1(1)			1(1)								5(1)	7(3)
Vocabulary				5(5)									5(5)
Listening	4(4)			2(2)									6(6)
Speaking					3(1)							4(1)	7(2)
Grammar	2(1)	8(1)		1(1)			4(4)		6(1)				21(8)
Total	9(8)	8(1)		12(12)	3(1)		6(6)		6(1)			9(2)	**53(31)**

MCQ: Multiple Choice Questions FB: Fill in the Blanks

LA: Long Answer Question

The numbers in brackets are the number of questions.

The numbers outside the brackets are the marks assigned to these questions

The English Language Acquisition Achievement Test for students of School of Open Learning (SOL) studying English Fluency in B.A. (Prog.) or B.COM (Prog.) for the final stage is given as Appendix 5.

3.5.5 Interaction Scale to Find out the Interaction of Students and the Self- learning Instructional Material

To find out the interaction between the students and the self-learning instructional material, the researcher developed an evaluation checklist or tool called Interaction Scale to determine whether the self-learning instructional material is appropriate for the students. The Interaction Scale for Students is attached as Appendix 7.

The checklist was to be filled by the students who were part of the experimental group and studied English Language Acquisition skills through the developed self-learning instructional material. The items in the checklist are divided into five groups on the basis of five different dimensions, exploring different aspects of self-learning instructional material. These 5 groups are: (1) Layout, design, and presentation; (2) Content, topics, and language; (3) Language teaching methods and activities; (4) Four language skills - listening, speaking, reading, and writing); and (5) Sub-skills - Vocabulary, Grammar, and Conversational skills. Groups 1 to 4 contain 7 items each related to their respective topics, and Group 5 has 6 items.

The students had to read the items in the checklist about the Self-Learning Instructional material and indicate the level of their agreement by marking 0-4. The items are checked on the basis of a 5-point Likert Scale in which 0 = strongly disagree, 1 = disagree, 2 = uncertain, 3 = agree, and 4 = strongly agree. The students were also requested to write any comments and suggestions for the self-learning instructional material in the space provided in the tool.

3.5.6 Self-Learning Instructional Material for English Language Acquisition Skills (SLIM)

The researcher had gone through a process of developing the self-learning instructional material that involved various phases, as shown in Fig. 3.5. The steps in designing the self-learning instructional material for English language acquisition are given in the flow chart:

Phase 1	Identification of students' needs
Phase 2	Specifying the syllabus in broad terms on the basis of need analysis (multi strand syllabus – Topic based + skill-based syllabus) • Specify the theme • Specify the English language skills to be taught related to the theme • Specify the objectives of units
Phase 3	Selecting and sequencing the course content • Selecting authentic resources to give maximum exposure to language • Script Designing • Integration of Activities
Phase 4	Assessment of material • Conducting pilot testing • Modification in the material
Phase 5	Final draft of the self-learning instructional material

Fig. 3.5 Phases of Development of Self-Learning Instructional Material

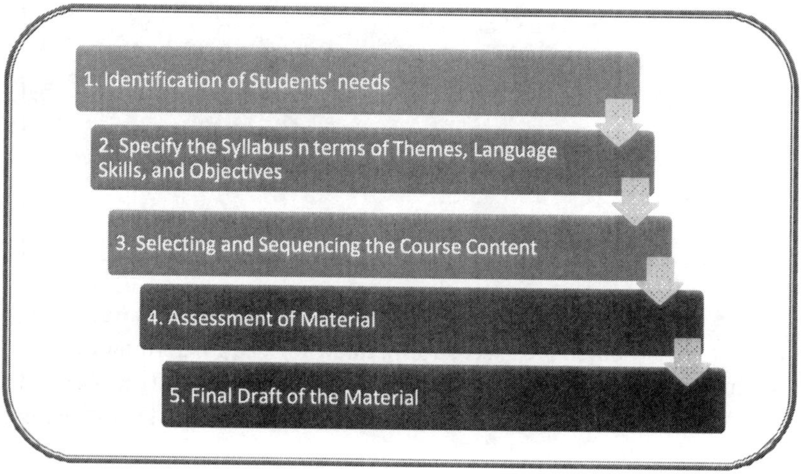

The self-learning instructional learning material is developed in five phases:

Phase 1: first of all, the need analysis for the English language acquisition skills of SOL students is to be done so that accurate needs can be addressed in the developed material;

Phase 2: On the basis of the students needs, the researcher selected the themes on which English language skills are taught. Five themes were selected that could address the needs of the students. These five themes are Travel, Health and Food, Entertainment, the Workplace, and Technology. Following that, English language skills are chosen to be taught in conjunction with these themes. The researcher selected to teach four macro skills: Reading, Writing, Listening, and Speaking, and two micro-skills: Vocabulary and Grammar. The selected themes and language skills are shown in Fig. 3.6.

Fig. 3.6: Planning of Five Themes and Six Skills in Self-learning Instructional Learning Material

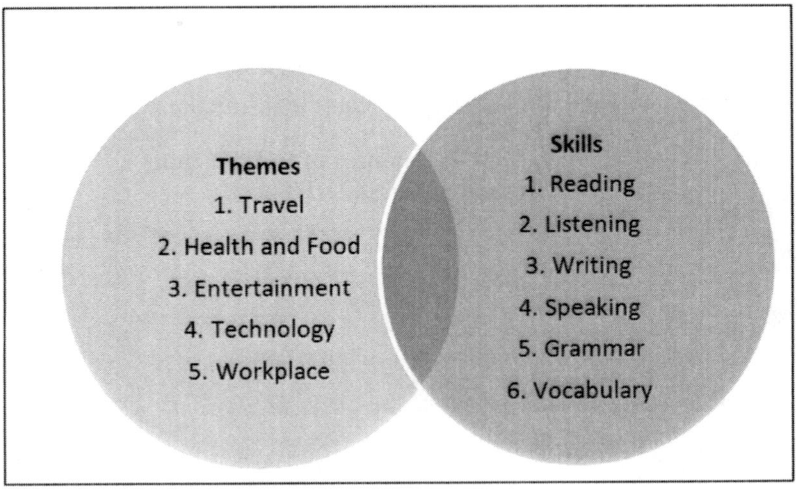

Then the researcher planned to take these five themes as five units. In each unit, the objectives were formulated for each macro and micro skill which are given in Table 3.12. With these objectives, students would be able to know that what they can do with these developed skills using the specified theme.

Table 3.12: Objectives for Each Unit

Objectives	Units
Unit 1: Travel	explore a travel diary mainly describing the events of a journey and the experiences and discoveries of the writer; • listen the important details in narratives like descriptions of a holiday; • practice some phrases and sentences to start, extend, and end the conversation; • compose a paragraph on their personal travel experience in some details; • construct some simple and negative sentences; • demonstrate the skill of questioning using 'wh' words; • communicate using vocabulary related to travel
Unit2: Entertainment	uncover the life of a storyteller in a short extract taken from a popular book • comprehend the children's animated film in English based on a classic text; • make use of contractions while listening and speaking English; • compose coherent and cohesive sentences in a paragraph on a topic familiar to them; • frame sentences in context of right time and state of action (tenses); • identify the contractions in a conversation
Unit Food 3: Health And Food	Justify their decision to buy any packaged item on the basis of newspaper article; • follow detailed directions or simple technical information, such as operating instructions for everyday equipment; • Participate in a conversation while placing an order at a restaurant Writing: Compose formal and informal emails; • Communicate clearly using imperative sentences and causative verbs; • Give a presentation using prescribed phrases or sentences on any familiar topic; • Solve crossword for the vocabulary related to food
Unit 4: Technology	outline the important points and its sub-points in the article published in e newspaper; • recall the information listened through an episode broadcast on a radio channel; • participate in a conversation where someone asks you some short questions; • design a work report and a newspaper report; • distinguish the use and structure of active and passive forms of sentences; • restructure the sentences using common phrasal verbs while listening and speaking
Unit 5: Workplace	apply the ways discussed in the article that help them in their online interview • communicate effectively while appearing in an interview; • participate in an office meeting; • compose their CV and covering letter along with it; • practice using gerunds and infinitives in their real-life situations for speaking about different topics like their habits, opinions, etc.; • comprehend the meaning of official terms used while interacting at a workplace

Phase 3: Selecting and Sequencing the Course Content

After selecting the theme, skills, and objectives, the researcher planned to select and sequence the units' contents. The self-learning instructional material is developed using the Communicative Language Teaching approach in three steps:

1. **Selecting authentic resources to give maximum exposure to language**: In this step, the researcher chose authentic material for the content that is available in students' daily lives on a particular theme from different sources like books, newspapers, cartoon magazines, TV, podcasts, radio, YouTube videos, etc. This material gives exposure to different macro and micro skills like reading, listening, speaking, and writing in an integrated manner.

For example,

- In Unit 1, for exposure to listening skills, a link to a YouTube video is given - https://youtu.be/Jl1u2aGm5bg -
- In Unit 1, a YouTube video link is given https://www.youtube.com/watch?v=KY0K5f06adg - Through this, students are exposed to how to have a conversation using different types of sentences, which covers the Speaking skill.
- In Unit 2, an introduction from 'All-Time Favourites' by Ruskin Bond is used as the material for developing reading skills.
- For a Grammar topic, a graphic story from the children's magazine is used.

- Another Grammar topic is introduced through the text written on the labelling on the packaging and on the bottles.

2. Script Designing

After exposure to the selected authentic material, details of the concept or topic are explained through the examples taken from the exposed material so that students can have language use along with language learning. Many more solved examples from different situations are also given to broaden the topic. Many language concepts have been taught or presented in the form of tables and timelines.

3. Integration of Activities

Many different practice exercises are created to provide a full understanding of the topic. These activities provide opportunities through which the students can use the taught concept while having a conversation in English. These activities are varied in nature, which helps to boost motivation and interest in using English in their daily lives.

Phase 4: Assessment of Self-Learning Instructional Material

After having a rough draft of the material, it was shown to the subject experts from the English and Education disciplines of various private and government universities. An opinionnaire was developed by the researcher to check the effectiveness of the material and was also given to the experts along with the material. Then their valuable suggestions and recommendations were incorporated into the self-learning instructional material. The description of the tool is already given. The percentage of assessment of this tool by subject experts was found to be above seventy per cent.

Phase 5: Final Draft of Self-Learning Instructional Material

After the validation, the final draft of the self-learning instructional material for English language acquisition skills is ready by incorporating the suggested changes.

3.6 EXPERIMENTAL PROCEDURE

The samples in the present study were 60 students studying BA (Prog.) 1st semester in the School of Open Learning, University of Delhi, and they took "English Fluency" as a Generic Paper. For the experimental group, which was treated to Self-learning instructional material for English language acquisition skills, a total of 30 students were taken from the batch of BA (prog.) 1st semester that the researcher taught in the School of Open Learning. The control group, which was treated to traditional teaching with the existing self learning material, also consists of 30 students. All the PCP classes for both groups were taken by the researcher herself. The experiment was conducted in four phases:

Phase I: Administration of the Pre-Test

Phase II: Conducting the Teaching Programme

Phase III: Administration of Post-Test

Phase IV: Interaction Scale

The first phase involves testing the previous knowledge of all 30 groups in both groups. It was done through the self-developed pre-achievement English Language Acquisition tool. In the second stage, the Experimental group was given treatment through the teaching of self-learning instructional material for 10 Sundays, and the control group was taught traditionally using the existing self-learning material. To check the efficiency of the treatment, i.e., the self-learning instructional material for English language acquisition, which was given to the experimental group, students in both the groups were tested on achievement with the achievement test. A detailed design of the experiment has been given in the Table 3.14:

Table 3.13: A Detailed Design of the Experiment

S. No	Phase	Duration	Experimental Group	Control Group
1.	Pre-Test	1 day	Achievement test in English language acquisition skills	Achievement test in English language acquisition skills
2.	Treatment	8 days	Teaching English with self-learning instructional material	Teaching English through traditional method
3.	Post-Test	1 day	Achievement test in English language acquisition skills	Achievement test in English language acquisition skills
4.	Interaction Scale	1 day	Interaction Scale	No test

3.6.1 Pre-Test Phase

Before starting the experiment, the researcher got the opportunity to teach the "English Fluency" paper to the BA (Prog.) 1st-semester students in one of the PCP centers of SOL. During that time, the researcher made a rapport with the students and asked them to participate in this pre-test-experiment-post-test. Many students agreed, and they were oriented to the tests to be used with them and also to the methodology of the treatment to be followed, i.e., Self-learning instructional material for English language acquisition skills and the conventional method. After that, the researcher himself gave both groups the achievement test for English language acquisition skills. Before conducting the test, the instructions needed to be carried out were explained to the students in a clear manner in verbal mode. The administration of these tests was carried out as per the norms and instructions contained in their manuals. Students had to mark or write their answers in the space provided in the questionnaire. For listening tasks, the researcher called every student one by one, took the listening test, and evaluated their listening skills. The answer sheets were scored with the help of a scoring key, which indicated their current level of English language acquisition skills. This took a whole week.

3.6.2 Conducting the Experimental Programme

First, the instructional treatment was given to the experimental group in the form of teacher-directed instructions along with the self-learning instructional material to determine its effectiveness. The instructional treatment was given for about 8 Sundays, which included 5 units on five themes, and a post-test was administered in the sixth week. On the other side, the control group was taught through the lecture method using the existing self-learning material followed by teacher-directed instructions. For maximum precision and to prevent teacher biases, the researcher herself administered the treatment to both groups.

3.6.2.1 Teaching through Self-Learning Instructional Material in English Language Acquisition Skills

At the start of the experiment, students in the experimental group received an introduction to the self-learning instructional material. The innovative method used for teaching and learning in this module inspired students to learn. For that, all the objectives mentioned in all the themes were well-explained, so that students got encouragement to take part. This self-learning instructional material, which the teacher used to deliver the classes, was based on a different syllabus than the one that SOL used for their self- learning material. To accomplish the formulated goals, the teacher conducted the lessons in accordance with the recommendations of the prepared lesson plans in the module. Through the use of the internet on the mobiles, exposure to listening skills was provided in the class and the teacher explained each concept with the help of tables, concept maps, timelines, real-life examples, etc. Then the different activities for these concepts were also explained to make them easier for students to do. Students were also encouraged to do the speaking activities as group activities in the class to boost their confidence. The teacher tried to develop the right attitude towards learning the English language. As a result, the

Experimental Group received a total of eight classes over the course of eight weeks.

3.6.2.2 Teaching through Lecture Method of Teaching

On the other hand, a traditional method focused on whole-class instruction was employed to teach the students in the control group. Regular teaching techniques, like the lecture method, were used in this situation. The existing self-learning material was used to teach, which was based on the SOL curriculum, to make students more efficient and fluent in their English language skills. All the topics given on writing skills, grammar topics, and the suggested texts were well explained through the lecture method. The drill exercises were given as the home task. After every class, the students were encouraged to read the self-learning material provided by SOL at home, and whatever difficulties they faced in understanding the concepts, they could ask in the next class. The teacher gave a suitable response to each inquiry. The format of the question paper was also discussed, as students were very confused about this area, and they were also given the drill exercises on the basis of the format of the question paper. Last year, question papers were discussed to give students more clarity on the types of questions that would come in the upcoming exams.

3.6.3. Post-Test phase

As the treatment was completely given to the experimental group, the subjects' English language acquisition skills were assessed to determine the effect of the treatment. The Achievement Test in English Language Acquisition Skills was administered to both the experimental and control groups. The same achievement test was used to assess the pre test. All the students in both groups—the control group and the experimental group— were subjected to a post-test. In this way, post-test scores were obtained on the achievement test in English language acquisition skills for both groups.

3.7 STATISTICAL TECHNIQUES EMPLOYED

In this current study, the collected data was statistically analyzed using the following techniques:

1. Descriptive statistics such as mean and SD were worked out on the scores of achievement.
2. ANOVA was applied to test the assumption of homogeneity of variance for pre-test scores

3. Two-way Analysis of covariance (ANCOVA) with a 2x2 factorial design was employed to study the main effects and interactional effects of independent variables (Treatment and Gender) on the dependent variable (Achievement in English language acquisition skills).

3.8 PRECAUTIONS OBSERVED

The following precautions were taken over the duration of experiment (Pretest- Treatment-Posttest) for ensuring efficacy and high precision in experimental conditions, which may have contributed to the results

- During the time of experimentation, no stress was imposed on the students. The experiment was conducted in a natural setting.
- To avoid any teacher bias, both the experimental and control groups were taught by the researcher herself.
- For creating a harmonious and enjoyable environment for teaching and learning, rapport with the students was established.
- It was confirmed that the topics covered in the experimental phase had not been previously taught to the students.
- It was ensured that the importance of the content of the material was maintained and was not altered during the instructional treatment.
- Teaching was done for the complete 55 minutes that were given to teach a SOL class during PCP.

3.9 CONSTRAINTS FACED DURING EXPERIMENT

At the time of data collection, the researcher faced many challenges and difficulties during the experiment, which are mentioned below:

- A lot of effort was put into convincing the authorities about the importance of this experiment. Many formalities were done to get written permission from the authorities and make them agree to cooperate. The investigator spoke with the Principal and the authority and briefed them on the programme's purpose.
- SOL students are not very regular in the PCP classes. It was ensured that every participant in both groups would attend all the classes by giving them counseling from time to time during the experiment.
- The researcher contacted many colleges for allotment of the teaching classes of BA (Prog.) 1st semester students for the 'English Fluency' paper. Finally, the researcher was able to get a college for conducting this experiment.

- It was a time taken effort to convince the authorities of the colleges of the extra time that was required to conduct the experiment as the PCP classes were held on Sundays only.
- In the beginning, it was very difficult to convince the students to participate, as they came from very distant places and could not spare much time for the experiment. But the researcher was able to convince them by maintaining their interest in the experimental treatment.
- The SOL students were not making good efforts to participate in the activities in the beginning, but gradually they performed in the class with great enthusiasm.
- Many students did not have basic knowledge of English language, and they had many misunderstandings about various concepts.
- A WhatsApp group was also created to build rapport with the students and solve their technical problems if they had any.

Despite these challenges, the experiment to examine the effects of self-learning instructional material on SOL students' English language acquisition skills ran quite smoothly.

CHAPTER - IV

DATA ANALYSIS

The identification and description of the problem, review of related literature, tools used for data collection, and procedure for data collection have been presented in the previous chapters. In this chapter, the researcher discusses the analysis and interpretation of data and its results as well. In this research, the analysis and interpretation of data were based on the data that was collected from the 60 students of BA (Prog), 1st-semester students studying "English Fluency" as a generic paper in the School of Open Learning, and 30 English language experts and educators at the University of Delhi. The analysis and interpretation were done on the data collected through a need analysis questionnaire, an achievement test, an opinion questionnaire for the subject experts and educators, and an interaction scale for the students in the experimental group. In this study, the self-learning instructional material for English language acquisition skills, the conventional method, and gender were the independent variables, and the achievement test in English language acquisition skills was the dependent variable.

To see the effectiveness of the self-learning instructional material for English language acquisition skills and the conventional method of teaching, the scores of students were obtained before starting the experiment and after giving the treatment in the experiment. So for the same group, pre-test and post-test scores were obtained in English language acquisition skills through an achievement test. The pre-test achievement scores were subjected to descriptive statistics to get the mean, SD, and normality test, and One way ANOVA to test the assumption of Homogeneity of Variance. The post-test achievement scores were subjected to a 2×2 Analysis of Covariance (ANCOVA). It was concluded that hypotheses will be rejected or accepted at 0.01 and 0.05 levels of significance. The results will be compared quantitatively and presented graphically for better understanding.

This chapter has been divided into six sections:

- The first section (4.1) presents the needs analysis of the student's English language acquisition skills.
- The second section (4.2) presents the opinions of subject experts and educators on the effectiveness of self-learning instructional material for English language acquisition skills.
- The third section (4.3) presents the comparison of achievement scores between the control and experimental groups before the experimental group treated with the treatment
- The fourth section (4.4) displays the analysis of the comparison of the adjusted mean scores of achievement in English language acquisition skills of students taught through self-learning instructional material and lecture methods (with existing study material) by considering their pre-achievement in English language acquisition skills as covariates.
- The fifth section (4.5) presents the analysis of comparison of the adjusted mean scores of achievement in English language acquisition skills of male and female students by considering their pre-achievement in English language acquisition skills as covariates.
- The sixth section (4.6) shows the analysis of the comparison of the adjusted mean scores of achievement in English language acquisition skills of male and female students taught through self-learning instructional material and lecture methods (with existing study material) by considering their pre-achievement in English language acquisition skills as covariates.
- The seventh section (4.7) explains that strategies used in self-learning instructional material have a significant effect on students' achievement in English language acquisition skills; therefore, it is hypothesized that there is a positive attitude among the students towards the self-learning instructional material.

4.1 NEED ANALYSIS OF THE STUDENTS' ENGLISH LANGUAGE ACQUISITION SKILLS

Need Analysis in English language acquisition skills is an attempt to collect information in order to build a comprehensive understanding of the needs or problems faced by students when they try to communicate in English. This need analysis will help, further, to design a syllabus or new self-learning instructional material for this Communicative Language

Course in English. In this, the researcher collected information about some specific language functions that the students needed to learn. So the self-learning instructional material can be designed based on the student's needs and is expected to make the student proficient and more confident in using English for communication.

Participants in this present study were 120 undergraduate 1st-year students studying BA (P) and B.COM (P) in the School of Open Learning, University of Delhi. The participants in the sample were divided into three streams: Language through Literature, English Fluency, and English Proficiency, which are offered to students who have studied English up to classes XII, X, and VIII, respectively. The researcher decided to take 40 students from each group for the quantitative study and one senior faculty member teaching in SOL for the qualitative study.

Data were collected using two tools: (1) the questionnaire for the students and (2) the telephone interview with a senior professor working at this college. Students received questionnaires to help researchers learn more about the actual difficulties they encounter when using the English language in their daily lives. A telephone interview was also conducted to get information from the senior professor. The collected data was analyzed and presented in the form of a Percentage and Pie chart in the tables below.

4.1.1 Quantitative data

The questionnaire contained 10 multiple-choice questions related to the student's actual needs in English communication skills. The students were given many options to tick to get the maximum amount of information. The questions and their responses are presented below from the Tables 4.1.1 to 4.1.7:

Table 4.1.1: Representation of Feedback of Students about the Number of Years they Studied English at School

S. No	Statement	Levels	Classes				Pie Chart
			1- 12	1-10	6-8	6-10	
(i)	For how many years have you studied English in your school?	LTL	90%	10%	0	0	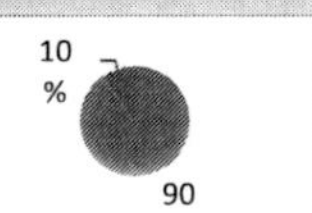
		EF	100%	0%	0	0	
		EP	90%	0%	10%	0	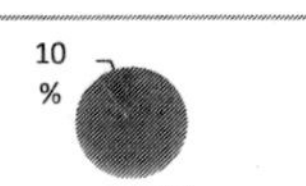

It is interpreted from the Table 4.1.1 that 90% students in LTL group, 100% in EF group, and 90% in EF group have studied the English language for 12 years (from class 1 to 12). It does not follow the criteria set by the University of Delhi. The criteria are students who have studied the English language till class 8, class 10, and class 12 get English C, English B, and English A respectively.

Table 4.1.2: Representation of Feedback of Students about their Socio-Economic background (Medium of Study in School)

S. No	Statement	Levels	Options		Pie Chart
			English	Hindi	
(ii)	In which medium did you study in your school?	LTL	60%	40%	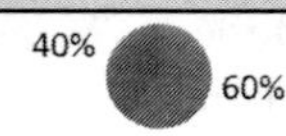
		EF	70%	30%	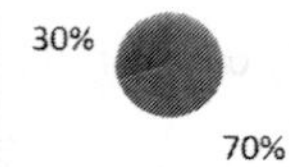
		EP	20%	80%	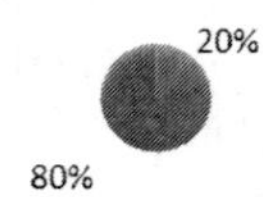

Table 4.1.3: Representation of Feedback of Students about their Socio-Economic background (from Which School they Passed Class XII)

S. No	Statement	Levels	Options		Pie Chart
			Government school	Private School	
(iii)	You passed your Class XII from	LTL	80%	20%	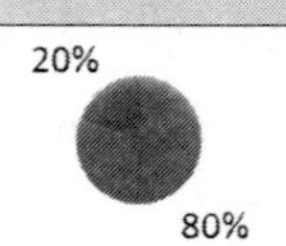
		EF	50%	50%	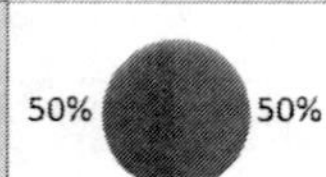
		EP	90%	10%	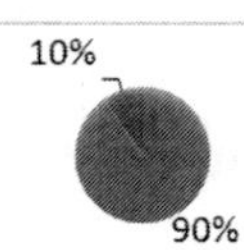

Table 4.1.2 and 4.1.3 give some information about the students' socio-economic and educational background. It reveals that 60% students in LTL group and 70% students in EF group studied in English medium schools, whereas only 20% students in EP group had studied from the English medium schools.

In LTL and EP groups, 80% and 90% students completed their higher secondary education from government schools respectively but on the contrary only 50% students passed from the Government schools.

Table 4.1.4: Representation of Feedback of Students about their Needs to Communicate in English

S. No	Statement	Levels	Options			Pie Chart
			Colleges or University	Home	Society	
(iv)	Where do you need to communicate in the English language	LTL	90%	20%	40%	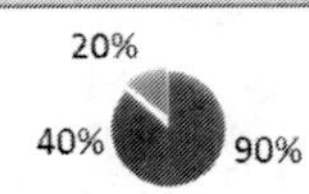
		EF	60%	20%	70%	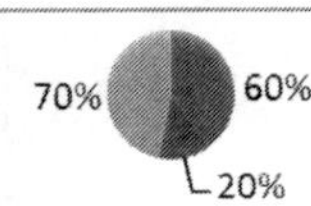
		EP	60%	40%	40%	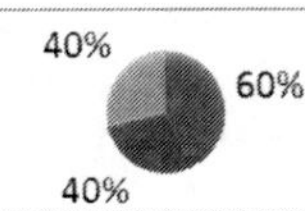

The situations and conditions where these students need to use English language is made known from the Table 4.1.4. 90% students in LTL group, 60% in EF group, and 60% in EP group feel that they need to communicate in English in colleges and universities. The second place is society where 40% students in LTL group, 70% in EF group, and 40% in EP group need to be proficient in English language. At their home, only 20%, 20%, and 40% students in LTL, EF, and EP group respectively need to use English language in their conversation.

Table 4.1.5: Representation of Feedback of Students about the Status of their Speaking and Grammar Skills basics

S. No	Statement	Levels	Options			Pie Chart
			Yes	No	May be	
(v)	Are you able to use the English language proficiently?	LTL	30%	0%	70%	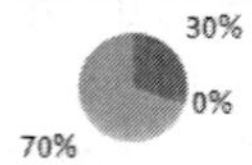
		EF	50%	20%	30%	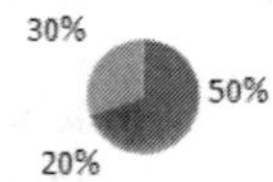
		EP	20%	20%	60%	
(vi)	Do you confidently answer someone who asks you something in English?	LTL	60%	30%	10%	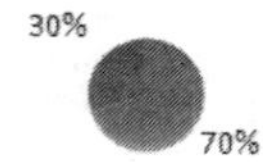
		EF	60%	30%	10%	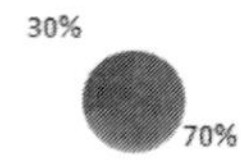
		EP	20%	60%	20%	
(vii)	Do you know the basics (about noun, pronoun, adjective, verb, adverb, simple sentences) of the grammar of the English Language?	LTL	60%	0	40%	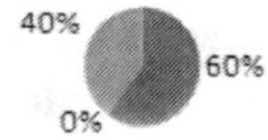
		EF	70%	20%	10%	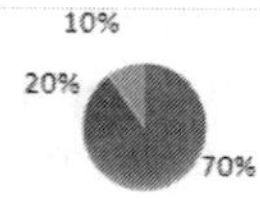
		EP	50%	0	50%	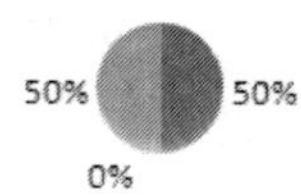

Table 4.1.5 shows that only 30% students in group LTL, 50% in EF, and 20% in EP are confident that they can use English language for communication proficiently whereas 70%, 30%, and 60% students in LTL, EF, and EF respectively are not sure about it. It also reveals that in LTL and EF, 60% of students can give answers confidently in English when

someone asks them something in English. In contrast to these two groups, in EP, only 20% of students can answer confidently. 30%, 30%, and 60% students in LTL, EF, and EP respectively are not able to answer in English confidently and rest of the students are not sure about it. In LTL, EF, EP, 60%, 70% and 50% students know basic grammar respectively whereas 40%, 10%, and 50% students in LTL, EF, and EP respectively are not clear in their mind about it.

Table 4.1.6: Representation of Feedback of Students about the Status of their Listening Skill

S. No	Statement	Levels	Options					Pie Chart
			Everything	Mostly	some	A little	Very Little	
(viii)	When people speak to you in English, how much are you able to understand?	LTL	20%	60%	20%	0	0	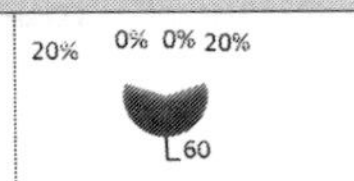
		EF	30%	50%	10%	10%	0	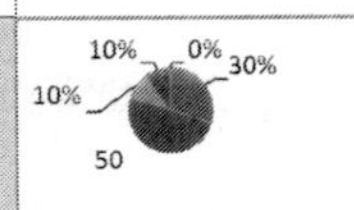
		EP	10%	30%	40%	10%	10%	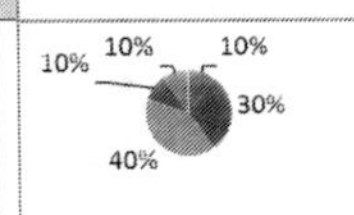

Table 4.1.6 illustrates that a fewer number of students (20% in LTL, 30% in EF, and 10% in EP group) comprehend fully when people speak to them in English. Many students (60% in LTL, 50% in EF, and 30% in EP group) understand most of the English speech of the speaker. In EF and EP groups, 10% of students in each group have very poor listening skills.

Table 4.1.7: Representation of Feedback of Students about their the Most Proficient and the Least Proficient Skill English Language Skill

S. No	Statement	Levels	Options				Pie Chart
			Listening	Reading	Speaking	Writing	
(ix)	Tick the English language skill in which you are the least proficient	LTL	10%	10%	50%	30%	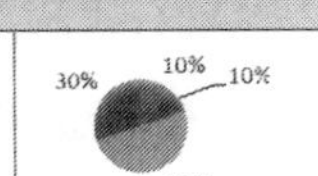
		EF	10%	20%	50%	20%	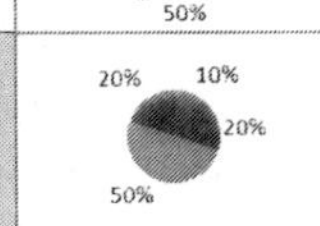
		EP	10%	0%	40%	30%	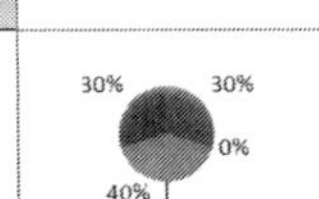

(x)	Tick the English language skill in which you are the most proficient	LTL	10%	70%	10%	0	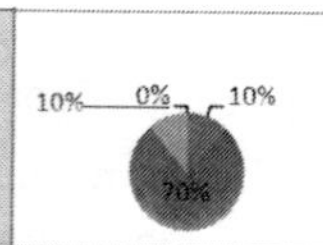
		EF	10%	60%	10%	20%	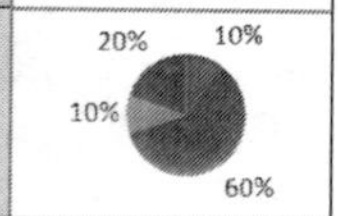
		EP	10%	50%	0	40%	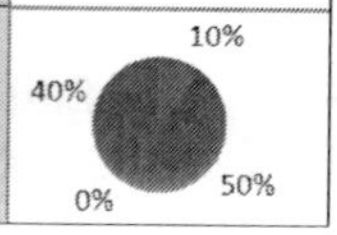

Table 4.1.7 informs that in LTL and EF groups, 50% students and 40% in EP group are least proficient in speaking. It also enlightens that 70% students in LTL, 60% in EF, and 50% in EP group are proficient in reading skills. Listening skills and writing skills cannot be ignored as only 10% and 0% students in LTL, 10% and 20% in EF, 10% and 40% in EP group feel that they are most proficient in these two skills.

(xi) What problem do you face while answering anyone in English?

Ans. Many students feel that they have a short vocabulary while using English as communication. They face problems in speaking English as they hesitate a lot, feel nervous, and do not have enough confidence to speak fluently. One or two students face problems on the part of pronunciation and a little bit of grammar.

(xii) Write about the situations when you need to communicate in English in your life.

Ans. Most students need to communicate in English while receiving any call from colleges and institutions, for introducing themselves to others, have a conversation with the person who is well versed in English, working in their offices, moving around in society and with their friends, and for their career advancement.

4.1.2 Qualitative Data

Some questions were asked in a telephone interview with senior professors who are teaching currently in Department of English, School of Open Learning, University of Delhi.

1. On what basis have you divided the students of B.Com. (p) and BA (p) into three groups?

Ans. *Students who have studied the English language till class 8 get English C. Students who have studied the English language until class 10 get English B. Students who have studied the English Language until class 12 get English A.*

2. What kind of educational background do these students have?

Ans. *Students who are not eligible for regular college at the University of Delhi take admission at the School of Open Learning. They have no other choice. These students come from low socio-economic backgrounds, whose parents are illiterate, and they received their secondary education from a government school. It does not mean that these students are not intelligent, but they did not get the right amount of exposure to English language skills. The condition for the same is very pathetic at the elementary stage; then what could you do at the higher education level?*

3. What is their level of proficiency in the English language?

Ans. *These students have the worst language skills, even though they do not have study skills and social skills. They do not have the right attitude for studying and learning on their own. They do not know how to study with the self-learning instructional material.*

4. In spite of SOL students' low socio-economic and educational backgrounds, what are the other problems for the students?

Ans. *There is a common syllabus for students studying at regular colleges and SOL students, which is a big disadvantage for SOL students. A committee that did not include any SOL faculty members decided on the syllabus. This syllabus does not suit the needs of SOL students, as they have different educational backgrounds as compared to regular students.*

Enough Faculties are not there in SOL. Currently, there are only four permanent teachers in the Department of English. The student-teacher ratio is very high. SOL gives the facilities of the PCP (Personal Contact Program), where the student-teacher ratio is 25: 1 where students are supposed to study their self-learning instructional material before coming to this PCP and discussing their problems with the teacher. But in actuality, PCP has converted into a class of 100-150 students, where students come into the class as a blank slate. And the teacher has to complete the whole syllabus in just a few days.

SOL does not have enough faculties to teach so many students at a time. Because of these poor facilities, this year's enrollment in BA (Eng. Hons.) has come down very significantly.

5. **What kind of material do you suggest for these students so that they can use English well in their real lives?**

Ans. *There should be a practice workbook where small paragraphs are given for exposure to English language skills. Creative assessment should be used where we can evaluate how much students are able to understand from any reading passage, poetry, etc. Questions should be different from the usual pattern, like creative questions, which encourage students to write their own views after understanding the context.*

The current study was carried out to determine the actual needs of the undergraduate students to make them proficient in communication in English. After analyzing the qualitative and quantitative data, it was found that the current, Communicative Language Course in English is not apt for the students of SOL, as the students studying in SOL have come from low socioeconomic and educational backgrounds (different from regular colleges) and have the worst language skills. Another disclosure is that these SOL students need the training to study the self-learning instructional material so that they can benefit from PCP programs conducted to solve their problems. Most students feel that they are proficient in reading skills, and the skills on which they need to work are speaking, writing, and then listening. These students complain that they have a short vocabulary while talking in English, and they hesitate a lot, feel nervous, and do not have enough confidence to speak English fluently. Assessment should be creative so that accurate assessment can be done for all four skills of the English language.

4.2 Analysis of Opinions of Subject Experts and Educators towards the Effectiveness of the Self-Learning Instructional Material for English Language Acquisition Skills

In order to validate the self-learning instructional material for English language acquisition skills for BA (Prog.) 1st-semester students, the opinionnaire was given to 16 subject experts and teacher educators. These subject experts include subject experts working in different schools and colleges in the Department of English and teacher educators working in the Department of Education from the various educational institutions in North India. They had to give their opinions about the SLIM on various parameters. These parameters were constructed based on four aspects:

A. the aspect of the **authenticity of the material,** which has five parameters,
B. the aspect of the **presentation of the content,** which has six parameters,
C. the aspect of **utility for students,** which has six parameters
D. and the aspect of **activities for assessment,** which also has six parameters.

The opinions for each parameter are based on the three-point scale, i.e., A: stands for agree, DA: stands for disagree, and UD: stands for undecided. Opinions are given a score of 1, 0 or none for agree, disagree, and undecided. The total value of the score indicates the effectiveness of developed self-learning instructional material for English language acquisition skills. The total score varies from 0 to 35, showing the least effectiveness to the highest effectiveness of the self-learning instructional material. Section or part-wise analysis was done by the researcher to know the opinions of the experts and educators on self-learning instructional material for English language acquisition skills. The opinions of subject experts are presented in the form of percentages and Pie charts in Tables 4.2.1, 4.2.3, 4.2.5, and 4.2.7. Group-wise opinion has been presented in the form of percentage in Tables 4.2.2, 4.2.4, 4.2.6, and 4.2.8 and presented graphically in the pie chart in Figures 4.2.1, 4.2.2, 4.2.3, and 4.2.4. The total opinion about the effectiveness of Self-Learning Instructional Material for English language acquisition skills for SOL students has been presented graphically in Table 4.2.9 and Figure 4.2.5.

To illustrate the opinions of subject experts and teacher educators on the effectiveness of Self-Learning Instructional Material for English Language Acquisition Skills for SOL students studying 1st semester BA (prog.) and B.Com (Prog.), the researcher has divided the analysis into four groups.

For the 'authenticity of the content' presented in the self-learning instructional material, Table 4.2.1 revealed that 100% of the subject experts have acknowledged that this self- learning instructional material has authentic content that explores simple resources and real-time situations where learners have lots of opportunities to practice English. Furthermore, 94% of subject experts have agreed that authentic content from diversified resources like newspapers, podcasts, and cartoon movie clippings is used in this self-learning instructional material. It can further be revealed from the table that 88% of subject experts appreciated that this self-learning instructional material teaches all the skills of the English language using resources that make the concept easily understandable and meaningful for the students and that make the learning process engaging and motivating for the students. It can be interpreted from the Table 4.2.2 and Fig. 4.2.1 that 93.75% of experts agreed, only 1.25% disagreed, and the rest 5% remain undecided about the statements given regarding the authenticity of the content. The subject experts appreciated that the self-learning instructional material for English language acquisition skills uses simple and varied authentic resources that put students into real-time situations to practice English language skills. This makes the learning process meaningful for the students, and hence they can engage themselves fully in their learning. Overall, the authenticity of the content was interpreted as the strong point of this self-learning instructional material, which therefore highlights the acceptance of self-learning instructional material for English language acquisition skills.

Table 4.2.1: Parameter-wise Representation of the Opinion of Subject Experts about the Effectiveness of Self-Learning Instructional Material for English Language Acquisition Skills with Respect to 'Authenticity of the Content'

No.	Statement	A	DA	UD	Pie Chart
	Part A: Authenticity of the Content				
A.1	Diversified resources like newspapers, podcasts, and cartoonmovie clippings are used	15 (94%)	0 (0%)	1 (6%)	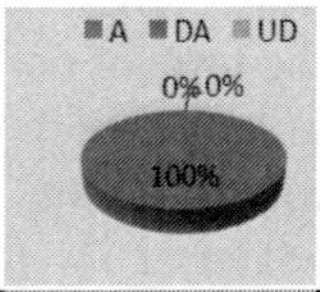
A.2	Exploring real-time situations where learners can speak English	16 (100%)	0 (0%)	0 (0%)	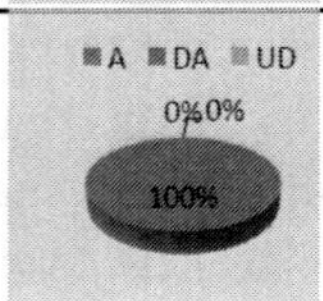
A.3	Simple resources for learners topractice English	16 (100%)	0 (0%)	0 (0%)	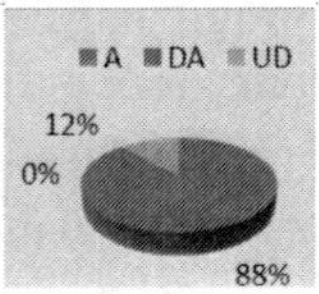
A.4	Resources are making teaching-learning process engaging and motivating for the students	14 (88%)	0 (0%)	2 (12%)	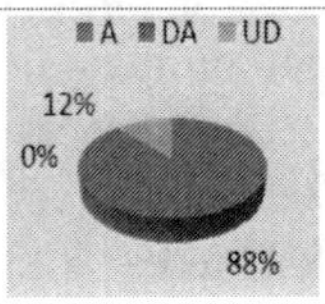

A.5	Making concepts easily understandable and meaningful	14 (88%)	1 (6%)	1 (6%)	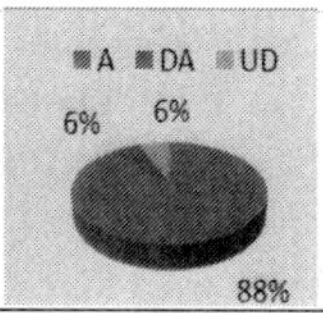

Table 4.2.2: Experts Overall Opinion about Effectiveness of Self-Learning Instructional Material for English Language Acquisition Skills with Respect to 'Authenticity of the Content'

Opinion (In Percent)	Agree	Disagree	Undecided
Authenticity of theContent'	93.75%	1.25%	5%

Fig. 4.2.1: Expert Overall Opinion about Authenticity of the Content

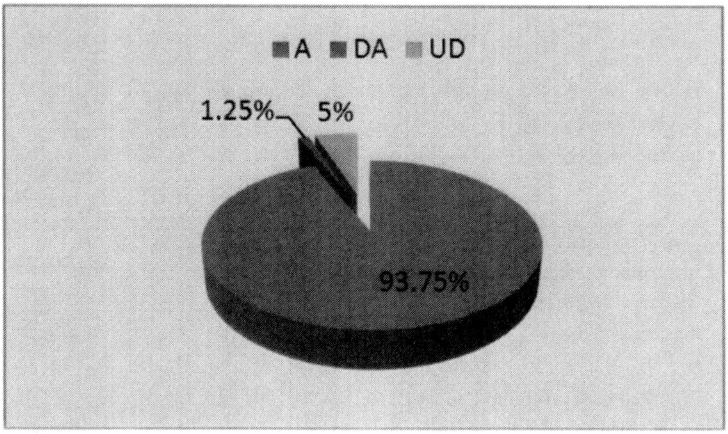

The second aspect, Presentation of the Content, of the opinionaire is presented in Table 4.2.3, which shows that 100% of the experts recognized that the workbook format of the material is easy and handy for the students. The table format presentation for many topics makes it easier for students to understand those topics. 94% of experts and educators opined that the structure of the units in the self-learning instructional material is logical and systematically constructed. Further, it is interpreted that 88% of the experts approved that all the English language skills are integrated using themes that are well-chosen, relevant, and useful for students. Also, 75% of the experts approved that the language of the material was appropriate for the level of the students. It has been shown in Table 4.2.4 and Fig. 4.2.2 that 91% of experts agreed, only 7% disagreed, and the rest 2% remain undecided about the parameters given in Aspect B, i.e., Presentation of the Content.

Table 4.2.3: Parameter-Wise Representation of Opinion of Subject Experts about the Effectiveness of Self-Learning Instructional Material for English Language Acquisition Skills with Respect to 'Presentation of the Content'

No.	Statement	A	DA	UD	Pie Chart
	Part B: Presentation of the Content				
B.1	Themes are well chosen, relevant, and useful for students	14 (88%)	2 (12%)	0 (0%)	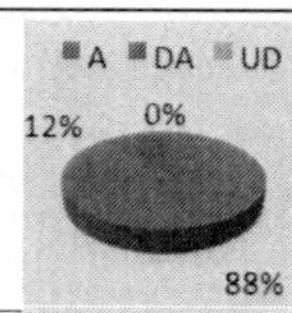
B.2	All the language skills are integrated	14 (88%)	2 (12%)	0 (0%)	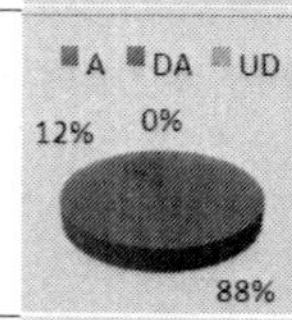
B.3	The structure of the units is logical and systematically constructed.	15 (94%)	0 (0%)	1 (6%)	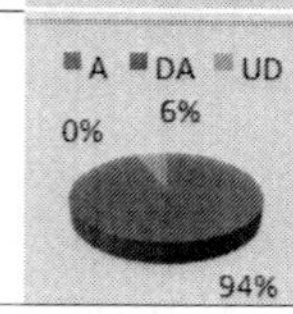
B.4	Table format presentations for many topics make it easier for students to understand them	16 (100%)	0 (0%)	0 (0%)	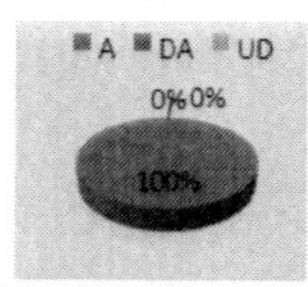
B.5	The language of the material is as per the level of the students	12 (75%)	3 (19%)	1 (6%)	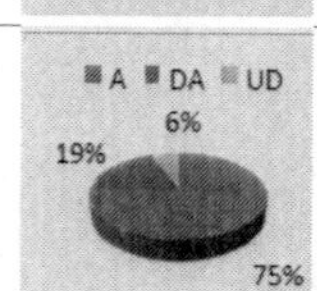
B.6	The workbook format is easy andhandy	16 (100%)	0 (0%)	0 (0%)	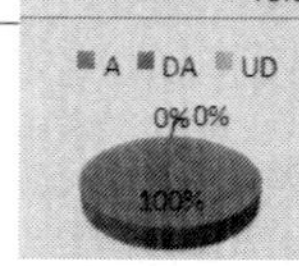

Table 4.2.4: Experts Overall Opinion about Effectiveness of Self-Learning Instructional Material for English Language Acquisition Skills with Respect to 'Presentation of the Content'

Opinion (In Percent)	Agree	Disagree	Undecided
Presentation of theContent'	91%	7%	2%

Fig. 4.2.2: Expert Overall Opinion about Presentation of the Content

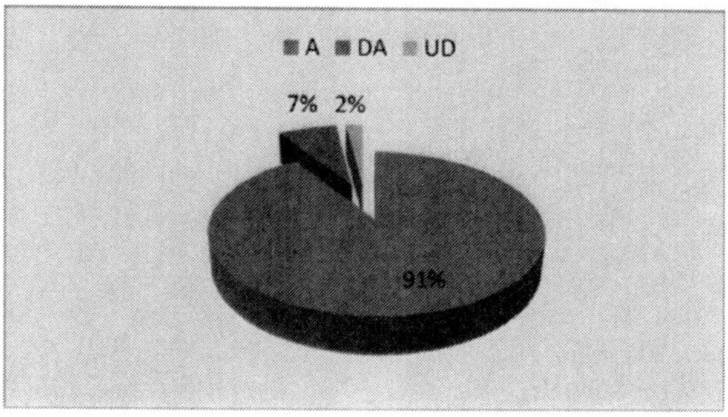

For the third aspect of the opinionnaire, Table 4.2.5 reveals that 100% of experts have acknowledged that the concepts taught in the self-learning instructional material are used in students' real-time situations. 94% of experts have agreed that self-learning instructional material helps clarify many concepts related to all skills of language and motivates students to make learning effective. 81% of experts agreed that this self- learning instructional material is interesting for students as it provides varied exposure to all the skills of the English language in an integrated form. It has been further discovered that 75% of experts opine that this SLIM makes the academic performance of students better. This SLIM meets the needs of learners with a variety of learning styles, according to 62% of experts. It has been further shown in Table 4.2.6 and Fig. 4.2.3 that 84% gave their agreement, only 3% of experts disagreed, and the rest, 13%, remain undecided about the parameters given in Group B, i.e., 'Utility for the Students'. Furthermore, it has been revealed that it is highly useful for the students as it presents all the skills in integrated forms in varied learning styles to make it interesting and motivational for the students.

Table 4.2.5: Parameter-Wise Representation of Opinion of Subject Experts about the Effectiveness of Self-learning Instructional Material for English Language Acquisition Skills with Respect to 'Utility for the Students'

No.	Statement	A	DA	UD	Pie Chart
	Part C: Utility for the Students				
C.1	Use the concepts taught in their real-time situations	16 (100%)	0 (0%)	0 (0%)	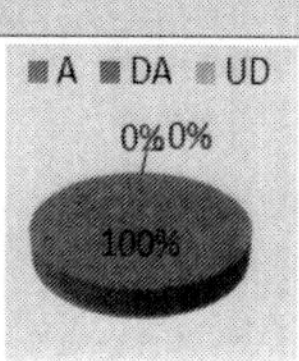

C.2	Helping in clarifying many concepts related to all skills of language	15 (94%)	1 (6%)	0 (0%)	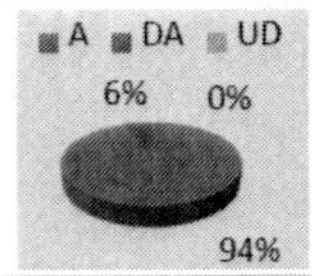
C.3	Motivates students to make learning effective	15 (94%)	1 (6%)	0 (0%)	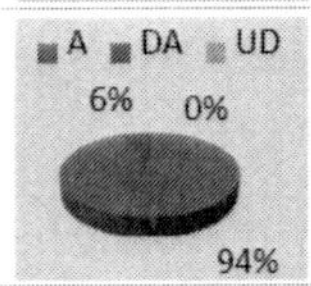
C.4	Students to make academic performance better	12 (75%)	2 (12%)	2 (12%)	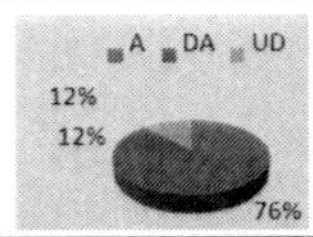
C.5	It is interesting for students to get varied exposure	13 (81%)	0 (0%)	3 (19%)	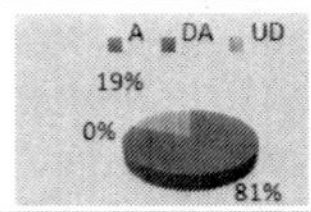
C.6	Caters the needs of varied learning styles.	10 (62%)	0 (0%)	6 (38%)	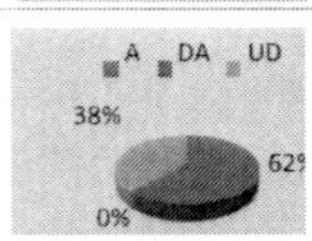

Table 4.2.6: Experts Overall Opinion about Effectiveness of Self-Learning Instructional Material for English Language Acquisition Skills with Respect to 'Utility for the students'

Opinion (In Percent)	Agree	Disagree	Undecided
Presentation of the Content'	91%	7%	2%

Fig. 4.2.3: Expert Overall Opinion about Utility for the Students

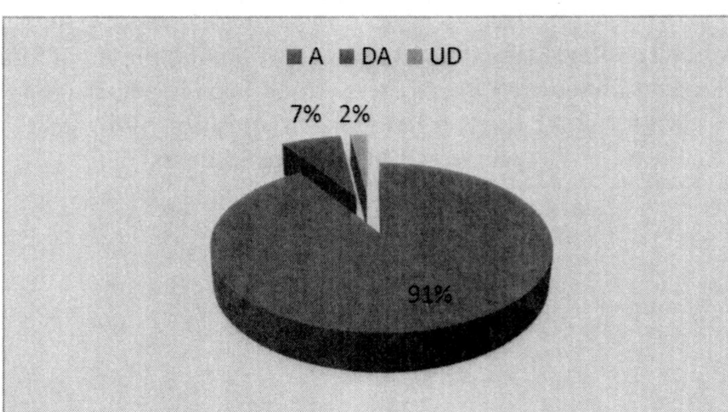

For Group 4 Activities of Assessment, it has been interpreted from Table 4.2.7 that 88% of experts approve that activities are assessing each skill of the English language. 81% of the experts agreed that activities given in SLIM are creative, engaging, interesting, motivational, and give students varied experiences. 62% of experts opined that activities are as per the levels of students, not above or below their level, whereas 58% of experts acknowledged that students can do self-assessment through these activities. It has been further shown in table 4.2.8 and fig. 4.2.4 that 77% of experts agreed, only 6% disagreed, and the rest, 17%, remain undecided about the parameters given in group 4, i.e., 'Activities of Assessment'. Furthermore, it has been illustrated that the SLIM is highly useful for both students and teachers, as it has many varieties of activities for all the skills of the English language through which teachers can assess the learning of the students and students can also assess themselves.

Table 4.2.7: Parameter-Wise Representation of the Opinion of Subject Experts about the Effectiveness of Self-learning Instructional Material for English Language Acquisition Skills with Respect to 'Activities for Assessment'

No.	Statement	A	DA	UD	Pie Chart
	Part D: Activities for Assessment				
D.1	Different types of creative activities are given for assessment	13 (81%)	0 (0%)	3 (19%)	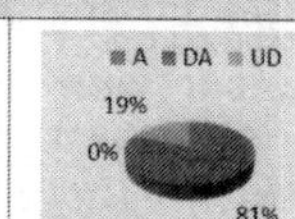
D.2	Activities give students a varied experience.	13 (81%)	1 (6%)	2 (13%)	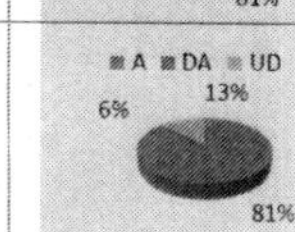
D.3	Activities are engaging, interesting, and motivational	15 (81%)	0 (0%)	1 (6%)	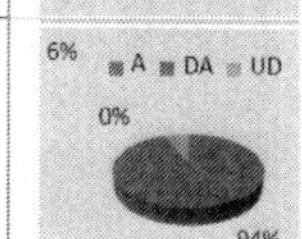
D.4	Activities are given as per students' level	10 (62%)	3 (19%)	3 (19%)	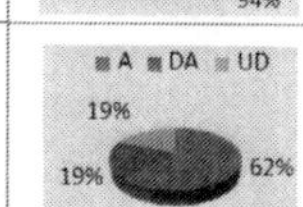
D.5	Activities assess every skill of the language	14 (88%)	0 (0%)	2 (12%)	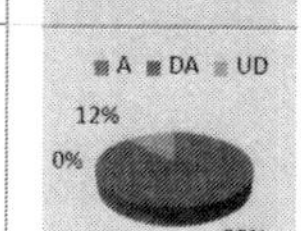
D.6	Students can assess themselves through the given activities	9 (58%)	2 (12%)	5 (30%)	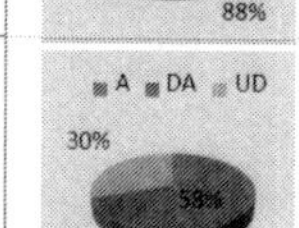

Table 4.2.8: Experts Overall Opinion about Effectiveness of Self-Learning Instructional Material for English Language Acquisition Skills with Respect to 'Activities for Assessment'

Opinion (In Percent)	Agree	Disagree	Undecided
Activities forAssessment	77%	6%	17%

Fig. 4.2.4: Expert Overall Opinion about Activities for Assessment

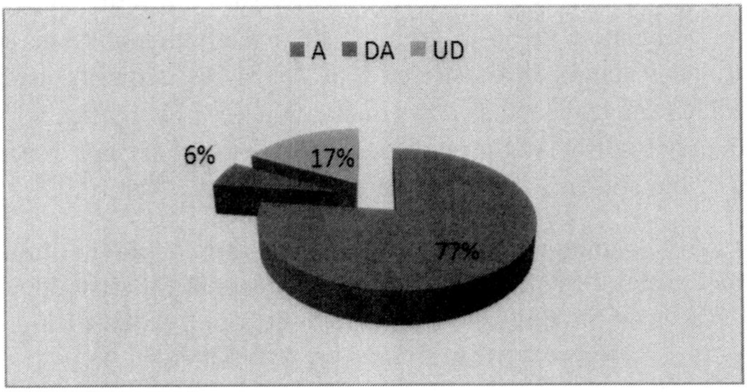

Table 4.2.9: Total opinion of Experts about Effectiveness of Self-Learning Instructional Material for English Language Acquisition Skills

Opinion (In Percent)	Agree	Disagree	Undecided
Total Opinion	84%	6%	10%

Fig. 4.2.5: Total Opinion of Experts about the Effectiveness of Self-learning Instructional Material for English Language Acquisition Skills of Undergraduate Students of SOL

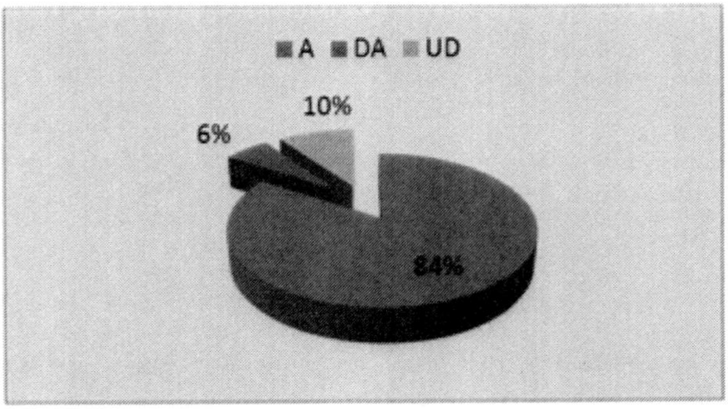

A=Agree, DA=Disagree, UD=Undecided

The total opinion of experts on the overall effectiveness of the Self-Learning Instructional material has been analyzed and illustrated in Table 4.2.9 and in the form of a pie chart in Fig. 4.2.5. It has been interpreted from Table 4.2.9 that 84% of the experts agreed on the effectiveness of Self-Learning Instructional Material for the English language acquisition skills of undergraduate students in SOL. Only 6% of experts disagreed, and the rest (10%) are undecided about the parameters given in the scale. It has been further indicated that most of the language experts and teacher educators favour the effectiveness of this Self-Learning Instructional Material. They also commented that the SLIM is creatively designed and well prepared. The exercises or activities are comprehensive, and students will surely benefit from them, especially from the vast vocabulary. It can be concluded that it is highly helpful for students as well as teachers. It provides exposure and opportunities through authentic resources to practice all the skills, i.e., reading, listening, writing, speaking, conversation, and vocabulary, in their integrated forms. The concepts are presented in graphical forms like tables, concept maps, etc. to make more understandable for the students The SLIM is based on interesting activities that are creative, engaging, motivational, and helpful in assessing the learning.

4.3 Analysis of Achievement of Achievement Scores of Control and Experimental Group before the Experimental Treatment

To achieve the objectives, the researcher developed self-learning instructional material for the acquisition of English language skills, and then an experiment was conducted to see its effectiveness on the achievement in English language acquisition skills of BA (Prog.) 1st semester students of the School of Open Learning.

For the experiment, the selected 60 students studying the 'English Fluency' course were administered a pre-test for English language acquisition skills. Then all 60 students were divided into two groups: the Control Group and the Experimental group. The pre- test was administered to all the students in both groups. Then the pre-test achievement scores were subjected to descriptive statistics to get the mean, SD, and normality test and One way ANOVA to get the Homogeneity test of Variance.

After doing the experiment and getting the post test scores, the data was analysed through ANCOVA to get the mean, standard deviation, and significance of the difference between the means of pretest scores and posttest scores. To use ANCOVA as a statistical tool for analysing data, the assumptions of normal distribution of data and homogeneity of variance must be satisfied for the pretest achievement scores of both groups. Therefore, the results of mean, standard deviation, skewness, and kurtosis have been presented for pre test scores and post test scores in both groups in the Table 4.3.1.

Table 4.3.1: Summary of Mean, SD, Skewness, and Kutosis of Pre-Test Scores and Post-Test Scores in Both Groups

	Pre-Test	Post-Test
Mean	21.94	25.52
SD	7.68	8.40
N	60	60
Skewness	.408	.092
Kurtosis	-.505	-.704

From Table 4.3.1, it has been revealed that the values of mean and standard deviation for pre-test scores come out to be 21.94 and 7.68, respectively, whereas the values of mean and standard deviation for post-test scores have been found to be 25.52 and 8.40, respectively. The values of skewness for the pre-test and post-test have been found to be 0.40 and 0.09, whereas the values of kurtosis have been found to be -0.5 and -0.7 respectively. The values are within range. Therefore, the data is considered to be normal, as depicted in Figure 4.3.1.

Fig. 4.3.1: Pre-Test and Post-Test of Students Achievement in English Language Acquisition Skills

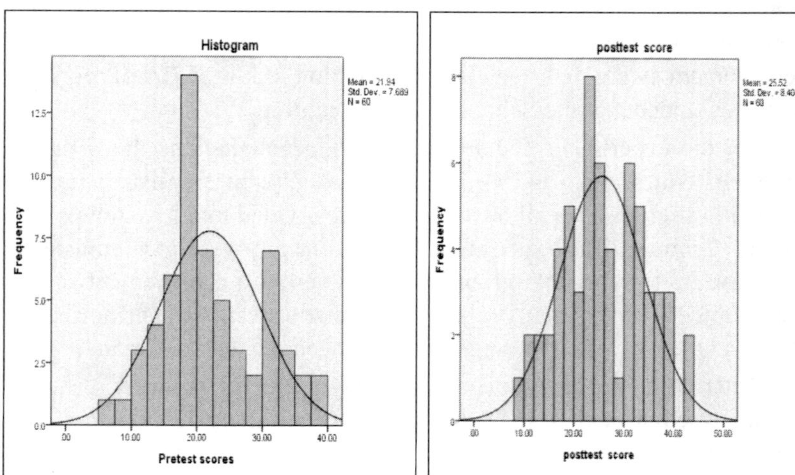

The normality of the data had also been confirmed with the Test of Normality called the Shapiro-Wilk Test, and its result has been presented in Table 4.3.2.

Table 4.3.2: Test of Normality – Shapiro-Wilk Test for Pre-test Score

Data	Statistics	Df	Sig.
Pretest Scores	0.96	60	0.55

It has been revealed from Table 4.3.2 that the p-value is 0.55, which is greater than 0.05. It indicates that the data is normally distributed.

Homogeneity of variance means that whatever the differences are in one group, the same magnitude of difference is there in another group. To check the condition of variance, the data was analysed with One-Way ANOVA, and the results are presented in Table 4.3.3.

Table 4.3.3: Summary of Test of Homogeneity of Variances of Pre-test Scores

Levene Statistic	Df1	Df2	Sig.
.589	1	58	.446

From Table 4.3.3, it can be seen that the F-Value for homogeneity of variance is 0.589, which is significant at the 0.05 level with df = 1/58. It indicates that there are equal variances across the groups. Thus, the null hypothesis that there are equal variances across the groups is not rejected, or there is no difference between the variances of the two groups. Thus, the two samples come from populations with the same variance.

4.4 Teaching Strategy-Wise Comparison of Adjusted Mean Scores of Achievement of Students by Taking Their Pre-Achievement in English Language Acquisition Skills as Covariate

The first objective was to compare the adjusted mean scores of achievement in English language acquisition skills of students taught through self-learning instructional material and lecture methods (with existing study material) by considering their pre-achievement in English language acquisition skills as a covariate. The data was analyzed with the help of One-Way ANCOVA, and the results are given in Table 4.4.1.

Table 4.4.1: Summary of One-Way ANCOVA of Achievement of students by taking pre-achievement as their covariate

Sum of Variance	Df	SSy.x	MSSy.x	Fy.x-Value
Instructional Strategy	1	278.79	278.79	9.53**
Error	57	1667.24	29.25	
Total	60	43233.00		

From Table 4.4.1, it can be seen that the adjusted Fy.x-Value is 9.53, which is significant at the 0.01 level with df = 1/57. It was indicated that there is a significant difference in adjusted mean scores of achievement between students taught through self-learning instructional material and the lecture method (with existing study material) by considering their pre-achievement in English language acquisition skills as a covariate. Thus, the null hypothesis that there is no significant difference in adjusted mean scores of achievement between students taught through self-instructional learning material and the lecture method (with existing study material) by considering their pre-achievement in English language acquisition skills as a covariate is rejected. Further, the adjusted mean score of students treated through self-learning instructional material is 27.68, which is significantly higher than the Lecture method group, whose adjusted mean score of achievement is 23.35. Because of this existing difference in achievement scores in the post-test of both groups, a pair-wise comparison has been done, and the results are presented in Table 4.4.2.

Table 4.4.2: Post-hoc Test for Difference between Post Achievement Test Mean Scores

Name of the Group	Mean Difference	Std. error	Sig.
Control Group (I) – Experimental Group (J)	I – J = -3.962	1.421	.007*
Experimental Group (J) – Control Group (I)	J – I = 3.962	1.421	.007

*Significant at 0.01 level

Table 4.4.2 reveals that the mean difference between the control group, which was taught through the lecture method using the existing material, and the experimental group, which was taught through the self-learning instructional material, is 3.962. The significant value of both groups, i.e., the control group and the experimental group is .007 > 0.01, which is significant at the 0.01 level of significance. By comparing the means of the control group and the experimental group, it is interpreted that the self- learning instructional material developed by the researcher has improved the English language acquisition skills of BA (Prog.) 1st semester students of SOL, as compared to the students who were taught through the lecture method using existing material. The comparison of the adjusted mean scores of achievement of students taught through self- learning instructional material and lecture methods (with existing study material) by considering their pre-achievement in English language acquisition skills as covariate is given in Graph 4.4.1.

Graph 4.4.1: Estimated Marginal Means of Post-test Score

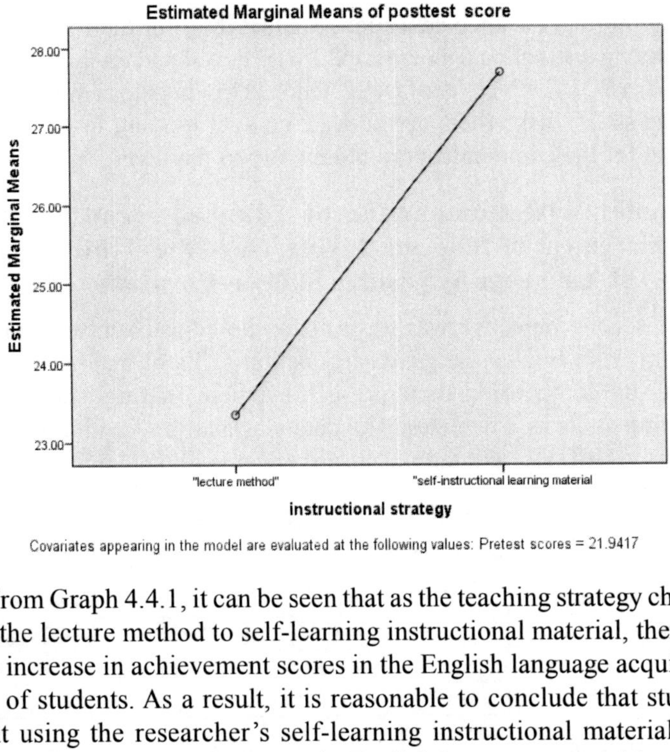

From Graph 4.4.1, it can be seen that as the teaching strategy changes from the lecture method to self-learning instructional material, there is a sharp increase in achievement scores in the English language acquisition skills of students. As a result, it is reasonable to conclude that students taught using the researcher's self-learning instructional material have demonstrated better performance in English language acquisition skills when compared to students who received instruction using the lecture method and preexisting material. Hence, the self-learning instructional material was found to be significantly better at facilitating achievement in the English language acquisition skills of students in comparison to the lecture method when pre-achievement was taken as covariate.

The self-learning instructional material developed by the researcher has improved the English language acquisition skills of BA (Prog.) 1st semester students of SOL, as compared to the students who were taught through lecture method using existing material. This result is consonance with the study of Aalaei (2016); Sreehari (2012); Mehta (2015); Rana (2017). The Self-Learning Instructional Material (SLIM) developed using Communicative Language Teaching beneficial to students of distance education. Many researchers have done research on the effectiveness of CLT to enhance English language skills. They implemented activities based CLT. Only Naz (2016) had modified the existing SLM for the distance education School of Aligarh Muslim University. Otherwise no study has been done so far related to development of self-learning instructional material using communicative language teaching for students studying through distance education. Significantly for the first time any self- learning instructional material (SLIM) is developed for those students studying in SOL, University of Delhi which helps them to acquire English language skills, make them confidence, and get training to use English language for the communication in their day-to-day lives.

4.5 Gender-Wise Comparison of Adjusted Mean Scores of Achievement of Students Taking Their Pre-Achievement in English Language Acquisition Skills as Covariate

The second objective was to compare the adjusted mean scores of achievement in English language acquisition skills of male and female students by considering their pre-achievement in English language acquisition skills as covariates. The data was analyzed with the help of One-Way ANCOVA, and the results are given in Table 4.5.1.

Table 4.5.1: Summary of One-Way ANCOVA of Achievement of Students by Taking Pre-Achievement as their Covariate on Gender Basis

Sum of Variance	Df	SSy.x	MSSy.x	Fy.x-Value
Gender	1	0.065	0.065	0.002 (ns)
Error	57	1945.96	34.14	
Total	60	43233.00		

Ns – not significant

From the table 4.5.1, it can be seen that the adjusted F-Value for Gender is 0.002, which is not significant. It indicates that there is no significant difference in adjusted mean scores of achievement in English language acquisition skills between Male and Female students when their pre-achievement is taken as covariate. So there was no significant effect of Gender on achievement in the English language acquisition skills of students when their pre-achievement was taken as covariate. Thus, the null hypothesis that there is no significant difference in the adjusted mean scores of Achievement in English language acquisition skills of male and female students by considering their pre- achievement in English language acquisition skills as covariates is not rejected. It may be said that both male and female students were found to possess achievement English language acquisition skills at the same level when their pre-achievement was taken as covariate. The result is not in the favour of the result shown in the study of Owen & Razali, (2018) that illustrates difference in mean score between male and female students but the difference between gender was not statistically different.

4.6 Effect of Interaction between Instructional Strategy and Gender on the Achievement of Students by Taking Their Pre-Achievement in English Language Acquisition Skills as Covariate

The fourth objective was to compare the adjusted mean scores of Achievement in English language acquisition skills of male and female students taught through self- instructional learning material and lecture methods (with existing study material) by considering their pre-achievement in English language acquisition skills as covariate. The data was analyzed with the help of One-Way ANCOVA, and the results are given in Table 4.6.1.

Table 4.6.1: Summary of One-Way ANCOVA of the Effect of Interaction Between the Instructional Strategy and Gender on the Achievement of Students by Taking Pre-Achievement as Their Covariate

Sum of Variance	Df	SSy.x	MSSy.x	Fy.x-Value
Gender*Instructional Strategy	1	3.81	3.81	0.126 (ns)
Error	55	1663.31	30.24	
Total	60	43233.00		

Ns – not significant

From Table 4.6.1, it can be seen that the adjusted F-Value for the interaction between the Instructional Strategy and Gender is 0.126, which is not significant. It reflects that there is no significant difference in adjusted mean scores of achievement in English language acquisition skills of Male and Female students taught through Self-learning Instructional material and lecture methods using existing material by taking their pre- achievement as their covariate. So there was no significant effect of interaction between Instructional Strategy and Gender on the achievement in English language acquisition skills of students by taking their pre-achievement as their covariate. Thus, the null hypothesis stated that there is no significant difference in the adjusted mean scores of Achievement in English language acquisition skills of male and female students taught through self-learning instructional material and lecture method (with existing study material) by considering their pre-achievement in English language acquisition skills as covariate is not rejected. It may be said that achievement in English language acquisition skills of students was found to be independent of interaction between Instructional Strategy and Gender when their pre-achievement was taken as their covariate. From the literature review, it was found that no study has seen the effect of interaction between instructional strategy and gender on the achievement of students in English language acquisition skills.

4.7 Interaction Analysis of Self-Learning Instructional Strategy on Students' Achievement in English Language Acquisition Skills

This section deals with the interaction analysis of the Self-Learning Instructional strategy with students. The researcher's review of the literature informs us that the self- learning instructional strategy has a significant impact on students' achievement in English language acquisition skills. Therefore, it is hypothesized that there is a positive attitude among the students towards the self-learning instructional material.

The attitude of the students towards the self-learning instructional material was obtained through an Interaction Feedback Questionnaire. This questionnaire was given to all 30 students in the experimental group. The questionnaire consists of five parts according to the weightage given to five aspects: Layout, Design, and presentation contain seven statements; Content, Topic, and Language have 7 statements; Language Teaching Methods and Activities contain 7 statements; The four language skills—Listening, Reading, Speaking, and Writing also contain 7 statements; and Sub-skills—Vocabulary, Grammar, and Conversational Skill have 6 statements.

The assessment method for each statement or parameter was based on a five-point scale: SD: stands for Strongly Disagree, D stands for Disgree, UNC stands for Uncertain, A stands for Agree, and SA stands for Strongly Agree. Section or part-wise analysis was done by the researcher to know the opinions of the students about the Self-Learning Instructional material for English language Acquisition Skills.

The statement-wise students' feedback for the self-learning instructional material is presented in the form of percentages and pie graphs in tables 4.7.1, 4.7.2, 4.7.3, 4.7.4, and 4.7.5. The overall parameter-wise students' feedback is presented in the form of pie chart in the Figures 4.7.1, 4.7.2, 4.7.3, 4.7.4, and 4.7.5.

This section presents the analysis of the feedback of 30 students in the experimental group towards the effectiveness of Self-learning Instructional Material on their English Language Acquisition Skills. For this purpose, the researcher has divided the analysis into five groups.

Table 4.7.1: Statement-wise Representation of Feedback of Students about the Effectiveness of Self-Learning Instructional Material for English Language Acquisition Skills with Respect to 'Layout, Design, and Presentation'

S.N	Statement	SD	D	UNC	A	SA	Pie Chart
	Part A: Layout, Design, and Presentation						
1.	Units are designed and presented in an harmonious organization	7 (23%)	1 (3%)	5 (17%)	5 (17%)	12 (40%)	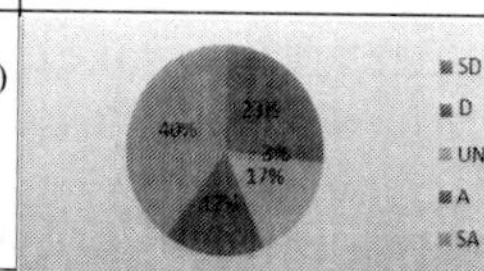
2.	Contains a detailed list of contents including unit titles, language skills, and activities related to them	0 (0%)	8 (27%)	2 (6%)	12 (40%)	8 (27%)	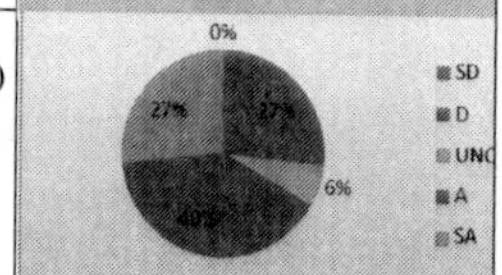
3.	Objectives of each unit are Clearly stated in the beginning.	2 (6%)	0 (0%)	8 (27%)	12 (40%)	8 (27%)	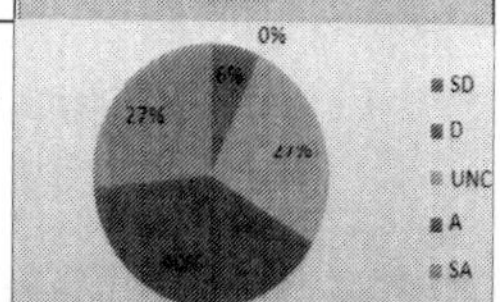
4.	The content and Learning activities are well-sequenced with clear headings and subheadings	0 (0%)	4 (13%)	5 (17%)	15 (50%)	6 (20%)	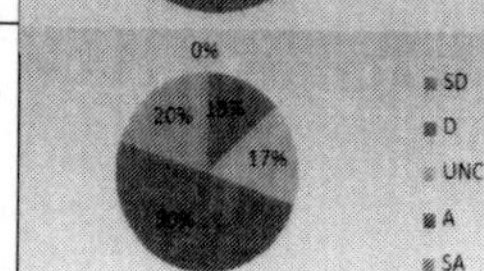
5.	Illustrations and other non-textual materials like tables, diagrams, hyperlinks, and timelines are purposeful and clear	1 (3%)	3 (10%)	2 (7%)	9 (30%)	15 (50%)	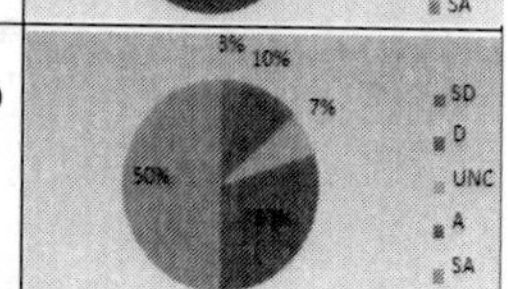
6.	Instructions for each activity are stated clearly for the students to follow.	0 (0%)	5 (17%)	5 (17%)	10 (33%)	10 (33%)	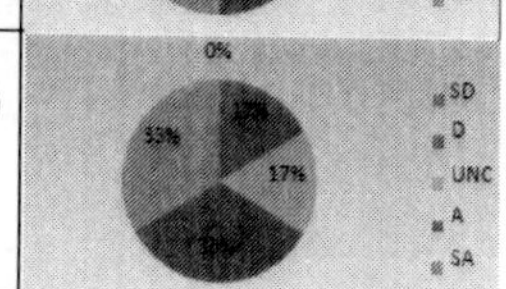
7.	Each unit offers a variety of exercises and activities to practice the target language skills to help the students to communicate in English in real life.	1 (3%)	3 (10%)	2 (7%)	12 (40%)	12 (40%)	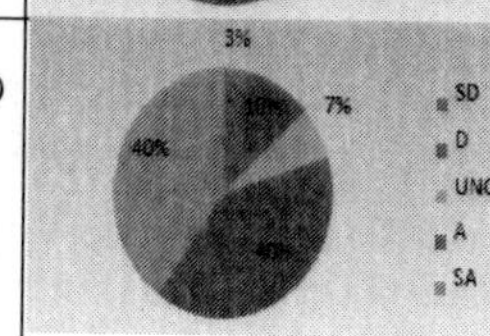

For the 'layout, design, and presentation' in the self-learning instructional material, Table 4.7.1 revealed that around 60% of the students agree that units are designed and presented in an harmonious organization in which list of contents including unit titles, language skills, and activities related to them and objectives of each unit are clearly stated. But 26% of the students disagree with it. It means we need to revise the layout and presentation of the content of the self-learning instructional material. 70% of the students feel that the content and learning activities are well-sequenced with clear headings and subheadings, and illustrations and other non-textual materials like tables, diagrams, hyperlinks, and timelines are purposeful and clear. More than 70% of the students vote that each unit offers a variety of exercises and activities to practice the target language skills and it was easy for them to follow the instructions stated in each activity. From Fig. 4.7.1, it has been interpreted that overall 70% of the students appreciated the layout, design, and presentation of the self-learning instructional material, 11% disagree and 5% strongly disagree and the rest 14% of the students are undecided with the parameters for the layout, design, and presentation of the self- learning instructional material.

Fig. 4.7.1: Overall Feedback of Students about the Effectiveness of Self-Learning Instructional Material for English Language Acquisition Skills with Respect to 'Layout, Design, and Presentation'

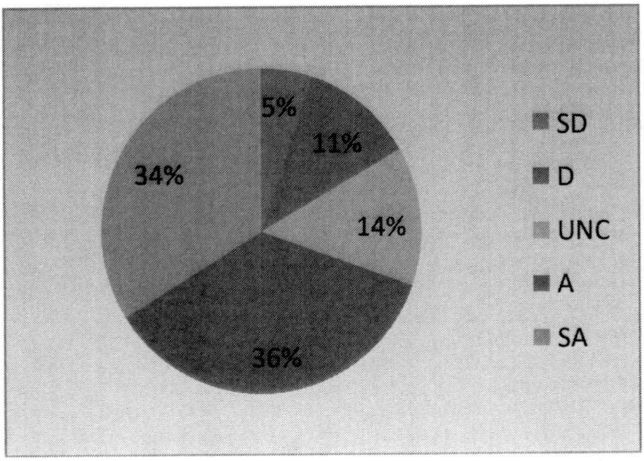

The second aspect, 'Content, Topic, and Language' of the feedback interaction scale is presented in Table 4.7.2, which shows that 60% of the students recognized that the topics of the units are interesting and up-to-date. Further, it is interpreted that around 70% of the students' experience that the content and language used in the topics is appropriate to the students' level and gives exposure to the authentic language. It also covers all four skills in an integrated and balanced way. It has been shown in fig. 4.7.2 that 71% of students agreed, only 16% disagreed, and the rest 11% remain undecided about the parameters given in Aspect B, i.e., Content, Topic, and Language.

Table 4.7.2: Statement-wise Representation of Feedback of Students about the Effectiveness of Self-Learning Instructional Material for English Language Acquisition Skills with Respect to 'Content, Topic, and Language'

No.	Statement	SD	D	UNC	A	SA	Pie Chart
Part B: Content, Topic, and Language							
1.	The topics of the units are up-to-date and interesting	6 (20%)	2 (7%)	2(7%)	10 (33%)	10 (33%)	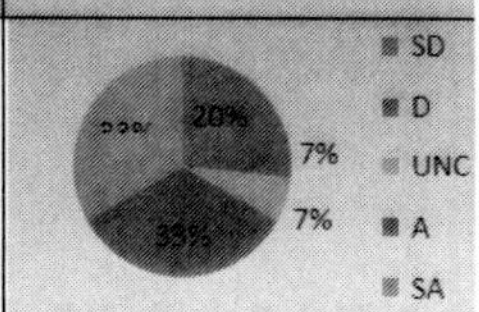
2.	The topics, content, and language used are appropriate to the students' level	2 (7%)	7 (23%)	3 (10%)	9 (30%)	9 (30%)	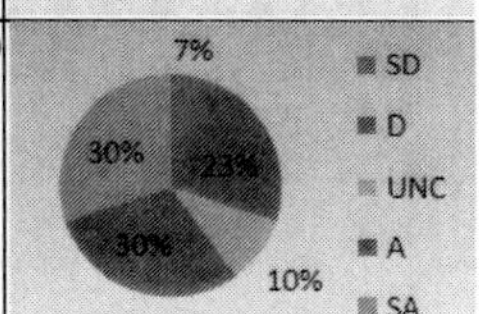
3.	The content and language gives exposure to real language	0 (0%)	3 (10%)	7 (23%)	10 (34%)	10 (33%)	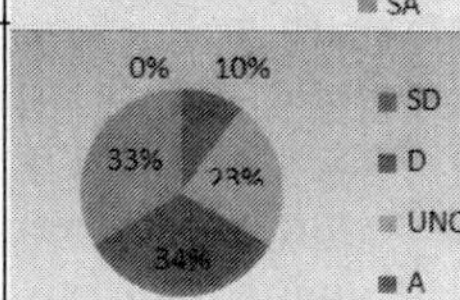
4.	The content is relevant to the students' needs and interest	1 (3%)	2 (7%)	3 (10%)	12 (40%)	12 (40%)	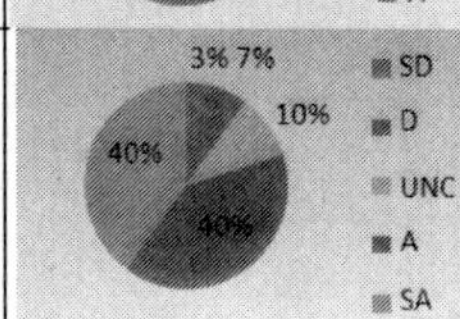
5.	The content covers all 4 language skills - listening, speaking, reading, and writing with an appropriate balance and in an integrated manner	1 (3%)	0 (0%)	3 (10%)	6 (20%)	20 (67%)	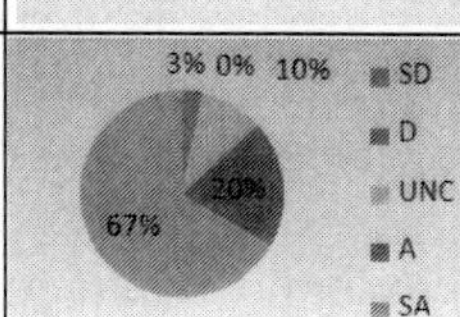
6.	Language used for Instructions for each activity is clearly understandable for the students to follow.	0 (0%)	3 (10%)	2 (7%)	10 (33%)	15 (50%)	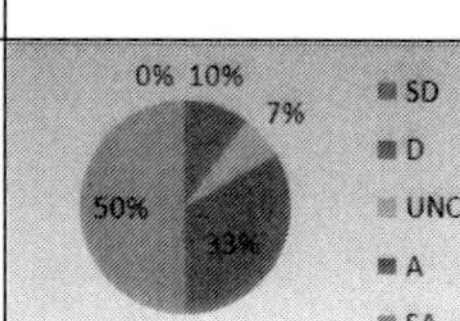

7.	The language used in the textbook is authentic and up-to-date.	0 (0%)	2` (7%)	4 (13%)	16 (53%)	8 (27%)	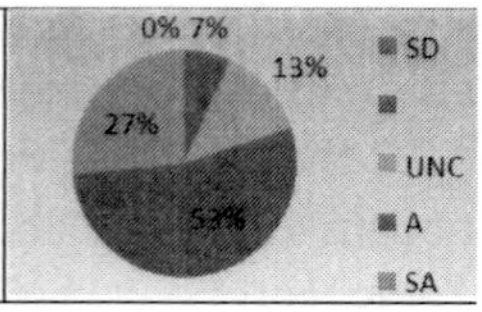

Fig. 4.7.2: Overall Feedback of Students about the Effectiveness of Self-Learning Instructional Material for English Language Acquisition Skills with Respect to 'Content, Topic, and Language'

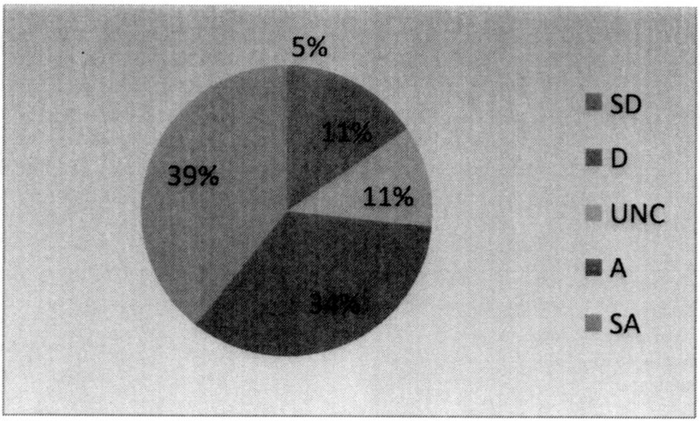

For the third aspect of the feedback interaction scale, Table 4.7.3 reveals that around 70% of the students have highly appreciated the creative and student-centered teaching approach. They felt that this language teaching method stimulate interaction and negotiation which encourage learners to apply their learned skills and also enhances the students' autonomy. They participated actively in the activities that used varied authentic resources. They enjoyed using the technology for learning. It has been further shown in Fig. Table 4.7.3 that 76% of the students gave their agreement, only 13% of experts disagreed, and the rest, 11%, remain undecided about the parameters given in Group C, i.e., 'Language Teaching Method and Activities'. Furthermore, it has been revealed that it is highly useful for the students as it encourages learners to participate fully in the teaching learning activities that matched with their interest and provide variety in presenting real-life examples for language learning.

Table 4.7.3: Statement-wise Representation of Feedback of Students about the Effectiveness of Self-Learning Instructional Material for English Language Acquisition Skills with Respect to 'Language Teaching Method and Activities'

No.	Statement	SD	D	UNC	A	SA	Pie Chart
Part C: Language Teaching Method and Activities							
1.	Stimulate interaction and negotiation	7 (23%)	0 (0%)	5 (17%)	8 (27%)	10 (33%)	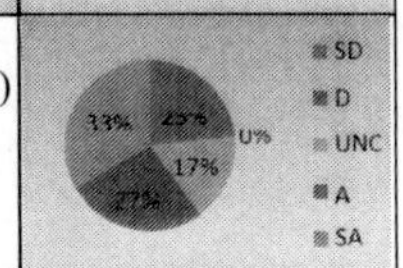
2.	Creative and student-centered approach to teaching and learning	0	6 (20%)	2 (7%)	10 (33%)	12 (40%)	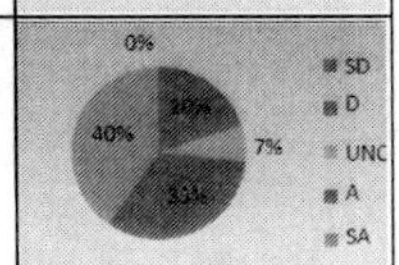
3.	Encourage learners to apply their developing language skills	0 (0%)	3 (10%)	7 (23%)	8 (27%)	12 (40%)	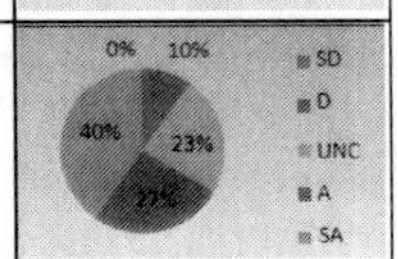
4.	Use varied authentic resources to produce teaching and learning activities	1 (3%)	3 (10%)	3 (10%)	11 (37%)	12 (40%)	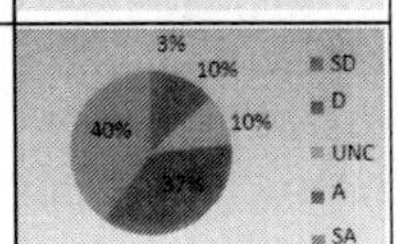
5.	The activities encourage student participation and enable them to appropriately use language in different real situations	2 (7%)	0 (0%)	3 (10%)	10 (33%)	15 (50%)	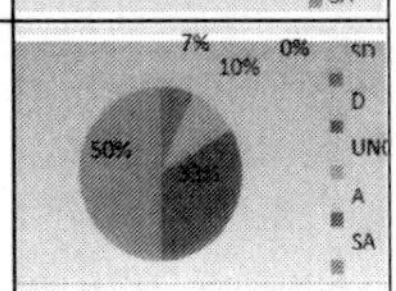
6.	The activities enhance the students' autonomy-become independent Learners responsible for their own learning	1 (3%)	2 (7%)	0 (0%)	12 (40%)	15 (50%)	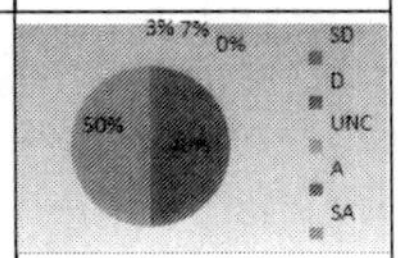
7.	Self-learning instructional material encourages the use of technology in learning English	0 (0%)	2 (7%)	3 (10%)	10 (33%)	15 (50%)	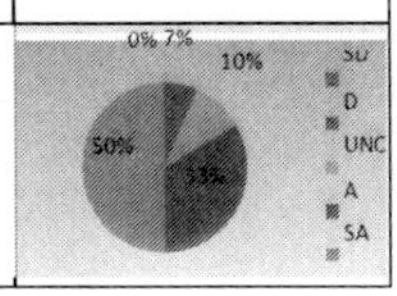

Fig. 4.7.3: Overall Feedback of Students about the Effectiveness of Self-Learning Instructional Material for English Language Acquisition Skills with Respect to 'Language Teaching Method and Activities"

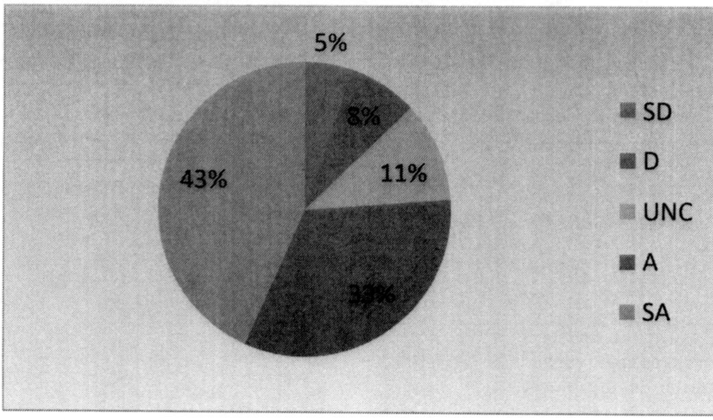

For Group 4, 'Four Language Skills: Listening, Speaking, Reading, and Writing', it has been interpreted from Table 4.7.4 that 64% of the students agree that all the four skills – listening, speaking, reading, and writing - are integrated and appropriate for the students' level. The material used in listening, speaking, reading, and writing tasks are authentic and interesting. 80% of students acknowledged that the self-learning instructional material has a variety and sufficiency of tasks related to four skills and relevant and important topics are covered. 90% of the students opine that various exercises are provided for practice in the balanced weightage for all four language skills. It has been further shown in Table 4.7.4 and Fig. 4.7.4 that 77% of experts agreed, only 11% disagreed, and the rest, 12%, remain undecided about the parameters given in group 4, i.e., 'Four Language Skills: Listening, Speaking, Reading, and Writing'. Furthermore, it has been illustrated that the students appreciated the self- learning instructional material as it is highly useful for students.

Table 4.7.4: Statement-wise Representation of Feedback of Students about the Effectiveness of Self-learning Instructional Material for English Language Acquisition Skills with Respect to 'Four Language Skills: Listening, Speaking, Reading, and Writing'

No.	Statement	SD	D	UNC	A	SA	Pie Chart
Part D: Four Language Skills: Listening, Speaking, Reading, Writing							
1.	The material used in listening, speaking, reading, and writing tasks are authentic and interesting both in terms of content and language.	7 (23%)	3 (10%)	1 (3%)	10 (34%)	9 (30%)	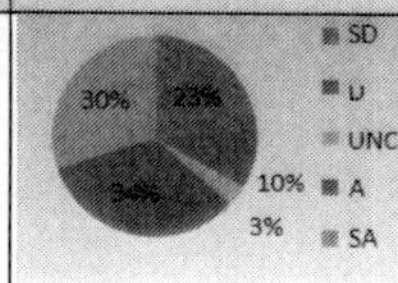
2.	Listening, speaking, reading, and writing tasks are appropriate for the students' level	0	7 (23%)	3 (10%)	10 (34%)	10 (33%)	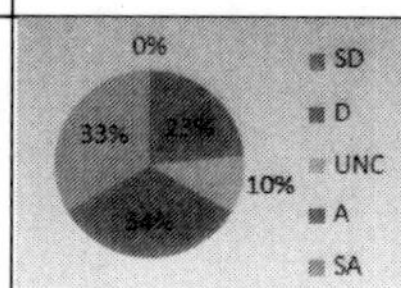
3.	All the four skills are integrated with each other into the practice.	0 (0%)	1 (3%)	9 (30%)	10 (34%)	10 (33%)	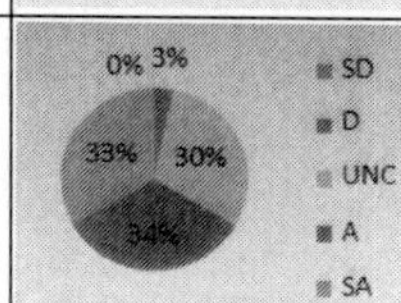
4.	It has a variety and sufficiencyof listening, speaking, reading, and writing tasks.	1 (3%)	1 (3%)	2 (7%)	14 (47%)	12 (40%)	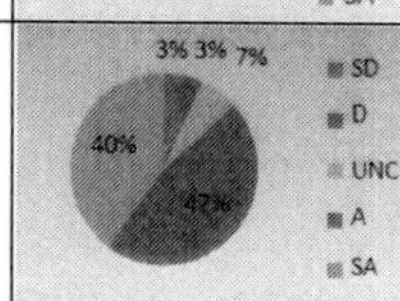
5.	Relevant and important topics are chosen and covered for the four skills	0 (0%)	0 (0%)	6 (20%)	4 (13%)	20 (67%)	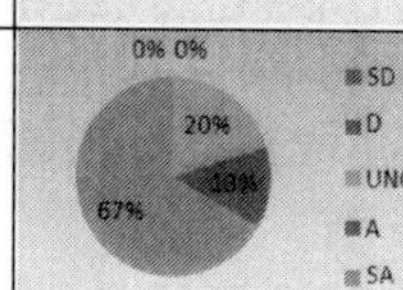
6.	Various exercises are provided for practice for all four language skills	1 (3%)	0 (0%)	2 (7%)	7 (23%)	20 (67%)	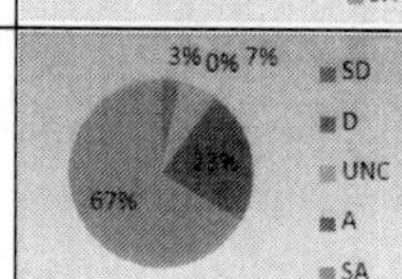
7.	All language skills - listening, speaking, reading, and writing are given balanced weightage	1 (3%)	0 (0%)	2 (7%)	15 (50%)	12 (40%)	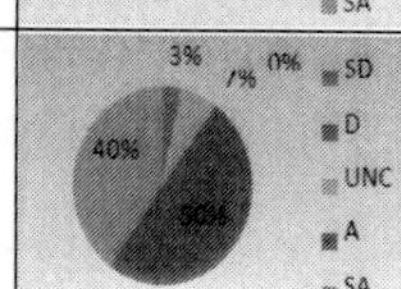

Fig. 4.7.4: Overall Feedback of Students about the Effectiveness of Self-Learning Instructional Material for English Language Acquisition Skills with Respect to 'Four Language Skills: Listening, Speaking, Reading, Writing'

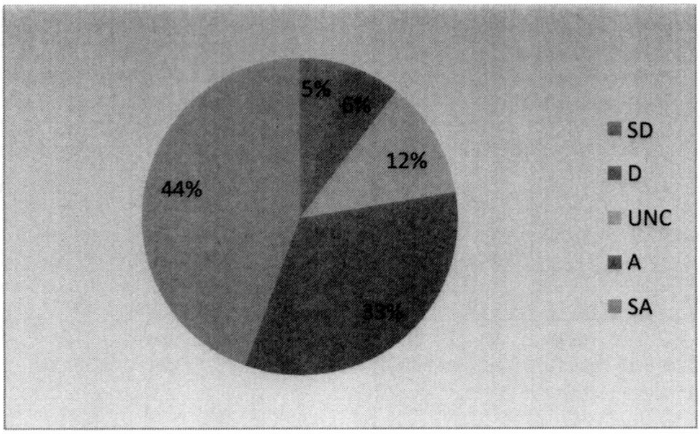

For Group 5, 'Sub-Skill – Vocabulary, Grammar, and Conversational Skills', it has been revealed from Table 4.7.5 that around 60% of the students experience that different activities are given to help the students understand the meaning of vocabulary items and use them correctly in context and the grammatical items are introduced explicitly in meaningful contexts with the integration with other skills using clear examples and explanations. 80% of the students agreed that the forms and examples of vocabulary and grammatical items are given in the tabular form in the self-learning instructional material gives more clarity whereas 86% of students acknowledge that conversational items are useful, boost up the confidence and motivate students to use English in their daily life activities. It has been further shown in Table 4.7.5 and Fig. 4.7.5 that 74% of experts agreed, only 12% disagreed, and the rest, 14%, remain undecided about the parameters given in group 5, i.e., 'Sub-Skill – Vocabulary, Grammar, and Conversational Skills'. Furthermore, it has been illustrated that the students gave very positive feedback for the self-learning instructional material. They feel that it is highly motivational for them to actively participate in their learning. Many activities are given for their self-assessment. It covers many things related to the English language acquisition skills. Even students are suggesting that this king of material should be created more and some of them suggest that more activities can be given for practice the English language acquisition skills.

Table 4.7.5: Statement-wise Representation of Feedback of Students about the Effectiveness of Self-Learning Instructional Material for English Language Acquisition Skills with Respect to 'Sub-Skill – Vocabulary, Grammar, and Conversational Skills'

No.	Statement	SD	D	UNC	A	SA	Pie Chart
Part E: Sub-Skill – Vocabulary, Grammar, and Conversational Skills							
1.	Different activities are given to help the students understand the meaning of vocabulary items and use them correctly in context	6 (20%)	3 (10%)	2 (7%)	7 (23%)	12 (40%)	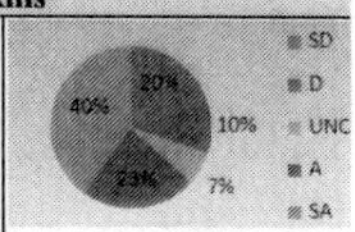
2.	The grammatical items are chosen appropriately and sufficiently according to the students' level.	0	7 (23%)	5 (17%)	10 (33%)	8 (27%)	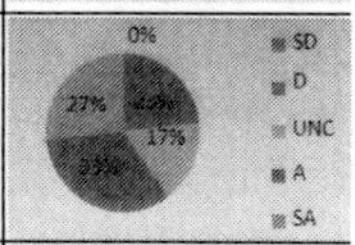
3.	The grammatical items are introduced explicitly in meaningful contexts with the integration with other skills using clear examples and explanations.	0 (0%)	2 (7%)	8 (27%)	10 (33%)	10 (33%)	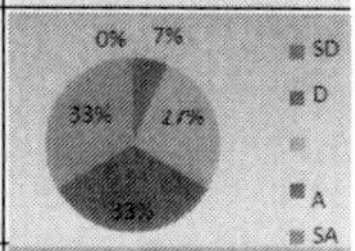
4.	The forms and examples of vocabulary and grammatical items are given in the tabular form which gives more clarity	1 (3%)	0 (0%)	5 (17%)	12 (40%)	12 (40%)	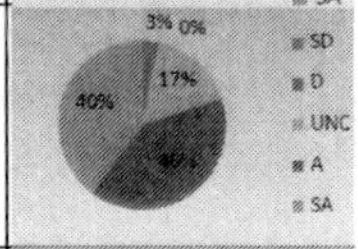
5.	Different varied authentic resources are used for giving practicing exercises	0 (0%)	1 (3%)	2 (7%)	10 (33%)	17 (57%)	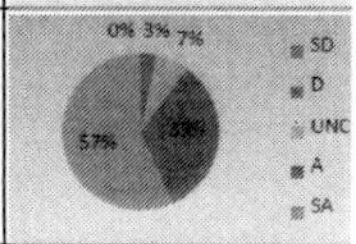
6.	Conversational items are useful, boost up the confidence and motivate students to use English in their daily life	0 (0%)	1 (3%)	3 (10%)	7 (23%)	19 (64%)	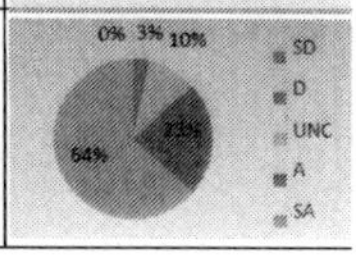

Fig. 4.7.5: Overall Feedback of Students about the Effectiveness of Self-Learning Instructional Material for English Language Acquisition Skills with Respect to 'Sub-Skill – Vocabulary, Grammar, and Conversational Skills'

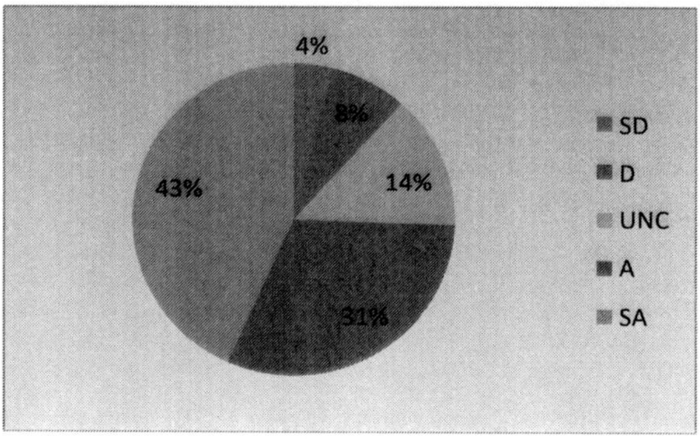

The self-learning instructional material for English language proficiency is built around engaging communicative language teaching exercises that are inspiring, motivating, and useful for gauging students' learning. Because the created materials were appealing to the students, they actively participated in the teaching and learning process, which helped them communicate more clearly.

These findings are consistent with a wide range of earlier studies, including those by Yang (2010), Irmawati (2012), Shawer (2013), Kholis (2014), and many others. By using the communicative approach, the students have made tremendous progress in their learning of the English language. As they are aware that they are still learning and that it will improve their communication skills, students report feeling more motivated to learn English. The study's conclusions suggested that Communicative Language Teaching (CLT) speeds up students' acquisition of English, boosts their self-esteem, and improves their communicative proficiency in English.

CHAPTER - 5

FINDINGS, EDUCATIONAL IMPLICATIONS, & SUGGESTIONS FOR FURTHER STUDY

Any research is not complete without its results and conclusions. A conclusion summarizes and analyzes the finding and arrives at a reasoned conclusion that is compatible with the finding. A finding in research is an empirical fact supported by data that has been acquired and does not merely depend on opinion (even that of an expert). In this chapter, the researcher presents the major findings and conclusions. Implications of this study and suggestions for further study have also been discussed afterwards. Based on the analysis and interpretation of the results, which have already been discussed in the previous chapter, the researcher set up the Conclusions of the current study. The educational implications of this study have been identified. Additionally, there have been some suggestions for further research in the area of this study.

5.1 FINDINGS OF THE STUDY

The effectiveness of the self-learning instructional material for English language acquisition skills over traditional methods of teaching has been found in the current study. On the basis of the discussion on the analysis and interpretation of data, conclusions have been drawn. For further research in this area and related to this study, many educational implications and suggestions have been discussed. Some of the significant conclusions in the current study are as follows:

5.1.1 Need Analysis for Students' English Language Acquisition Skills

The current study was carried out to find out the actual needs of the undergraduate students studying at the School of Open Learning, University of Delhi, to make them proficient in communication in English. After analyzing the qualitative and quantitative data, it was found that the existing

Communicative Language Course in English is not apt for the students of SOL, as the students studying there have come from low socioeconomic and educational backgrounds (different from regular colleges) and have the worst language skills. Another disclosure that came out is that SOL students need training to study the self-learning instructional material for their course so that they can take maximum benefit from PCP programs conducted to solve their problems. Most students feel that they are proficient in reading skills, and the skills on which they need to work are speaking, then writing, and then listening. These students complain that they have a short vocabulary while talking in English, and they hesitate a lot, feel nervous, and do not have enough confidence to speak English fluently. Assessment should be creative so that accurate assessment can be done for all four skills of the English language.

5.1.2 Opinions of Subject Experts and Opinions about the effectiveness of Self- Learning Instructional Material for English Language Acquisition Skills

In this, the researcher did a section-wise analysis of the opinionnaire to know the expert opinion about the acceptance of self-learning instructional material. The findings from the analysis show that most language experts and teacher educators favour the effectiveness of this Self-Learning Instructional Material. It is also determined that the SLIM is creatively designed and well prepared, the activities are comprehensive, and students will surely benefit from it, especially the vast vocabulary. It can be concluded that it is highly helpful for students as well as teachers. It provides exposure and opportunities through authentic resources to practice all the skills in integrated forms. The concepts are presented in graphical forms like tables, concept maps, etc. to make them more understandable for the students The SLIM is based on interesting activities that are creative, engaging, motivational, and helpful in assessing the learning.

5.1.3 On the basis of objectives, the following findings have been presented after analyzing the data:

Objective No. 1

To compare the adjusted mean scores of Achievement in English language acquisition skills of students taught through self-learning instructional material and lecture methods (with existing study material) by considering their pre-achievement in English language acquisition skills as covariate.

Findings:

The self-learning instructional material was found to be significantly better at facilitating achievement in the English language acquisition skills of students in comparison to the lecture method when pre-achievement was taken as a covariate.

Objective No. 2

To compare the adjusted mean scores of Achievement in English language acquisition skills of male and female students by considering their pre-achievement in English language acquisition skills as covariates

Findings:

Both Male and Female students were found to possess English language acquisition skills at the same level when their pre-achievement was taken as a covariate.

Objective No. 3

To compare the adjusted mean scores of Achievement in English language acquisition skills of male and female students taught through self-learning instructional material and lecture methods (with existing study material) by considering their pre-achievement in English language acquisition skills as a covariate

Findings:

The achievement in English language acquisition skills of students was found to be independent of the interaction between Instructional Strategy and Gender when their pre-achievement was taken as their covariate.

Objective No. 4

To analyze the perception of students towards the newly developed self-learning instructional material.

Findings:

There is a positive attitude of the students towards the self-learning instructional material. Students gave positive responses for the SLIM like it was very helpful for them to develop English language skills, it motivates them to actively participate in the activities, Exercises are very helpful for the self-assessment. Students suggested for more material like SLIM which covers many conceptual topics related to all English language skills. Two students also suggested that more exercises can be given in SLIM.

5.1.4 Conclusion

Self-Learning Instructional Material is the foundation of distance education. Maila and Pitsoe (2012), as cited in Rahman, Jahan & Panda (2018), observe that SLMs are required to carry out the functions of a face-to-face teacher. "These materials should be self-paced, flexible, auto-instructional, economical in time and effort, more interesting and exciting, and may be developed within the accessible resources". SLMs must perform in a manner that inspires students to finish their coursework and prepares them for increasingly independent study.

So, Self-Learning Instructional Material in distance education plays a vital role. In the context of English as a second language, it should offer the learners the platform to get the maximum exposure to their English language acquisition skills since, in the contemporary era, it's very important to have good communication skills in the globalized language, English. Rawung & Lynne Li (2008) also argued that in this changing and competitive world, many educational reforms are taking place, especially in English language education, to make people participate effectively in communication through the English language with the world globally. For this, the learners need to get the right exposure to all four skills of the English language—reading, listening, writing, and speaking—in an integrated form with the help of varied authentic resources. This becomes more challenging when the students are learning through distance education, where only self-learning instructional material is the main communication agent between teachers and students.

5.2 LIMITATIONS OF THE STUDY

Each research project has its limits, which are brought on by limitations in methodology or research design and hence impact the entire investigation. Although it is crucial to present the study's limits as it explains how the restrictions on any research could affect the conclusions of the study, the limitations of the present study are given as follows:

- It was very difficult for the researcher to convince students to participate in the pilot testing of this experimental research. As students are studying through distance learning, it is very difficult for them to find spare time to participate and fill out the pre-achievement test.
- Most of the time, students in SOL centers are not very regular during PCP classes. It was very challenging to motivate students

to come to all the classes for this research to be completed. The researcher had to motivate them from time to time.

- The research was done on the students coming to only one centre of the School of Open Learning, University of Delhi.
- The self-learning instructional material was based on a process-oriented theme- based approach. Initially, it was difficult for the students to understand the format and the way of studying this newly-developed SLIM. Once they get used to doing the study this way, they enjoy it later.
- To provide an exploration of listening skills, the researcher took the help of internet sources. It might be difficult for the students and teachers to make arrangements for that.
- An orientation session about the SLIM was given in the beginning to the students to give them an idea of What to do, How to do it, and What to expect from the SLIM.
- Teaching Speaking Skills requires great assistance from the teachers. So the main focus in PCP classes should be on giving the students a platform to enhance their speaking skills.
- After the class, the researcher connects with the students through other mediums like WhatsApp so that they can send their audio files and videos to assess their speaking skills and rectify the difficulties they faced.

5.3 EDUCATIONAL IMPLICATIONS OF THE STUDY

The objectives of teaching at the primary, secondary, and tertiary levels are different. At the tertiary or higher level of education, students need to excel in their skills and master their respective subjects. A good communication skill in English is the most demanded skill in every field, as we cannot ignore the rise of the English language as a global language. Most universities offer English language courses at the undergraduate level to fulfill this objective. This task becomes more challenging when education is done through distance learning. In distance learning, where students are from different socio-economic backgrounds with a multitude of educational and cultural backgrounds, they are getting exposure through the Self-Learning Instructional Material and have little opportunity for face-to-face learning in the Personal Contact Programme. So, good Self-learning instructional material is the first pre-requisite for distance education. For English language teaching, new research, innovations, and theories give the idea of teaching the English language in a challenging environment where the present infrastructure, class size, availability of teachers, quality of teachers, training of teachers, etc. should be incorporated.

In the present study, the researcher has developed self-learning instructional material for English language acquisition skills for undergraduate students who are studying through distance learning and also checked its effectiveness on the achievement of their English communication skills. While teaching those students, the researcher observed that the actual needs of students for enhancing their English communication skills had not been addressed, and they were not satisfied and confused with the existing syllabus and the available self-learning material at the School of Open Learning, University of Delhi. In distance mode, SLM is the only platform for giving exposure to students of various skills in the English language. Many things need to be taken care of while developing self-learning instructional material. The present study has various educational implications in the field of English language teaching for adult students through distance learning. Some of those implications are listed below:

- This study aims first to remove the apprehensions that the students who study at the School of Open Learning at the University of Delhi cannot communicate in good English. Generally, because of a lack of exposure, students in SOL are looked down upon by society when they finish their education.
- This study will be helpful for getting the actual scenario and status of the English acquisition skills of the students at SOL.
- As the self-learning instructional material was found to be significantly better at facilitating achievement in the English language acquisition skills of students in comparison to the lecture method when pre-achievement was taken as a covariate, this study implies that the actual practical approach to Communicative Language Teaching (CLT) is useful in teaching the English language for communication purposes to SOL students to get the desired results.
- This study also entails that this study will be helpful to learners who actually want to achieve their life goals but are not able to communicate in English, which has become a hindrance in their path as both Male and Female students were found to possess English language acquisition skills at the same level when their pre-achievement was taken as a covariate.
- This study will give other teachers, educators, and administrators the stimulus to experiment with this approach in their classes.

They will be motivated by this research and gain confidence to rely on the CLT approach. It is emphasized with the findings that the achievement in English language acquisition skills of students was found to be independent of the interaction between Instructional Strategy and Gender when their pre-achievement was taken as their covariate.

- The positive attitude of the students towards the self-learning instructional material signifies that SLIM will be helpful to SOL students who are not good in English for many reasons, like the non-availability of good teachers in their schools, not getting the right exposure, non-supportive parents, a lack of confidence, a lack of motivation, and a focus on only getting good marks by memorizing. This research will give these learners avenues to communicate well in society in English.
- The researcher's self-learning instructional material is based on a variety of themes drawn from the needs and circumstances of the students in real life. These varied themes help the students connect the content to their own lives and, as a result, motivate them to learn.
- All the skills of any language cannot be learned in isolation. If we look into our lives, listening, speaking, reading, and writing— all these skills and sub-skills— are integrated. So in this self-learning instructional material, all the skills are taught in an integrated way to give students a real-life and meaningful learning experience of the English language.
- This is a saddening fact that listening is the most ignored skill out of all the skills, especially in the existing syllabus of English communication in SOL for undergraduates and its SLM. There are various activities for listening skills in each unit to give the students exposure to the English language through authentic resources.
- This study implies that to learn any language, you have to live it. So this self- learning instructional material developed by the researcher gives students of SOL the opportunity to live the English language through various authentic resources and practice exercises.

5.4 SUGGESTIONS FOR FURTHER RESEARCH

As every research project is not complete in all aspects, this current research also has many limitations. Every researcher has to deal with the limitations of time and space (in terms of resources); therefore, the current study opens up many platforms for further studies, which are listed below:

- The present study has been carried out on limited topics related to English language skills; more studies may be conducted on other topics related to English language skills.
- The present study has been conducted on BA (prog.) 1st-semester students who studied 'English Fluency' as a generic paper. This study can be conducted on students who have other English language subjects like 'Language through Literature', 'Communication in Everyday Life', and many more.
- The present study was done for the students of the School of Open Learning, University of Delhi. This study may be experimented on regular students studying in different affiliated colleges of the University of Delhi or on students studying through distance mode in other universities.
- A comparison can be made between the self-learning instructional material for English language acquisition skills and other methods of teaching.
- Other research may be conducted to investigate the effectiveness of self- learning instructional material for the English language skills of students belonging to disadvantaged groups like backward classes, physically disabled, and gifted students.
- This study can be further explored in relation to other variables like creativity, intelligence, learning style, class size, cognitive style, etc.
- This study can be tested on the students of rural, tribal groups where students have very low confidence in using English language for communication.
- The self-learning instructional material could also be used for other courses where English is the compulsory subject.
- Other teaching approaches and methods can also be used to develop self- learning instructional material for students, and then further studies can be conducted to investigate their effectiveness.

The list is not complete yet. There are many other areas in this field that have not been explored due to limitations in space and time. Attempts in these directions can be explored more through research.

BIBLIOGRAPHY

- Aalaei, N. (2017). The Effect of Using Communicative Language Teaching on Developing English Speaking and Listening Skills of Iranian Secondary School Students. *Journal of Applied Linguistics and Language Research. 4*(8), 256-266.
- Abbas, F., Aslam, S. & Yasmeen, R. (2011). Communicative Language Teaching: a Modified Version. *Language in India, 11*(4), 331-341.
- Abdelmageed, N. A. T., & Omer, M. A. A. (2020). The Effectiveness of Using Communicative Language Teaching Approach (CLT) in Developing Students' Speaking Skills from Teacher's Perceptions. *European Journal of English Language Teaching.*
- Afsyah, S. (2019). WhatsApp application in English Language Teaching (ELT) context: Media to describe people. *Utamax: Journal of Ultimate Research and Trends in Education*, *1*(1), 23-28.
- Ahmadi, D. M. R. (2018). The use of technology in English language learning: A literature review. *International journal of research in English education*, *3*(2), 115-125.
- Ahmed, R. Z., & Bidin, S. J. B. (2016). The effect of task based language teaching on writing skills of EFL learners in Malaysia. *Open Journal of Modern Linguistics*, *6*(03), 207.
- Al-Mutairi, M. A. (2020). Kachru's Three Concentric Circles Model of English Language: An Overview of Criticism & the Place of Kuwait in It. *English Language Teaching*, *13*(1), 85-88. doi: 10.5539/elt.v13n1p85.
- Al Zoubi, S. M. (2018). The Impact of Exposure to English Language on Language Acquisition. *Journal of Applied Linguistics and Language Research*, *5*(4), 151-162.
- Ananthi, T. (2018). Teaching Creative Writing in English among the Under-graduate Students. *Language in India*, *18*(10), 13-16.
- Ansari, M. S. (2015). Speaking Anxiety in ESL/EFL Classrooms: A holistic Approach and Practical Study. *International Journal of Education Investigation*, *2*(4), 38-46.
- Anuradha, V. (2020). *An Experimental Study on Teaching English Language through an Innovative Method*. [Doctoral Thesis, Dr. M.G.R. Educational and Research Institute]. http://hdl.handle.net/10603/338988.

- Aromdee, R., & Jansem, A. (2012). Using Authentic Materials Based on Communicative Language Teaching to Develop Factory Workers 'Basic EFL Literacy at AIP Co., Ltd.: A Case Study. *" Current Issues and Future Directions in Media, Communication and Language" ICLC 2012*, 34.
- Asrul, A., & Dahlan, S. (2022). The Use of Communicative Language Teaching (CLT) Method in Improving Students' English Vocabulary. *Journal of Languages and Language Teaching, 10*(4), 541-550.
- Aykut, A. (2008). Implementing a holistic teaching in modern ELT classes: Using technology and integrating four skills. https://mpra.ub.uni-muenchen.de/20707/1/MPRA_paper_20707.pdf.
- Aydoðan, H., & Akbarov, A. A. (2014). The Four Basic Language Skills, Whole Language & Integrated Skill Approach in Mainstream University Classrooms in Turkey. *Mediterranean Journal of Social Sciences, 5*(9), 672.
- Baby Vijila, R. (2008). Effectiveness of Task Based Communicative Activities in Developing the Writing Skills of the Teacher Trainees. [Doctoral Thesis, Alagappa University]. http://hdl.handle.net/10603/194997.
- Bedadur, N. V. (2018). Authentic material and the communicative approach to language teaching. *Learning Curve*, (31), 42-45.
- Bellal, M., & Nader, F. (2014). "E-shop": a collaborative learning activity. *Procedia-Social and Behavioral Sciences, 152*, 214-218.
- Bhakte, S. (2019). Communicative English. *International Journal of Research and Analytical Reviews, 6*(1).
- Brown, D. B. (2014). *Mobile learning for communicative language teaching: An exploration of how higher education language instructors design communicative MALL environments*. The University of Memphis.
- Ceper-Tangerang, B. (2016). *The Effectiveness of Using Short Story towards Students' Reading Comprehension of Narrative Text.* [Doctoral dissertation, State Islamic University].
- Chang, S. C. (2011). A contrastive study of grammar translation method and communicative approach in teaching English grammar. *English language teaching, 4*(2), 13.
- Chen, S., & Wang, J. (2019). Effects of Task-Based Language Teaching (TBLT) Approach and Language Assessment on Students' Competences in Intensive Reading Course. *English Language Teaching, 12*(3), 119-138.
- Cheng, L., Yunus, M. M., & Mohamad, M. (2016). Issues Contributing to Low Performance of English in a National School in Song, Sarawak. *Proceedings of the ICECRS, 1*(1), v1i1-519. https://doi.org/10.21070/picecrs.v1i1.519
- Chipili, D. (2013). The use of short stories for CLT in senior ESL classes in Zambia. [Master's dissertation, University of South Africa, Pretoria]. http://hdl.handle.net/10500/9293.
- Celce-Murcia, M., Brinton, D., & Snow, A. (2014). *Teaching English as a Second or Foreign Language* (4th ed.). Boston, MA: Heinle ELT.

- Christ, T. W., & Makarani, S. A. (2009). Teachers' attitudes about teaching English in India: An embedded mixed methods study. *International Journal of multiple research approaches*, *3*(1), 73-87.
- Chawla, D. (2017). *Creating Learning Materials for Open and Distance Learning*. (2005).
- Commonwealth of Learning.
- Dao, P., Iwashita, N., & Gatbonton, E. (2017). Learner attention to form in ACCESS task-based interaction. *Language Teaching Research*, *21*(4), 454-479. https://doi.org/10.1177/1362168816651462
- Department of Distance and Continuing Education, School of Open Learning, Campus of Open Learning. https://web.sol.du.ac.in/info/sol
- Derbel, E. M. I. R. A., & Al-Mohammadi, S. (2015). Chapter Ten Integration of Language Skills and Culture in English Language Teaching: Rationale and Implications for Practice. *Issues in English education in the Arab world*.
- Dim, M. H. (2013). Developing the Task-based Strategies Syllabus to Enhance Communicative English Ability of Burmese Migrant Students. *Language in India*, *13*(11).
- Dörnyei, Z. (2009). The 2010s Communicative language teaching in the 21st century: The 'principled communicative approach'. *Perspectives*, *36*(2), 33-43.
- Dos Santos, L. M. (2020). The Discussion of Communicative Language Teaching Approach in Language Classrooms. *Journal of Education and e- Learning Research*, *7*(2), 104-109. Examine the Role of Print Rich Environment in Developing Early Writing. *Journal of Teaching English and Literature, 34*, 13-18.
- Dr. Jayaram, K. and Dr. Dorababu, K. K. 2015. "Self Learning Material in Distance Education System", *International Joyrnal of Current Research*, 7, (10), 21929-21934.
- Eddie, A. A., & Aziz, A. A. (2020). Developing Primary Students' Spoken Interaction Skill through Communicative Language Teaching. *International Journal of Academic Research in Business and Social Sciences*, *10*(2), 303-315.
- Efendi, M. Y. (2022). Designing Supplementary Speaking Materials Based On Communicative Language Teaching (CLT). *EDULEC: EDUCATION, LANGUAGE AND CULTURE JOURNAL*, *2*(2), 150-160.
- Elliot, A. J., & Hulleman, C. S. (2017). Achievement goals. In A. J. Elliot, C. S. Dweck, & D. S. Yeager (Eds.), *Handbook of competence and motivation: Theory and application* (pp. 43–60). The Guilford Press.
- Ellis, R. (2015). *Understanding Second Language Acquisition*. Oxford: Oxford University Press, 1985.
- Exploring Key Issues in Material Development. N. P. Sudharshana in conversation with Brian Tomlinson. (2021). *Fortell, 42*, 167-174. https://www.fortell.org/wp-content/uploads/2021/04/Fortell.January-2021-167-174.pdf

- Farooq, M. U. (2015). Creating a Communicative Language Teaching Environment for Improving Students' Communicative Competence at EFL/EAP University Level. *International Education Studies*, 8(4), 179-191.
- Fithriani, R., Dewi, U., Daulay, S. H., Salmiah, M., & Fransiska, W. (2019). Using Facebook in EFL writing class: Its effectiveness from students' perspective. *KnE Social Sciences*, 634-645.
- *Five Components of Effective Oral Language Instruction*, Professional Development Service for Teachers, Dublin. https://pdst.ie/sites/default/files/Oral%20Language%20Booklet%20PDF.pdf
- Gatbonton & Segalowitz (2005). Rethinking Communicative Language Teaching: A Focus on Access to Fluency. *Canadian Modern Language Review.* 61(3):325-353. DOI: 10.1353/cml.2005.0016.
- Ghofur, A., S. Degeng, I. N., Widiati, U., & Setyosari, P. (2017). The Effect of Communicative Language teaching and Audio-Lingual method on English Speaking Skill Across Different Learning Styles. *KnE Sciences, 1*(3), 1-7. https://doi.org/10.18502/kss.v1i3.719.
- Gomathy, C. K. (2018). A Study on the Effect of Digital Literacy and Information Management. International *Journal of Scientific Research and Review,* 7(2). https://www.researchgate.net/publication/332111175_A_STUDY_ON_THE_EFFECT_OF_DIGITAL_LITERACY_AND_INFORMATION_MANAGEMENT
- Gudepu, M. D. (2013). Applications of Communicative Language Teaching Techniques in Reading Classes: A Special Focus on Junior Colleges in Telangana Region (India). *World Journal of English Language*, *3*(2), 57.
- Gupta, D. (2005). ELT in India: A brief historical and current overview. *Asian EFL Journal*, *7*(1), 197-207.
- Gupta, D. (2004). CLT in India: Context and methodology come together. *ELT journal*, *58*(3), 266-269.
- Gupta, M., & Lata, P. (2014). Development of objective type achievement test in science (Biology) for x class students. *International Journal of Social Science and Interdisciplinary Research*, *2*(8), 49-62.
- Hedia, M. M. H. (2022). The effectiveness of communicative language approach in enhancing English speaking skills of EFL adult learners in Egypt. *Insights into Language, Culture and Communication*, *2*(1), 49-68.
- Ho, Y. Y. C. (2020). Communicative language teaching and English as a foreign language undergraduates' communicative competence in Tourism English. *Journal of Hospitality, Leisure, Sport & Tourism Education*, *27*, 100271.
- Hiep, P. H. (2007). Communicative language teaching: Unity within diversity. *ELT journal*, *61*(3), 193-201.
- Irmawati, N. D. (2012). Communicative Approach: An Alternative Method Used in Improving Students' Academic Reading Achievement. *English Language Teaching*, *5*(7), 90-101.
- Iqbal, J. (2019). Effectiveness of Self Instructional Material of Distance Education. *Pakistan Journal of Distance & Online Learning, 5*(1), 71-90.

- Jailakumari, G. (2006). Effectiveness of Tasks Based Communicative Activities in Learning English Grammar by the Teacher Trainees. [Doctoral Thesis, Alagappa University]. http://hdl.handle.net/10603/196762.
- Jain, S. (2017). *Effectiveness of Programmed Learning and Computer Assisted Instruction as self learning techniques in teaching of English grammar at secondary level.* [Doctoral Thesis Maharishi Dayanand University]. http://hdl.handle.net/10603/207046.
- John, S. (2020). Effective CLT Activities for the Teaching of English to Adult Learners. In *Journal of English Language Teachers' Interaction Forum, 11*, 23.
- Kakoty, A. (2013). The Impact of Language learning Strategies Instruction on Assamese ESL Learners. [Doctoral Thesis, North-Eastern Hill University]. http://hdl.handle.net/10603/194877.
- Kaushik, R. (2022). Teachers' Perceptions of English Language and Communication Skills of Commerce Undergraduates. *Fortell, 10*, 169-180. https://www.fortell.org/wp-content/uploads/2022/10/January-2022-Print-copy-169-180.pdf
- Kumar, N. U., Philip, P., & Kalaiselvi, A. (2013). The application of CLT to teaching English as a second language-an assessment of practice in India. *International Journal of Humanities and Social Science Invention*, *2*(5), 24-29.
- Krashen D. S. (1982). *Principles and Practice in Second Language Acquisition*. Pergamon Press Inc: University of Southern California.
- Kholis, A. (2014). *Communicative Language Teaching(CLT) in Teaching Listening to the Eight Grade Students of Bilingual Program at SMP N 2 Ponorogo in Academic Year 2013/2014.* [Doctoral dissertation, IAIN Ponorogo].
- Lightbown, P. M., & Spada, N. (2006). *How Languages Are Learned* (3rd ed.). Oxford: Oxford University.
- Lu, J., & Auman, A. E. (2011). The Impact of Educational Reform on China's Magazines for Teaching English. *International Journal of Education*, *3*(1), 1.
- Madhkhan, M., & Mousavi, S. M. (2017). The Effect of Implementation of TBLT in Reading Comprehension Classes of Iranian EFL Learners. *English Language Teaching*, *10*(11), 119-128.
- Manathunga, M. A. (2021). A Study on the Use of Communicative Language Teaching Approach to Teach English in Schools in Rathnapura District, Sri Lanka. http://repository.rjt.ac.lk/bitstream/handle/123456789/5175/114.pdf?sequence=1
- Meganathan, R. (2015). Teacher Learning in In-Service Professional Development Insights from Two In-Service Training Programmes. *Journal of Indian Education, 1*, 105-131. Available at www.ncert.nic.in.
- Mehta, N. K. (2015). Communicative approach in learning English language: Effectiveness at middle school level (with special reference to government middle school of Ujjain city in the state of Madhya Pradesh, India). *Limbaj ºi context. Revista internaþionalã de lingvisticã, semioticã ºi ºtiinþã literarã*, (2), 113-118. https://ibn.idsi.md/ro/cautare?find=811.111%27243%28540%29.

- Ministry of Education, Government in India. (2018). *All India Survey on Higher Education 2017-18.* https://www.education.gov.in/sites/upload_files/mhrd/files/statistics-new/AISHE2017-18.pdf
- Ministry of Education, Government in India. (1953). *The Report of Secondary Education Commission*. https://tnschools.gov.in/wp-content/uploads/2022/01/Report-of-the-secondary-education-commission-October-1952-June-1953.pdf
- Ministry of Education, Government in India. (1953). *The Report of University Education Commission*.

  https://www.educationforallinindia.com/1949%20Report%20of%20the%20University%20Education%20Commission.pdf
- Ministry of Human Resource Development, Government of India. (2020). *National Education Policy 2020*.

  https://www.education.gov.in/sites/upload_files/mhrd/files/NEP_Final_English_0.pdf
- Mishra, S., & Gaba, A. K. (2001). How do distance learners use activities in self-instructional materials?. *Indian Journal of Open Learning*, *10*(1), 40-51.
- Mittal P. & Lata P. (2022). Ideas and Means to Transform Distance Education. In Mishra M., Lata P. & Chopra P. (Eds.), *Emerging Trends in Education: An Overview* (pp. 65-70).
- National Council of Educational Research and Training (1966). *Report of the Education Commission, 1964-66*. http://www.academics-india.com/Kothari%20Commission%20Report.pdf
- National Council of Educational Research and Training. (2006). *Position Paper National Focus Group on Teaching of English. https://ncert.nic.in/pdf/focus-*group/english.pdf
- Newby D. (2011). *Competence and Performance in Learning and Teaching: theories and practices.* Retrieved from http://ejournals.lib.auth.gr/thal/article/view/5476/5373. DOI: https://doi.org/10.26262/istal.v19i0.5476.
- Nikmah, L., & Azimah, A. (2015). Using Authentic Material from Magazines to Enhance the Student's Reading Comprehension. *Lingua*, *7*(2), 138.
- Naz, T. (2016). Designing SLM Self Learning Material for Integrated Skills in English at Undergraduate Level in Aligarh Muslim University. [Doctoral Thesis, Aligarh Muslim University]. http://hdl.handle.net/10603/118104
- Nesa, M. (2019). Wiki-Based Blended Classroom Design: English as Second Language (ESL) Learning Activities. *Research Journal of English Language and Literature, 7*(3), doi: doi.org/10.33329/rjelal.73.401.
- Nunan, D. (1989). *Designing Tasks for the Communicative Classroom.*

  Cambridge: Cambridge University Press.
- Nunan, D. (2014). Task-based teaching and learning. *Teaching English as a Second or Foreign Language*, *4*, 455-470.
- Olaizola, M. A. (2119). The Arrival and Development of the English Language in India.

https://addi.ehu.es/bitstream/handle/10810/43444/TFG_Madrazo.pdf?sequence=1&isAllowed=y. Accessed on 23 January, 2022.

- Owen, E. A., & Razali, A. B. (2018). The Effect of Communicative Activities on Libyan Secondary School Students' Speaking Performance in Malaysia. *International Journal of Instruction*, *11*(4), 45-60.
- Panchabakesan, S. (2011). Problems and Prospectives in Distance Education in India in the 21st Century. *Problems of Education in the 21st Century*, *30*(1), 113-122.
- Panda, S., & Garg, S. (2019). *India* (pp. 27-42). Springer Singapore.
- Pandya Ashok P. (2020). *Teaching English language through movies An Experiment teaching English language through movies An Experiment.* [Doctoral Thesis, Saurashtra University]. http://hdl.handle.net/10603/348823
- Panambunan, E., Tulung, G. J., & Maru, M. G. (2016). Improving Students' Speaking Ability through Communicative Language Teaching of the Second Level Students at 'MEC'Megalia English Course. *Journal of English Language and Literature Teaching*, *1*(01).
- Pardede, P. (2020). Integrating the 4Cs into EFL Integrated Skills Learning. *Journal of English Teaching*, *6*(1), 71-85.
- Parmar, R. V. (2018). *Development and Effectiveness of Computer Assisted Instruction in English Grammar for Standard IX Students.* [Doctoral dissertation, Maharaja Sayajirao University of Baroda (India)].
- Patel, H. & Singh, D. S. (2021). Independent Learning and Self-Practice to Enhance English Language. *International Journal of Research Publication and Reviews, 2*(12), 1207-1209.
- Plúas Saico, A., & Zhou, Y. (2013). *Communicative language teaching CLT activities for encouraging an improvement in the students' oral expression from 1st course section AF at Eloy Alfaro high school academic year 2013– 2014.* (Bachelor's thesis, Guayaquil: ULVR, 2013.).
- Phoeun, M., & Sengsri, S. (2021). The Effect of a Flipped Classroom with Communicative Language Teaching Approach on Undergraduate Students' English Speaking Ability. *International Journal of Instruction*, *14*(3), 1025-1042.
- Prabhu, N. S. (1987). Second Language Pedagogy. Oxford: Oxford University Press.
- Rahmatillah, K. (2019). Communicative Language Teaching (CLT) through Role Play and Task-Based Instruction. *Script Journal: Journal of Linguistic and English Teaching*, *4*(1), 161-177.
- Rahmatuzzman, M. (2018). Communicative language teaching (CLT): Theory Vs reality in the context of secondary schools in Bangladesh. *Journal of Education and Social Sciences*, *10*(1), 24-32.
- Rana, M. (2017). *Communicative Language Teaching Versus Transmission Models of Teaching in a Government College: An Experimental Study.* [Doctoral dissertation, University of Management and Technology Lahore].

- Randolph, J. (2009). A guide to writing the dissertation literature review. *Practical assessment, research, and evaluation*, *14*(1), 13.
- Ravindran, R. (2021). The Predicament of Rural College Students during the Pandemic: An ELA Website for their Rescue. *Journal of English Language Teaching*, *63*(1), 38-42.
- Richards, J. C., & Rodgers, T. S. (1986). *Approaches and Methods in Language Teaching*. Cambridge: Cambridge University Press.
- Rohyani, E. (2019). *The Application of Communicative Language Teaching Approach Via Short Movies in the Speaking Practice at the Eleventh Grade Students of SMKN 2 Pacitan in the Academic Year of 2018/2019*. (Doctoral dissertation, STKIP PGRI PACITAN).

  http://repository.stkippacitan.ac.id/id/eprint/55
- Rowley, J., & Slack, F. (2004). Conducting a literature review. *Management research news*, *27*(6), 31-39.
- Sanaa, M. (2013). *Developing the Students' Speaking Skill through Communicative Language Teaching* [Master's thesis, Mohamed Khieder University of Biskra). http://archives.univ-biskra.dz/handle/123456789/4740
- Sawitri, Ajeng. 2012. A Set of English Reading Materials Using English Teen Magazines for the Seventh Grade Students of SMPN 5 Depok Sleman Yogyakarta. Yogyakarta: English Language Education Study Program, Department of Language and arts Education, Faculty of Teachers Training and Education, Sanata Dharma University.
- Sector, E. (2015). Bridging Communicative Language Teaching and Task-Based Language Teaching in Cambodia: Learners' Reactions to an Integrated Programme in the Non-Formal. *Contemporary task-based language teaching in Asia*, 46.
- Sengupta, A. (2021). Using Authentic Materials to Develop Students' Oral Competence: Moving Away from 'Product'to 'Process'. *Fortell, 42*.
- Septiyana, L. (2019). Designing English Speaking Materials Using Task Based Language Teaching (TBLT) For Islamic Economics Students. *IDEAS: Journal on English Language Teaching and Learning, Linguistics and Literature*, *7*(2).
- Setiyorini, T. J., Yulia, Y., & Robiasih, H. (2022). Communicative language teaching method at improving students' macro and micro-skills of reading comprehension in intensive reading course. *EduLite: Journal of English Education, Literature and Culture*, *7*(2), 233-250.
- Shahid, C. ., Abbasi, I. A. ., & Bhutto, S. (2022). Improving Communicative Competence through CLT Approach in Second Language Learning at the Undergraduate Level. *Pakistan Journal of Humanities and Social Sciences*, *10*(4), 1472–1486. https://doi.org/10.52131/pjhss.2022.1004.0305
- Shawer, S. (2013). Preparing adult educators: The need to develop communicative language teaching skills in college-level instructors. *Journal of Literacy Research*, *45*(4), 431-464.

- Singh, M., Randhawa, V., & Singh, A. P. (2011). Designing, Validation and Evaluation of Self Instructional e-Module on Photography for Online Learning. *Vol, 11*, 13-17.
- Siswita, F., & Al-Hafizh, M. (2014). Teaching Writing Recount Text to Senior High School Students by Using "Reading-Writing Connection Strategy". *Journal of English Language Teaching*, *2*(2), 62-72.
- Spada, N., Jessop, L., Tomita, Y., Suzuki, W., & Valeo, A. (2014). Isolated and integrated form-focused instruction: Effects on different types of L2 knowledge. *Language teaching research*, *18*(4), 453-473.
- Sreehari, P. (2012). Communicative Language Teaching: Possibilities and Problems. *English Language Teaching*, *5*(12), 87-93.
- Sung, K. Y. (2010). Promoting communicative language learning through communicative tasks. *Journal of Language Teaching and Research*, *1*(5), 704.
- S. Vadivel. (2018). Is English a Subject or Language?-Practical analysis. Inclusive and Equitable Quality Education in ELT, 124. https://www.researchgate.net/publication/331889703_Is_English_a_Subject_or_Language-Practical_analysis
- Sultana, N. (2016). Evaluation of Self-Instructional Print Material of Distance Education System. *Bulletin of Education and Research*, *38*(2), 95-111.
- Suwannoppharat, K., & Kaewsa, A. (2015). Utilization of content-theme-based instruction: an overhaul of english language learning for non-native English learners. *International Journal of English Language Education*, *1*(3), 115-126.
- Tati, J. S., Paul, C., & Golingi, L. B. (2013). English language Speaking Anxiety among Community College Learners: How can it be Overcome?. *Social Sciences*, *2*(3), 38-53.
- Thakur, A. (2021). Language Learning: A Matter of Correct Attitude and Soft Skills. *Journal of English Language Teaching, 63*(1).
- Tiarina, Y., Syarif, H., Jufrizal, J., & Rozimela, Y. (2019). Students' Need on Basic English Grammar Teaching Material based on Interactive Multimedia: An Innovative Design. *COUNS-EDU: The International Journal of Counseling and Education*. https://doi.org/10.23916/0020190419310
- Tikkakoski, S. (2016). *Communicative language teaching as English pronunciation teaching method: Developing exercises.* [Bachelor's thesis, S. Tikkakoski). https://urn.fi/URN:NBN:fi:oulu-201602031107.
- Toro, V., Camacho-Minuche, G., Pinza-Tapia, E., & Paredes, F. (2019). The Use of the Communicative Language Teaching Approach to Improve Students' Oral Skills. *English Language Teaching, 12*(1), 110-118. doi: 10.5539/elt.v12n1p110.
- University Grants Commission. (n.d.). *Distance Education Bureau*. https://deb.ugc.ac.in/. Accessed on November, 2022.
- Ur, P. (1996). *A Course in Language Teaching: Practice and Theory* (4th ed.). Cambridge University Press, UK.
- Varghese, V., & Karki, P. (2018). An Analysis of Preferred Methods of Teaching and Learning English Language in Bangalore, India. *Journal on English Language Teaching*, *8*(4), 36-48.

- Wang, Y. H. (2010). Using communicative language games in teaching and learning English in Taiwanese primary schools. *Journal of Engineering Technology and Education*, *7*(1), 126-142.
- West, A. J. (2016). Adaptation of Communicative Language Teaching Methodology to an English Textbook for English Language Learning of NIDA Students. *PASAA: Journal of Language Teaching and Learning in Thailand*, *52*, 25-52.
- Yarlagadda, R., & Mantri, V. R. R. (2016). English for Employability – The Need for English Speaking Graduates in India. *Journal of English Language and Literature, 3*(1), 69-74. https://joell.in/wp-content/uploads/2016/03/THE-NEED-FOR-ENGLISH-SPEAKING.pdf
- Yesapogu, V. (2016). The Evaluation of English language in Indian Education and its Methodology: A Contemporary Application of Study. *International Journal on Studies in English Language and Literature (IJSELL), 4*(3), 35-43.
- Yung, K. W. H. (2023). Engaging exam-oriented students in communicative language teaching by 'packaging'learning English through songs as exam practice. *RELC Journal*, *54*(1), 280-290.
- Zhao, M. (2015). Implementation of Task-based Language Teaching in Classes of Second Language Acquisition. In *2015 International Conference on Education Technology, Management and Humanities Science (ETMHS 2015)* (pp. 183-187). Atlantis Press. https://doi.org/10.2991/etmhs-15.2015.42

Websites

- http://brilliantlearningsystems.com/six-principles-of-andragogy-malcolm-knowles/
- https://www.financialexpress.com/archive/25-of-indian-students-covered-by-distance-education-study/945204/
- https://elttguide.com/integrating-the-main-language-skills-in-efl-classes-why-and-how/
- Oai:addi.ehu.es:10810/43444.
- Semalty, A. (n.d.). Academic Writing [MOOC]. Swayam. https://onlinecourses.swayam2.ac.in/cec21_ge32/preview
- Dr. Yanthan, Z. (n.d.). Communication Skills [MOOC]. Swayam. https://onlinecourses.swayam2.ac.in/nou21_lb11/preview#:~:text=The%20course%20'Communication%20Skills'%20is,good%20personal%20profile%2C%20improve%20one's
- https://learnenglish.britishcouncil.org/
- https://tefllessons.com/english-language-teaching-materials/
- https://www.pdf-language-lessons.com/english/english-pdf-lessons/
- https://www.pdf-language-lessons.com/english/english-pdf-lessons/
- https://en.islcollective.com/
- https://www.fluentu.com/blog/educator-english/teaching-english-creatively/

APPENDIXES

Appendix - 1

NEED ANALYSIS QUESTIONNAIRE FOR STUDENTS OF SCHOOL OF OPEN LEARNING (SOL), UNIVERSITY OF DELHI STUDYING IN B.A (PROG.) AND B.COM (PROG.)

FOR RESEARCH PURPOSE ONLY

Supervised by: Dr. Parvesh Lata
Created by Payal Mittal

Name: ....

Age: ....

Name of the College: ....

Year/Semester: ....

Name of the English Course..
you are studying:

1. For how many years have you studied English in your school?
   a. Class I to Class XII　　b. Class I to Class X
   b. Class I to Class VIII　　d. Class VI to Class XII
   c. Class VI to Class X　　f. Class VI to Class VIII
   d. Others, mention it　　.......................................
2. In which medium did you study in your school?
   a. Hindi　　b. English
   b. If any other language, mention it ....
3. You passed your Class XII from
   a. Government School　　b. Private School
4. Are you working?:　　Yes / No
5. If yes, what are your responsibilities in which you are suppose to communicate in English...
6. If not, Where you need to communicate in English language
   a. At colleges or Universities　　b. At home
   c In society
7. Are you able to use English language proficiently?
   a. Yes　　b. No
8. When people speak to you in English, how much are you able to understand? (Tick one option).

a. Everything
b. Mostly
c. Some
d. A little
e. Very little

9. Do you confidently answer someone who asks you something in English?
   a. Yes
   b. No
10. What problem do you face while answering him/her in English?

    ....

    ....

    ....

    ....

    ....
11. How confident are you using English in these situations:
    a. Talk about my country or city with a friend
    b. Ask for directions on the street
    c. Making general conversation
    d. Introduce yourself or your job profile
    e. Ordering food in a restaurant
    f. While doing shopping
    g. Writing a letter of complaint
    h. Telephone calls
12. Tick the options that you are able to read and understand in English:
    a. Pick out any article or news of your interest in English newspaper or magazines
    b. the information (in English) written on labels on products
    c. emails, Facebook post, blog, information on websites
    d. Write emails, Facebook post, blog
    e. the information and guidelines giving in product manuals
    f. fill admission forms or any other form
    g. The information giving in the notices put on the college or University websites
    h. Figure out my phone bill or electricity bill
13. Tick the options that you are able to read and understand
    a. English news broadcast on television
    b. English movies without using the subtitles in Hindi
    c. Advertisements in English on TV or Radio
    d. English jingles and songs
    e. Guidelines and instructions in English given for some specific events
14. Write about the situations when you need to communicate in your life.

    ....

    ....

15. According to your need, Order the given language skills from 1 to 6, start from 1 which is the most important and to 6 which is the least important.

a. Reading	b. Listening
b. Speaking	d. Writing
c. Vocabulary	e. Pronunciation

Appendix - 2

NEED ANALYSIS QUESTIONNAIRE FOR TEACHING FACULITIES IN THE DEPARTMENT OF ENGLISH, SCHOOL OF OPEN LEARNING (SOL), UNIVERSITY OF DELHI

Name of the Faculty: ....

Name of the Department: ....

Name of the University: ....

Here, the list of questions asked in the interview:

1. On what basis have you divided the students of B.Com. (p) and BA (p) into three groups?
2. What kind of educational background do these students have?
3. What is their level of proficiency in the English language?
4. In spite of SOL students' low socio-economic and educational backgrounds, what are the other problems for the students?
5. What kind of material do you suggest for these students so that they can use English well in their real lives?

Appendix - 3

Opionionnaire for Effectiveness of Self-Learning Instructional Material for English Language Learners

The aim of conducting this research effort is to assess the usability or effectiveness of the developed Self-Learning Instructional Material for English Language Learners. This effectiveness is measured by how easily and effectively a learner can use this material, given particular exposure, carry out fixed activities, in a defined set of environment. This effectiveness testing is being done to identify problem area and difficulties, weakness, and area of improvement while using the SLIM. The Self-learning instructional material should be enjoyable to use, interactive, motivational diversified and integrated for the learners. The researcher has developed the Self-learning instructional material for learning English language for SOL (School of Open Learning, University of Delhi) students of BA (Prog.) or B.Com (Prog.) 1st semester who have studied English language till their Class 12.

The opinionnaire is divided into four categories:

A. Authenticity of the Material .

B. Presentation of Content

C. Utility for Students

D. Activities for Assessment

The method of assessment of above each parameter is based on three point scale, i.e.

1. A: Stands for Agree
2. B: Stands for Disagree
3. C: Stands for Undecided

For the successful completion of the study your assistance is very important. Without your kind co-operation this work cannot be completed, therefore it is my humble request that kindly reply to each statement after due consideration. I assure that the information imparted by you shall be kept confidential and would be used purely for the academic purpose.

Yours Sincerely

(Payal Mittal)

Respondents' Personal Information

Name : ....
Designation: ....
College/Institute: ....
Gender: ....
Age: ....
Locality R/U: ....
Educational Qualification: ....
Teaching Experience: ....

Opionionnaire for Effectiveness of Self-Learning Instructional Material for English Learners

A. Authenticity of the Material

No.	Statements	A	DA	UD
A.1	Diversified resources like from newspaper to podcast, cartoon movie clipping are used			
A.2	Exploring real time situations where learnerscan speak English			
A.3	Simple resources for learners to practiceEnglish			
A.4	Resources are making learning processengaging and motivational			
A.5	Making concepts easily understandable and meaningful			

B. Presentation of Content

No.	Statements	A	DA	UD
B.1	Themes are well chosen, relevant, and useful for students			
B.2	All the language skills are integrated			
B.3	Structure of the units are logical and systematically made			
B.4	Table format presentation for many topics makes easier for students to understand them			
B.5	The language of the material is as per the level of the students			
B.6	Workbook format is easy and handy			

C. Utility for Students

No.	Statements	A	DA	UD
C.1	Use the concepts taught in their real time situations			
C.2	Helping in clarifying many concepts related to all skills of language			
C.3	Motivates students to make learningeffective			
C.4	Students to make academic performancebetter			
C.5	Interesting for students to get this exposure			
C.6	Caters the needs of varied learning styles of			

D. Activities for Assessment

No.	Statements	A	DA	UD
D.1	Different types of creative activities are given for assessment			
D.2	Activities give varied experience to students			
D.3	Activities are engaging, interesting, and motivational			
D.4	Activities are given as per students' level			
D.5	Activities are assessing every skill of the language			
D.6	Students can assessed themselves through the given activities			

- Any valuable suggestions to improve the SIM –

  ....
  ....
  ....
  ....
  ....
  ....
  ....

Signature

(Name of the Expert)

Appendix - 4

ENGLISH LANGUAGE ACQUISITION ACHIEVEMENT TEST
(Pre-Tryout Stage)

FOR RESEARCH PURPOSE ONLY

ENGLISH LANGUAGE ACQUISITION ACHIEVEMENT TEST

FOR STUDENTS OF SCHOOL OF OPEN LEARNING (SOL) STUDYING ENGLISH FLUENCY IN B.A. (PROG.) OR B.COM (PROG.)

Supervised by: Dr Parvesh Lata

Constructed by Payal Mittal

Name of Student:	**Max. Marks: 100**
Gender:	**Time:**
Name of the course:	

General Instructions: The following question paper consists of total 68 questions. The question paper is divided into 6 sections:

Section A – Reading Skills which has 15 questions

Section B – Listening Skills which has 15 questions.

Section C - Vocabulary Skills which has 11 questions

Section D – Grammar Skills which has 17 questions

Section E – Writing Skills which has 7 questions

Section F – Speaking Skills which has 3 questions

Section A has only multiple choice questions. Section B, C, and D has two types of question: Multiple choice questions and fill in the blanks. Section E and F has three types of questions: Multiple choice questions, fill in the blanks, and Long Question.

All questions are compulsory. The marks these questions carry are written against the questions.

Reading Skills

Read the text given below and answer the questions that follow.

Pakistani schoolgirl Malala Yousafzai wrote an anonymous diary about life under Taliban rule in north-west Pakistan. She was shot in the head by militants for daring to go to school. In 2014 she became the youngest person ever to win the Nobel Peace Prize.

Accepting the award in Oslo she said she was "humbled" and proud to be the first Pashtun and the first Pakistani to win the prize. She also joked that she was probably the first winner who still fought with her younger brothers.

Malala Yousafzai first came to public attention through that heartfelt diary, published on BBC Urdu, which chronicled her desire to remain in education and for girls to have the chance to be educated.

When she was shot in the head in October 2012 by a Taliban gunman, she was already well known in Pakistan, but that one shocking act catapulted her to international fame. She survived the dramatic assault, in which a militant boarded her school bus in Pakistan's north-western Swat valley and opened fire, wounding two of her school friends as well. The story of her recovery - from delicate surgery at a Pakistani military hospital to further operations and rehabilitation in the UK, and afterwards as she took her campaign global - has been closely tracked by the world's media. She was discharged from hospital in January 2013 and her life now is unimaginably different to anything she may have envisaged when she was an anonymous voice chronicling the fears of schoolgirls under the shadow of the Taliban.

In 2013, she was named one of TIME magazine's most influential people and was first nominated for the Nobel Peace Prize. The same year, she won the European Parliament's Sakharov prize for Freedom of Thought and released her autobiography "I Am Malala". Malala was only 11 years old when her anonymous diary captivated audiences. She wrote under a pseudonym - Gul Makai, the name of a heroine from a Pashtun folk tale.

Militants destroyed scores of girls' schools in the time the Taliban wielded power over the valley. They had an implacable attitude to female education and this was Malala's primary concern. In January 2009, as the school was closing for winter holiday she wrote: "The girls were not too excited about vacations because they knew if the Taliban implemented their edict [banning girls' education] they would not be able to come to school again. I am of the view that the school will one day reopen but while leaving I looked at the building as if I would not come here again."

Since her recovery, Malala's campaign for global education has taken her around the world. She documented the anxiety she and her friends felt as they saw students dropping away from class for fear of being targeted by militants, and as the girls began to attend school in plain clothes not uniform, so as not to draw attention to themselves. Eventually, Malala and her family, like many thousands of other Swat residents, fled the valley when a government military operation attempted to clear the region of militancy.

Malala consistently received support and encouragement in her activism from her parents. The idea for the blog was even that of her father Ziauddin, who ran a local private school. The campaign of Malala Yousafzai: ''I want every girl, every child to be educated''

In a lengthy profile published in Vanity Fair magazine, one teacher from Swat said that her father "encouraged Malala to speak freely and learn everything she could". And her identity as the girl blogger from Swat eventually became known as she became more vocal on the subject of the right of girls to education. It is a subject she never ceased to be passionate about even after she returned home once the militants had been run out of Swat.

In 2009 a documentary film was made about her. Many more honours followed: in 2011 she was nominated for the International Children's Peace Prize by The Kids Rights Foundation and in 2012 the Pakistani government awarded her the National Peace Award - subsequently renamed the National Malala Peace Prize - for those under 18 years old.

Her father, Ziauddin Yousafzai, has been an essential support in her campaign. She even confronted then US special envoy to the region, Richard Holbrooke, urging him to do something about the state of affairs for women who want an education.

When she finally returned to Swat, Malala took advantage of the improved security and went back to school. Malala and her family was the subject of threats and it was on 9 October 2012 that these were borne out.

The Taliban said that they targeted her for "promoting secular education" and threatened to attack her again.

Despite the attack, Malala remained a school girl determined to complete her education. The bullet hit Malala's left brow and instead of penetrating her skull it travelled underneath the skin, the length of the side of her head and into her shoulder. Amid the outpouring of global support she was flown to the UK and at the Queen Elizabeth Hospital in the city of Birmingham she received specialist treatment and had a titanium plate fitted as well as a cochlear implant in her skull to help her hear.

She attended Edgbaston High School and her father was given a job with the Pakistani consulate in Birmingham for three years. In 2017, she was accepted to study Politics, Philosophy and Economics (PPE) at Oxford's Lady Margaret Hall.

As she studied, she continued her campaign and has taken it around the world. A fund set up in her name helps children in education around the world. Among other trips, she travelled to Nigeria, meeting President Goodluck Jonathan to press for action to free the 200 girls held by Boko Haram Islamist militants.

It is all a far cry from the young girl who wrote in her diary: "Today, I also read my diary written for the BBC in Urdu. My mother liked my pen name Gul Makai. I also like the name because my real name means 'grief stricken'." Source: https://www.bbc.com/news/world-asia-23241937

Questions.

1. What did Malala write in her diary?
   a. How she was shot in the head by Taliban militants
   b. How she spent her childhood with her friends
   c. Anxiety and fears of school girls of Swat
2. Which incident in Malala's life took her to international fame?
   a. Shot by Taliban militants
   b. Won Nobel Prize in 2014
   b. Her diary published on BBC Urdu

3. Why did Taliban militants shoot Malala?
   a. Because she wrote a diary which was published on BBC Urdu
   b. She was promoting secular education
   c. She fought with her younger brothers
4. In which year, she was nominated first time for Nobel Prize?
   a. 2013 b. 2014
   c. 2009
5. What is the name of Malala's autobiography?
   a. Gul Makai b. I Am Malala
   c. Pashtun Folk Tale
6. What was Taliban's view about girls' education?
   a. They wanted Pakistani girls to be educated
   b. They wanted to stop co-education in Pakistan
   c. They wanted to ban girls' education in Pakistan
7. Why did the girls start to attend school in plain clothes, not in uniform?
   a. To look more beautiful
   b. Not to draw attention of Taliban militants to themselves
   c. This was a rule in schools
8. On which subject, Malala wrote in her blogs?
   a. The Rights of girls to education b. Her family
   b. Taliban Militant rule
9. Why did Pakistani government rename its National Peace Award to National Malala Peace Prize?
   a. Other countries pressurized Pakistan to do so
   b. Taliban militants asked them to do so
   c. To give honour to Malala Yousafzai
10. After her recovery, why did Malala meet President of Nigeria?
    a. Requesting him to do something for the women who want an education
    b. Press for action to free 200 girls held by Boo Harm Islamist militants
    c. To free Pakistan from Taliban militants
11. What is the meaning of 'Malala'?
    a. Gul Makai b. Grief stricken
    c. First Pashtun
12. The most fitting title for this biographical sketch of Malala Yousafzai would be
    a. Malala: A Nobel Peace Prize Winner
    b. Malala: A survival from Taliban Militant's Attack
    c. Malala: From a Pakistani Schoolgirl to a Social Activist
13. Malala Yousafzai won all of the awards except:
    a. Nobel Peace Prize in 2014
    b. European'sParliament's Sakharov Prize
    c. International Youth's Peace Prize by The Kids Rights Foundation

14. What was Malala's campaign?
    a. To write blogs
    b. To complete her education
    c. Promote Girls' education
15. The correct meaning of 'anonymous' is
    a. Unidentified
    b. Famous
    c. Grief stricken

Listening Skills

Click on the link given below and listen a story about Ishi and Misha and answer the questions that follow.

https://anchor.fm/payal56/episodes/Listening-Episode-for-pre-achievement-test-e1i1udi

1. Why were Ishi and Misha at home?
   a. It was Sunday,
   b. It was summer holidays
   c. It was winter holidays
2. If you were at Ishi's place, what would have you done?
   a. Taken Misha to Mall for shopping and rides
   b. A nature walk
   c. For a visit to monument site
3. How is it cooler outside in the verandah than inside under the fan?
   a. Because of Mother Nature
   b. Rain coming outside
   c. It was night
4. How do the leaves make our surroundings cool?
   a. Keeps the strong sunrays away
   b. Doesn't let the soil dry too fast
   c. Both (a) and (b)
5. The .... Gently blow in the breeze and move the cool air like a thousand small fans.
   a. Big leaves,
   b. Butterfly
   c. Flowers
6. What did Misha want to do at this nice and cool place?
   a. Pluck flowers
   b. Play with her sister
   c. Watch cartoons
7. Who is the eldest one?
   a. Ishi
   b. Misha
8. Why couldn't the flowers sooth the itch in its petal?
   a. It didn't have arms and legs
   b. It didn't want to do that
   c. It wanted Misha to do it for her
9. Whom did flower ask for help?
   a. Ishi
   b. Butterfly
   c. Misha

10. What did butterfly have through which he helped the white flower?
    a. Tiny hair on his feet
    b. Ointment in his hand that soothed the itching
    c. Massage the petal with his legs
11. How did the white flower help butterfly, in return?
    a. Offered her beautiful yellow nectar
    b. By asking some food from Misha
    c. By giving some water
12. What did Misha enjoy the most outside?
    a. Breeze cool air
    b. Make their own cartoon
    c. Seeing butterfly and flowers
13. What value did you learn from this story?
    a. Enjoy the beauty of Nature
    b. Enjoy summer vacations with your family
    c. Plants are our best friends
14. What can you do to make your environment cool in the summer?
    a. Cover your balcony with a shade
    b. Stay indoors all the time
    c. Plant more trees around your surroundings
15. What did Disha ask her sister to do everyday at the end?
    a. Making their own cartoons
    b. Playing with flowers and butterfly
    c. Watch TV in the verandah

Vocabulary Skills

1. Read the text below. Use the word given in capitals at the end of some of the lines to form a word that fits in the gap in the same line.

Though modern life has made people very busy in their day- to-day lives, people are still able to make time for .... The video and audio .... have come up with advent of various types of multimedia devices. Music is one of the most popular forms of enter-tainment and leisure today. Music helps to relax people, in the fast paced.............society, suffering from stress and tension. Music can improve the mood and can comfort a person who is feeling fidgety and .... These days we have various types of compact sized multimedia music players like iPod, MP4, and MP3. Nowadays we have constant .... of....................products that are more convenient and enjoyable.	ENTERTAIN ENJOY MODERN TIRED UPGRADE ELECTRIC

2. Good afternoon Sir! We have many food items in Beverages, which one would you...................?
   a. Love b. Prefer
   c. Give
3. His math's assignment was too difficult so he gave up. 'Gave up' means
   a. Stop trying b. Try to complete
   c. start
4. We may have to...................our trip to Mananli until September.
   a. Put on b. Put off
   c. Put in
5. Rashmi loves...................He has one after every meal.
   a. Deserts b. Desserts
6. I can't talk to you right now, I'll call you................ after the meeting.
   a. On b. Out
   c. Back
7. waiting at the reception.
   a. They'are b. They're
8. you have some more pasta?
   a. Will'not b. Won't
   c. Will n't
9. My sister's science exam was too difficult but she easily.
   a. Got over b. Got through
   c. Got off
10. Mark the most appropriate word which means 'the atmosphere of a place'
    a. Picturesque b Ambience
    c. Decorum

Grammar Skills

1. Put the verb into correct form.
   a. My mother (not/drink) tea very often.

   ....

   b. What time (the market/close) here?

   ....

   c. Hey! What (you/look) for? I can help you.

   ....

   d. When (the next train/come)?

   ....

   e. Radha isn't very happy with her performance. She (not/practice) much.

   ....

   f. It (take) me an hour to get to work in the morning. How long (it/take) you?

……………………………………………………………………………………………

2. Pick out the verb, adjective, noun, and adverb used for the word 'create' in the paragraph. Also write down pronoun, preposition, connector, and determiner used.

   Ridhima created an eco-friendly garden creatively. She is very creative as each of her creation is unique and beautiful. Her parents are proud of her talent.

   Noun: ………………… Verb:…………………..………

   Adjective: ………………… Adverb: ……………….....………

   Pronoun: ………………… Connector: ………….....…………..

   Determiner: …………… Preposition: ……………………

3. He to library yesterday.
   a. Went b. Has gone
   c. Had gone
4. When Tanya ……………….., I had been For her for 2 hours.
   a. Come, waiting, b. Came, wait
   c. Coming, waiting d. Came, waiting
5. Would you mind................... a glass of water?
   a. Bring b. brought
   c. bringing d. to bring
6. Do you fancy........................ to a restaurant on Saturday?
   a. To go b. Going
   c. Went
7. My sister.................. To school at 7:30 am every morning.
   a. Go b. Is going
   c. Goes
8. Identify the types of tenses:
   a. I have never to a foreign country.
      i. Present simple tense ii. Present perfect tense
      ii. Past simple tense
   b. They will have completed their homework by the time vacation gets over.
      i. Present Perfect tense ii. Future Perfect tense
      iii. Future Simple Tense
9. Tomorrow, the National Seminar.............. by Chief Minister.
   a. Was inaugurated b. Is inaugurated
   c. Will be inaugurated
10. My parents enjoy............. home-made food.
    a. To have b. Having
    c. Have
11. We submit the project report by today evening.
    a. Have to b. Ought to

c. Should

12. He................. be very tired. He has been working all day long.

a. Will b. Could

c. Must

13. She doesn't like cooking................ she cooked good food.

a. Therefore b. Nevertheless

c. Moreover

14. .... the lack of exercise, people are getting obese or having weight-related problems.

a. Due to b. Though

c. Despite of

15. Tick the correct passive form for: *I will clean my car every Sunday.*

a. The car will be cleaned by me every Sunday.

b. The car is cleaned by me every Sunday.

c. The car will be cleaned.

16. The policeman instructed the driver.............. the traffic light when it is red.

a. Not jump b. Does not jump

c. Do not jump

17. My parents join the summer camp.

a. Get me b. Make me

c. Let me

Writing Skills

1. Describe a famous person that you are interested in. You would write about:
   - Who this person is.
   - How you know about this person
   - What sort of life they had before they became famous
   - How this person became famous
   - Why you like this person.

....

....

....

....

....

....

....

....

2. Complete the paragraph using best linking words.

   Young people are under a lot of pressure to stay up to date with the latest trends. In the ....(Past/nowadays/brief), people were only influenced by advertisers............... (then/so/and) their friends or social circle. ....(During/nowadays/recently), they have social media that pressures them not only be fashionable, but also to share it online. .... (So/moreover/ because), they are being judged not only by their peers at home, but also online. So, they are under huge amount of pressure.

3. In CV, your professional experiences comes under the heading

   a. Skills
   b. Education
   c. Employment history

4. This report aims to describe how the event of 'Environmental Meet' in the school was a successful which was held on 21st April 2022. The event started at 9:00 am and the teachers, students, and guests participated enthusiastically in the event.

   In report writing, this paragraph will come under the heading

   a. Recommendation
   b. Body
   c. Introduction

5. A covering letter is sent along with CV because

   a. To explain why you think you are the right person
   b. To introduce the person who recommended you for that job
   c. To describe your skills in details

6. Complete the email Dear Sir

   ...., a B.A.(Prog.) 1 semester student, studying English Language Course in Section D. I have not submitted the assignment yet as I am the part of NCC Social group of our college. ...., I was much involved in various activities for NCC group and for that reason even I could not attend many of your classes. I was not aware of the last date of the assignment submission which was 21 April, 2022.

   .... to request you to accept my assignment. I have already completed my assignment and ready to submit it whenever you would suggest. I will be highly obliged if you .... to submit the assignment as it will help me to get the better score in the final exams.

   Yours Sincerely

   Vishal Singh

Speaking Skills

1. Ask for a presentation or ask questions in an interview.
2. How would you reply in these situations?

   a. When someone asks you - Are you free this weekend?

      ....

   b. How would start if you have to place an order to a restaurant?

      ....

   c. You meet your friend after a long time.

      ....

3. Let's play the game 'Bothering Brother'. I say something and you ask me, "why"....? Let's go.

    a. I don't want to work today. – Why don't you want to work today?
    b. Because I don't feel like it. – Why don't...........................?
    c. Because working is hard. Why...........................?

Appendix - 5

ENGLISH LANGUAGE ACQUISITION ACHIEVEMENT TEST
(Final Stage)

FOR RESEARCH PURPOSE ONLY

ENGLISH LANGUAGE ACQUISITION ACHIEVEMENT TEST FOR STUDENTS OF SCHOOL OF OPEN LEARNING (SOL) STUDYING ENGLISH FLUENCY IN B.A. (PROG.) OR B.COM(PROG.)

Supervised by: Dr Parvesh Lata
Constructed by Payal Mittal

Name of Student:

Max. Marks: 100

Gender:

Time:

Name of the course:

General Instructions: The following question paper consists of total 68 questions. The question paper is divided into 6 sections:

Section A – Reading Skills which has 7 questions

Section B – Listening Skills which has 6 questions.

Section C – Vocabulary Skills which has 5 questions

Section D – Grammar Skills which has 8 questions

Section E – Writing Skills which has 3 questions

Section F – Speaking Skills which has 2 questions

Section A has only multiple choice questions. Section B, C, and D has two types of question: Multiple choice questions and fill in the blanks. Section E and F has three types of questions: Multiple choice questions, fill in the blanks, and Long Question.

All questions are compulsory. The marks these questions carry are written against the questions.

Reading Skills

Read the text given below and answer the questions that follow.

Pakistani schoolgirl Malala Yousafzai wrote an anonymous diary about life under Taliban rule in north-west Pakistan. She was shot in the head by militants for daring to go to school. In 2014 she became the youngest person ever to win the Nobel Peace Prize.

Accepting the award in Oslo she said she was "humbled" and proud to be the first Pashtun and the first Pakistani to win the prize. She also joked that she was probably the first winner who still fought with her younger brothers.

Malala Yousafzai first came to public attention through that heartfelt diary, published on BBC Urdu, which chronicled her desire to remain in education and for girls to have the chance to be educated.

When she was shot in the head in October 2012 by a Taliban gunman, she was already well known in Pakistan, but that one shocking act catapulted her to international fame. She survived the dramatic assault, in which a militant boarded her school bus in Pakistan's north-western Swat valley and opened fire, wounding two of her school friends as well. The story of her recovery - from delicate surgery at a Pakistani military hospital to further operations and rehabilitation in the UK, and afterwards as she took her campaign global - has been closely tracked by the world's media. She was discharged from hospital in January 2013 and her life now is unimaginably different to anything she may have envisaged when she was an anonymous voice chronicling the fears of schoolgirls under the shadow of the Taliban.

In 2013, she was named one of TIME magazine's most influential people and was first nominated for the Nobel Peace Prize. The same year, she won the European Parliament's Sakharov prize for Freedom of Thought and released her autobiography "I Am Malala". Malala was only 11 years old when her anonymous diary captivated audiences. She wrote under a pseudonym - Gul Makai, the name of a heroine from a Pashtun folk tale.

Militants destroyed scores of girls' schools in the time the Taliban wielded power over the valley. They had an implacable attitude to female education and this was Malala's primary concern. In January 2009, as the school was closing for winter holiday she wrote: "The girls were not too excited about vacations because they knew if the Taliban implemented their edict [banning girls' education] they would not be able to come to school again. I am of the view that the school will one day reopen but while leaving I looked at the building as if I would not come here again."

Since her recovery, Malala's campaign for global education has taken her around the world. She documented the anxiety she and her friends felt as they saw students dropping away from class for fear of being targeted by militants, and as the girls began to attend school in plain clothes not uniform, so as not to draw attention to themselves. Eventually, Malala and her family, like many thousands of other Swat residents, fled the valley when a government military operation attempted to clear the region of militancy.

Malala consistently received support and encouragement in her activism from her parents. The idea for the blog was even that of her father Ziauddin, who ran a local private school. The campaign of Malala Yousafzai: ''I want every girl, every child to be educated''

In a lengthy profile published in Vanity Fair magazine, one teacher from Swat said that her father "encouraged Malala to speak freely and learn everything she could". And her identity as the girl blogger from Swat eventually became known as she became more vocal on the subject of the right of girls to education. It is a subject she never ceased to be passionate about even after she returned home once the militants had been run out of Swat.

In 2009 a documentary film was made about her. Many more honours followed: in 2011 she was nominated for the International Children's Peace Prize by The Kids Rights Foundation and in 2012 the Pakistani government awarded her the National Peace Award - subsequently renamed the National Malala Peace Prize - for those under 18 years old.

Her father, Ziauddin Yousafzai, has been an essential support in her campaign. She even confronted then US special envoy to the region, Richard Holbrooke, urging him to do something about the state of affairs for women who want an education.

When she finally returned to Swat, Malala took advantage of the improved security and went back to school. Malala and her family was the subject of threats and it was on 9 October 2012 that these were borne out. The Taliban said that they targeted her for "promoting secular education" and threatened to attack her again.

Despite the attack, Malala remained a school girl determined to complete her education. The bullet hit Malala's left brow and instead of penetrating her skull it travelled underneath the skin, the length of the side of her head and into her shoulder. Amid the outpouring of global support she was flown to the UK and at the Queen Elizabeth Hospital in the city of Birmingham she received specialist treatment and had a titanium plate fitted as well as a cochlear implant in her skull to help her hear.

She attended Edgbaston High School and her father was given a job with the Pakistani consulate in Birmingham for three years. In 2017, she was accepted to study Politics, Philosophy and Economics (PPE) at Oxford's Lady Margaret Hall.

As she studied, she continued her campaign and has taken it around the world. It is all a far cry from the young girl who wrote in her diary: "Today, I also read my diary written for the BBC in Urdu. My mother liked my pen name Gul Makai. I also like the name because my real name means 'grief stricken'."

Source: https://www.bbc.com/news/world-asia-23241937

Questions.

1. Why did Taliban militants shoot Malala?
   a. Because she wrote a diary which was published on BBC Urdu
   b. She was promoting secular education
   c. She fought with her younger brothers
2. In which year, she was nominated first time for Nobel Prize?
   a. 2013
   b. 2014
   c. 2009
3. On which subject, Malala wrote in her blogs?
   a. The Rights of girls to education
   b. Her family
   c. Taliban Militant rule

4. Why did Pakistani government rename its National Peace Award to National Malala Peace Prize?
   a. Other countries pressurized Pakistan to do so
   b. Taliban militants asked them to do so
   c. To give honour to Malala Yousafzai
5. The most fitting title for this biographical sketch of Malala Yousafzai would be
   a. Malala: A Nobel Peace Prize Winner
   b. Malala: A survival from Taliban Militant's Attack
   c. Malala: From a Pakistani Schoolgirl to a Social Activist
6. What was Malala's campaign?
   a. To write blogs b. To complete her education
   c. Promote Girls' education
7. The correct meaning of 'anonymous' is
   a. Unidentified b. Famous
   c. Grief stricken

Listening Skills

Click on the link given below and listen a story about Ishi and Misha and answer the questions that follow.

https://anchor.fm/payal56/episodes/Listening-Episode-for-pre-achievement-test-e1i1udi

1. How do the leaves make our surroundings cool?
   a. Keeps the strong sunrays away
   b. Doesn't let the soil dry too fast
   c. Both (a) and (b)
2. The .... Gently blow in the breeze and move the cool air like a thousand small fans.
   a. Big leaves, b. Butterfly
   c. Flowers
3. What did Misha want to do at this nice and cool place?
   a. Pluck flowers b. Play with her sister
   c. Watch cartoons
4. Why couldn't the flowers sooth the itch in its petal?
   a. It didn't have arms and legs b. It didn't want to do that
   c. It wanted Misha to do it for her
5. What did butterfly have through which he helped the white flower?
   a. Tiny hair on his feet
   b. Ointment in his hand that soothed the itching
   c. Massage the petal with his legs
6. How did the white flower help butterfly, in return?
   a. Offered her beautiful yellow nectar
   b. By asking some food from Misha
   c. By giving some water

Vocabulary Skills

1. Good afternoon Sir! We have many food items in Beverages, which one would you.......................?
   a. Love b. Prefer
   c. Give
2. We may have to......................our trip to Manali until September.
   a. Put on b. Put off
   c. Put in
3. Rashmi loves He has one after every meal.
   a. Deserts b. Desserts
4. you have some more pasta?
   a. Will'not b. Won't
   c. Will n't
5. My sister's science exam was too difficult but she....................easily.
   a. Got over b. Got through
   c. Got off

Grammar Skills

1. Put the verb into correct form.
   a. My mother (not/drink) tea very often.

      ....

   b. What time (the market/close) here?

      ....

   c. Hey! What (you/look) for? I can help you.

      ....

   d When (the next train/come)?

      ....

   e Radha isn't very happy with her performance. She (not/practice) much.

      ....

   f. It (take) me an hour to get to work in the morning. How long (it/take) you?

      ....

2. Pick out the verb, adjective, noun, and adverb used for the word 'create' in the paragraph. Also write down pronoun, preposition, connector, and determiner used.

   Ridhima created an eco-friendly garden creatively. She is very creative as each of her creation is unique and beautiful. Her parents are proud of her talent.

   Noun: .... Verb: ....
   Adjective: .... Adverb: ....
   Pronoun: .... Connector: ....
   Determiner: .... Preposition: ....

3. When Tanya ……………………, I had been For her for 2 hours.
   a. Come, waiting,
   b. Came, wait
   c. Coming, waiting
   d. Came, waiting
4 My sister................ To school at 7:30 am every morning.
   a. Go
   b. Is going
   c. Goes
5. Identify the types of tenses:
   a. I have never to a foreign country.
      i. Present simple tense
      ii. Present perfect tense
      ii. Past simple tense
   b. They will have completed their homework by the time vacation gets over.
      i. Present Perfect tense
      ii. Future Perfect tense
      ii. Future Simple Tense
6. He..................... be very tired. He has been working all day long.
   a. Will
   b. Could
   c. Must
7. Tick the correct passive form for: *I will clean my car every Sunday.*
   a. The car will be cleaned by me every Sunday.
   b. The car is cleaned by me every Sunday.
   c. The car will be cleaned.
8. The policeman instructed the driver.................... the traffic light when it is red.
   a. Not jump
   b. Does not jump
   c. Do not jump

Writing Skills

1. Describe a famous person that you are interested in. You would write about:
   - Who this person is.
   - How you know about this person
   - What sort of life they had before they became famous
   - How this person became famous
   - Why you like this person.

…………………………………………………………………………………………

…………………………………………………………………………………………

…………………………………………………………………………………………

…………………………………………………………………………………………

…………………………………………………………………………………………

…………………………………………………………………………………………

…………………………………………………………………………………………

…………………………………………………………………………………………

…………………………………………………………………………………………

2. In CV, your professional experiences comes under the heading
   a. Skills b. Education
   c. Employment history
3. A covering letter is sent along with CV because
   a. To explain why you think you are the right person
   b. To introduce the person who recommended you for that job
   c. To describe your skills in details

Speaking Skills

1. Ask for a presentation or ask questions in an interview.
2. How would you reply in these situations?
   a. When someone asks you - Are you free this weekend?

      ....

   b. How would start if you have to place an order to a restaurant?

      ....

   c. You meet your friend after a long time.

      ....

Appendix - 6

SCORING KEY FOR VALID ACHIEVEMENT TEST
(Final Stage)

Section A: Reading Skills

1. b	2. b	3. a	4. c	5. a, c
6. c	7. a			

Section B: Listening Skills

1. c	2. a	3. c	4. a	5. a
6.a				

Section C: Vocabulary Skills

1. b	2. b	3. b	4. b	5. b

Section D: Grammar Skills

1. a. does not drink	2. Noun – creation
b. does the market close	Adjective – creative
c. are you looking	Pronoun – she
d. does the next train come	Determiner – an
e. did not practice	Adverb – creatively
f. takes; does it take	Connector – as
	Preposition – of

3. a	4. c	5. a. (ii); b. (ii)	6. c	7. b
8.c				

Section E: Writing Skills

1. …………	2. c	3. a

Appendix - 7

Interaction Scale for Students

Instructions: The objective of this self-instructional material evaluation checklist or tool is to aid students to determine whether the self-instructional material is appropriate for the students. The items in the checklist are divided into five groups on the basis of five different dimensions, exploring different aspects of self-instructional material. These 5 groups are: (1) Layout, design, and presentation, (2) Content, topics, and language, (3) Language teaching methods and activities, (4) Four language skills - listening, speaking, reading, and writing, (5) Sub-skills - Vocabulary, Grammar, and Conversational skill.

Read the items in the checklist about the Self-Instructional material and indicate the level of your agreement by marking 0-4.

0 = strongly disagree

1 = disagree

2 = uncertain

3 = agree

4 = strongly agree

1. Layout, design, and Presentation						
No.	Items	0	1	2	3	4
1	Units are designed and presented in an harmonious organization					
2.	Contains a detailed list of contents including unittitles, language skills, and activities related to them					
3.	Objectives of each unit are clearly stated in thebeginning.					
4.	The content and learning activities are well-sequenced with clear headings and subheadings					
5.	Illustrations and other non-textual materials like tables, diagrams, hyperlinks, and timelines are purposeful and clear					
6.	Instructions for each activity are stated clearly for the students to follow.					
7.	Each unit offers a variety of exercises and activities to practice the target language skills to help thestudents to communicate in English in real life.					

2. Content, Topics, and language						
No.	**Items**	**0**	**1**	**2**	**3**	**4**
1.	The topics of the units are up-to-date andinteresting					
2.	The topics, content, and language used areappropriate to the students' level					
3.	The content and language gives exposure to reallanguage					
4.	The content is relevant to the students' needs andinterest					
5.	The content covers all 4 language skills - listening, speaking, reading, and writing with an appropriatebalance and in an integrated manner					
6.	Language used for Instructions for each activity is clearly understandable for the students to follow.					
7.	The language used in the textbook is authentic andup-to-date.					

3. Language Teaching Methods and Activities						
No.	**Items**	**0**	**1**	**2**	**3**	**4**
1.	Stimulate interaction and negotiation					
2.	Creative and student-centered approach toteaching and learning					
3.	Encourage learners to apply their developinglanguage skills					
4.	Use varied authentic resources to produce teachingand learning activities					
5.	The activities encourage student participation and enable them to appropriately use language indifferent real situations					
6.	The activities enhance the students' autonomy – become independent learners responsible for their own learning					
7.	Self-instructional material encourages the use of technology in learning English					

4. Four language skills - listening, speaking, reading, and writing						
No.	**Items**	**0**	**1**	**2**	**3**	**4**
1.	Listening, speaking, reading, and writing tasks areappropriate for the students' level					
2.	The material used in listening, speaking, reading, and writing tasks are authentic and interesting both in terms of content and language.					
3.	All the four skills are integrated with each other into the practice.					
4.	It has a variety and sufficiency of listening,speaking, reading, and writing tasks.					
5.	Relevant and important topics are chosen and covered for the four skills					
6.	Various exercises are provided for practice for allfour language skills					
7.	All language skills - listening, speaking, reading,and writing are given balanced weight age					

5. Sub-skills - Vocabulary, Grammar, and Conversational skill						
No.	**Items**	**0**	**1**	**2**	**3**	**4**
1.	Different activities are given to help the studentsunderstand the meaning of vocabulary items and use them correctly in context					
2	The grammatical items are chosen appropriately and sufficiently according to the students' level.					
3.	The grammatical items are introduced explicitly in meaningful contexts with the integration with other skills using clear examples and explanations.					
4.	The forms and examples of vocabulary andgrammatical items are given in the tabular form which gives more clarity					
5.	Different varied authentic resources are used for giving practicing exercises					
6.	Conversational items are useful, boost up the confidence and motivate students to use English intheir daily life					

Any Comment:

....

....

....

Any suggestion:

....

....

....

Appendix - 8

Self-Learning Instructional Material for English Language Acquisition Skills for Undergraduate Students

Author's Note

Dear Learners

This self-learning instructional material is set on different themes to enhance learner's learning experience and provide exposure to English language in different situations and with varied learning authentic resources. In this material, we have incorporated many English language skills— Listening, Reading, Writing, Vocabulary, Speaking, Conversational, Grammar, etc. This exposure will give you confidence and motivation to use these English language skills in your real life situations.

There are 5 units based on different themes – Travel, Health and Food, Entertainment, Working with Technology and Workplace. There are various activities related to these themes. The concepts are presented, taught, and practised in English language using these themes which you have to perform and make your earning more meaningful and enjoyable.

Unit 1: Travel

INDEX

Learning Objectives

After reading this Unit, the students will be able to:

- explore a travel diary mainly describing the events of a journey and the experiences and discoveries of the Writer
- listen the important details in narratives like description of a holiday
- practice some phrases and sentences to start, extend, and end the conversation
- compose a paragraph on their personal travel experience in some details
- construct some simple and negative sentences
- demonstrate the skill of questioning using 'wh' words
- communicate using Vocabulary related to travel

READING SKILLS

 **Let's Do**

Read the following article.

Get Daring with These Adventure Activities to do in India

By Parnashree Devi, Jun 29, 2021, Best of the Blog, Blog, Destinations, India, Travel

Owing to innumerable adventure activities to do in India, daredevils from all around the world love to visit the country. Whether you are on a road trip, traveling solo, on a group tour, or on family vacations, these escapades are worth trying. Until now, India used to beguile visitors with a spellbinding cultural confluence. But, with the changing trends, the country has managed to rank on the bucket list of adventure junkies as well. From river rafting in Rishikesh to scaling the heights of the Himalayas.

Trekking

Trekking in India is not only about conquering the heights of the mountains! Rather, it also involves trekking on the frozen Zanskar River. From difficult treks, easy treks, short treks to long treks, where else you will find so many trekking options. As a matter of fact, the fun-filled activity is a memorable affair of breathtaking terrains, high passes, surprising trails, etc.

- Tips: Choose a trekking level that suits you the best. Don't start with a difficult trek, if you're a novice. In addition to this, carry your necessary essentials with you.
- Location: There are many trekking destinations in India. However, the most popular ones are Ladakh, Sikkim, Garhwal, Himachal Pradesh, etc.

Camping

Don't take it lightly when we add camping to the list of must-do adventure activities in India. Escape into the golden sand dunes or set your camps under the stars.

Enjoy spending days besides a color-changing lake or cherish some tranquil moments at the picturesque destinations amidst snow-covered peaks. Because of such a variety of options, a majority of the adventure tour packages definitely include camping.

- **Tips:** Place your camp in close proximity to a village or a city. Don't contribute to enVironmental pollution.
- **Location:** Leh, Kullu & Manali, Rishikesh, Rajasthan, etc., are some of the best camping sites in India.

Mountaineering

Challenging the daredevil in you, Mountaineering is an eye-opening experience. Outstanding amongst the rest of the adventure activities in India, the arduous escapade is for the brave hearts and daring souls. Above all, the deed offers you some unforgettable memories. Be it the soul-soothing ambiance of the towering peaks or the awe- inspiring views, everything seems so magical.

- **Tips:** Before going mountaineering, brush up on your climbing skills. Brace yourself for altitude sickness and acclimatization. Carry necessary medications with you. Follow the 'No trace' policy.
- **Location:** Kufri, Nanda Devi, Kanchenjunga, Uttarakhand are some of the ideal places for trying your hands at mountaineering.

Hot Air Balloon Safari

Even words fall short to describe how it feels to have a bird's eye view of a destination. What's even better is to fly slowly over some of the best places to visit in India. Hot Air Balloon Safari offers you exactly this and much more. Another key point to note about this new adventure activity in India is that it is scary, fun, and thrilling all in one go.

- **Tips:** Go for this joy ride in the morning. Follow the safety instructions. Dress appropriately. Steady yourself for landing.
- **Location:** Hot Air Ballooning is quite famous in Goa, Rajasthan, Maharashtra and Uttar Pradesh.

Scuba Diving

Witnessing what lies deep down the azure waters is really exciting. For this reason, Scuba Diving, especially in the Andaman Islands is the most cherished adventure activity in India. Swim with colorful sea creatures, get a closer look at the fishes of all kinds, or marvel at the exotic corals. Get spellbound with the magical beauty of underwater life this summer season.

- **Tips:** Choose certified instructors to partake in Scuba Diving. Listen to the instructions provided before going for the activity. Even if you are not a swimmer, you can still enjoy scuba diving.
- **Location:** Lakshadweep Islands, Pondicherry, Andaman, Goa are perfect destinations for Scuba Diving.

Let's Assess

Activity 1: Comprehension Questions

After reading this article, answer the following questions.

(a) What was India, in the past, famous for the fascinated visitors from the different parts of the world?

Ans. ....

....

(b) What makes trekking a fun filled activity?

Ans. ....

....

(c) Why do the most adventure tour packages have camping as an activity?

Ans. ....

....

(d) Make out some differences between hot air balloon safari and paragliding?

Ans. ....

....

(e) In which adventurous activity, teamwork is important and why?

Ans. ....

....

(f) How is trekking different from mountaineering?

Ans. ....

....

Let's Reflect

Many times these activities are shown on the television in many shows and movies being enjoyed by people. Write the name of the show or movie for each activity mentioned in the article.

- Jungle safari: ....
- Paragliding: ....
- Scuba Diving: ....
- Whitewater rafting: ....
- Camping: ....

Let's Think

Complete the chart with the help of dictionary. One example has been done for you.

Word	Meaning	Part of Speech	Example of Usage
Daredevil	a reckless or careless person who enjoys doingdangerous things	Noun	Daredevils always wantto go on some adventurous trips.
Escapade			
Picturesque			

Acclimatisation			
Wilderness			
Ambience			

LISTENING SKILLS

Let's Do

A Visit to Bir Billing in Himachal Pradesh

A link is shared below for you. Using the link, watch the Video carefully. This Video is about an adventurous place, Bir Billing in Himachal Pradesh which Tanya has visited recently with the intention of Paragliding, but the trip turned into a serious series of adventures! Let's listen about a part of this adventure which includes cycling in Bir and visiting some amazing places.

Try to get the whole understanding of the video. If you are getting only the gist, you can watch it twice or thrice.

https://youtu.be/Jl1u2aGm5bg -

Let's Assess

Activity 2 : Complete the Paragraph

After watching this video, complete the given paragraph describing the experience of Tanya.

Tanya with her friends went to .... There, they visited the .... which is the .... monastery in Bir. That place has an educational institute for .... There are....................... ., there are classes, there are ....campuses who take lectures for monks and also the canteen. There they played .... with the monks. Inside the main prayer chamber of monastery ...., and .... was not allowed.

For lunch, they stopped at .... for eating chowmein, momos, maggi, chai, soda nibu water. That place was .... to Sherabling monastery. After that they cycled all.................................... to head towards their next ...., Dharamalya. It's all uphill and little.................................... ! It was raining .... they had to keep .... their bicycles to get there.

GRAMMAR SKILLS

|| SENTENCES ||

Let's Understand

When we speak in any language, we talk about a **person, thing, animal,** and **place.** The highlighted words in the previous sentence are called **subject.** In a sentence, 'subject' is the word about whom you talk about. The action that a subject does is called **verb.** The subject is doing some action with some object and that object is called **object** in that sentence.

For example: Krish visited a hilly place. In this sentence,

Subject	Verb	Object
Krish (about whom we are talking about)	Visited (action he isdoing)	a hilly place (doing action on this object)

|| DECORATING A SENTENCE ||

In the above example, 'Krish visited a hilly place', we can add more information about nouns (Krish, hilly place) in the same sentence. We do it by adding **adjectives, determiners, adverbs, and prepositions** to the sentence. Let us learn how to do it from the table given below:

Adjectives - describes thenoun	Noun – whomyou are talking about	Verb- what did they do	Determiner –comes beforenoun and tells about quantity of noun	Object (another noun)	Adverb– Howdid he do	Where and when it happens – preposition
10 years-old Adventurous	Krish	visited	a	hilly place	after a long time	by his car

Write the new decorated sentence:

<u>Adventurous Krish visited a hilly place after a long time by his car</u>.

Now stick out some more sentences with your new sentence. There is some more information given about Krish. Stick out these sentences with the help of pronoun and connectors with previous sentence.

Pronouns: These are the words that replace nouns. For example, he, she, it, you, they, we.

Connectors: These are the words through which we can join two sentences. For example, 'although', ' and',' but', 'since', 'which', 'so', 'therefore', 'as', 'while', 'unless', 'despite', etc. Some of the examples have been given below. More information about Krish has been added by using the connectors with the new sentence that we have made above:

Adventurous Krish visited a hilly place after a long time by his car.

He is not expert.	Adventurous Krish visited a hilly place after a long time by his car **although** he is not expert.	to show contrast
He visited a monastery	Adventurous Krish visited a hilly place **and** a monastery after a long time by his car.	to connect similar ideas
He did not enjoy too much there	Adventurous Krish visited a hilly place after a long time by his car **but** he did not enjoy too much there.	To show difference or contrast
During the summer vacations	**During** the summer vacations, Adventurous Krish visited a hilly place after a long time by his car	to show time
He would getbored in his vacations	Adventurous Krish visited a hilly place after a long time by his car **otherwise** he would get bored in his vacations	To show the effect or result
He is not satisfied	Adventurous Krish visited a hilly place after a long time by his car **yet** he is not satisfied	To show contrast

All the highlighted words in the above table are called connectors

Let's Apply

Activity 3: Identification of Parts of Speech

Read this paragraph and then choose the words from it for the categories given below and write them in the appropriate category. Do not write the same word more than once.

It was a high summer noon. Alice and her sister were sitting in a meadow studying their books. They were very happy indeed. All of a sudden, a White Rabbit ran past the sisters. It had a coat and a hat on. Pulling out a pocket- watch, the Rabbit looked at it closely and shouted,

"Dear oh dear! I am getting late."

"How strange a rabbit!" exclaimed Alice. Unable to control herself, she ran after the rabbit rashly.

Verb	Noun	Adjective	Adverb
Preposition	**Pronoun**	**Connector**	**Determiner**

Here the lists of adjectives (words that describes how the noun is), connectors (words that joins two sentences), Adverb (words that tell you how the action has been done), Determiners (words that tell about the quantity of noun), prepositions (words that tell about the location and place of the action done), Pronoun (words that can replace nouns), Verbs (action verbs) are given below. Read these lists carefully.

List of Adjectives

Appearance	Attractive, beautiful, clean, dazzling, elegant, fancy, fit, gorgeous, handsome, long, magnificent, muscular, short, skinny, ugly
Shape	Broad, curved, deep, flat, high, hollow, low, narrow, refined, round, shallow, skinny, square, Steep, straight, wide
Colour	Black, Blue, gray, green, lemon, orange, purple, red, white, yellow
Size	Big, fat, gigantic, great, huge, immense, large, little, massive, microscopic, miniature, short, small, tall, tiny
Condition	Better, careful, clever, dead, easy, famous, gifted, helpful, important, inexpensive, odd, poor, powerful, rich, shy, tender, unimportant, uninterested, wrong
Personality	Ambitious, brave, calm, delightful, eager, faithful, gentle, happy, jolly, kind, lively, nice, obedient, jealous, lazy, mysterious, nervous, obnoxious
Sound	Crashing, deafening, echoing, faint, harsh, hissing, howling, loud, melodic, noisy, purring, quiet, rhythmic, screeching, shrilling, squeaking, thundering, tinkling, whispering
Time	Ancient, brief, early, fast, future, late, long, modern, old, old-fashioned, quick, rapid, short, Slow, young
Taste	Bitter, creamy, delicious, disgusting, fresh,greasy, juicy, hot, nutritious,ripe,rotten,salty, sour, spicy, spoiled, stale, sweet, tangy, tasteless, tasty, yummy
Touch	Breezy, bumpy, chilly, cold, cool, damaged,damp, dirty, dry, fluffy, freezing,greasy, hot, icy, Loose,melted, rough, sharp, slimy, sticky, strong, tight, uneven, warm, weak, wet, wooden
Quantity	Abundant, billions, enough, few, full, hundreds, limited, little, many, most, numerous, scarce, some, substantial

List of Connectors

Addition (connecting similar ideas)	Time	Sequence	Contrast (to show difference)	Condition	Reason	Result
And	When	Then	But	As long as	Because	So
Moreover	While	After	However	Otherwise	Due to	Therefore
Also	As	Firstly	Though	Unless	As	As a result
As well as	As soon as	Next	Although		In order to	Consequently
		Finally	Nevertheless			
		Secondly	Despite			
			While			

List of Adverbs

How	When	To what extent	Where
Beautifully	after, afterwards, annually	Extremely,	abroad, anywhere, away
Gracefully	before	quite,	down
Eagerly	daily	rather, really	everywhere
Gracefully	never, now	terribly, too,	here, home
Happily	soon, still	very	in, inside
Really	then, today, tomorrow		out, outside
stylishly	weekly, when		somewhere
Well	yesterday		there
Urgently			underground, upstairs

List of Determiners

Definite article	Indefinite articles	Demonstratives	Pronouns and possessive determiners	Quantises	Numbers
The	a, an	this, that, these, those	my, your, his, her, its, our, their	a few, a little, much, many, a lot of, most, some, any, enough	one, ten, thirty

List of Preposition

Preposition of Time	Preposition of Place	Preposition of Manner
On, in, at, from¡K..to,past, till/until, by, since, for, ago, before	Under, over, in, on, in front of, behind, next to, at, between, near, above, below	Out of, along, onto, off, across, down, through, up, over, around

List of Pronouns

Subject Pronouns	Object Pronouns	Possessive Pronouns	Reflexive Pronouns
I, you, he, she, it, we, they	Me, you, him, her, it, us, you, them	Mine, yours, his, hers, its, ours, yours, theirs	Myself, yourself, himself, herself, itself, ourselves, yourselves, themselves

Let's Practice

Activity 4: Decorating your Sentence

Some words are given for the categories – pronouns, adjectives, adverb, connectors, preposition, verb, determiners. Use these words to make sentence in the space provided to you. In your sentence, you must use at least one word of each type.

Noun	Pronoun	Adjective	Verb	Adverb	Preposition	Determiner	Conjunction
Man	His	Old	Was, Sitting, Eating	Happily	Under	A, His	And
Passenger	He	Young, Red	Ran, Catch	Quickly	After	The	But
Sita, Exams	She	Ambitious	Studied, Score	Well, Hard	For	Her	Still

....

....

....

....

Note: You can choose more words from the list of adjectives, connectors, adverbs, determiners, prepositions, pronouns and then make your own sentences by following the same route.

Let's Understand

|| MAIN VERBS AND AUXILIARY VERBS ||

Read this sentence : Pranav **is** 22 years-old and **has** just **given** the exams of his last semester.

In this sentence, two types of verbs are highlighted – 'is' and 'has given'

- **Main Verb :** These verbs tell the action that the subject is doing.

  In the above sentence, 'give' is the main verb that tells about Pranav who has just completed the action – given his exams.

- **Auxiliary Verb :** The Verbs like 'to be', 'to do', 'to have' are called auxiliary verbs. In the above sentence 'is' is form of 'to be' verb.

Forms of Auxiliary Verbs

3 Auxiliary verbs	Its forms
To have	Has, have, having, had
To do	Do, did, does
To be	am, are, is, was, were, being, been

Auxiliary Verbs can be used in 2 different forms:

1. **Auxiliary verbs as main verbs:** In this, forms of auxiliary verbs are used as main Verbs. For example, Pranav **is** 22 years- old. In this sentence, 'is' is used a auxiliary verb.

2. **Auxiliary verbs with other verbs:** These verbs can also be used as helping verbs with other verbs to form different tenses and different grammatical forms. For example,
    - I have done my homework. – 'have' is used as helping verb with verb 'done' to form present perfect tense
    - I am jumping over the railings. – 'am' is used as helping verb with the verb 'jump' to form present continuous tense.

Modal Auxiliary verbs: There is another form of using the auxiliary verb called the modal auxiliary verbs. Some of the modal auxiliary verbs are 'can', 'could', 'must', 'might', etc., do not change their forms. They are used in the sentences along with the main verb. There are 9 modal auxiliary verbs: shall, should, can, could, will, would, may, might, must. We will learn about them later in this unit.

Examples of Auxiliary Verbs

Main Verbs	Auxiliary Verbs as Main Verbs	Auxiliary Verbs as Helping Verbs
Last night I **slept** in the car. I **wake** up early in the morning every day. I **decided** to make a plan for campaigning.	It **was** a real struggle for me to get the tickets. I **did** swimming this morning. My friend **has** beautiful dress.	I **am eating** the lunch. The river **was flowing** very fast. She does work very hard. Kids **have gone** to the park. She **has been reading** a book since morning.

Uses of Auxiliary Verbs

Auxiliary Verbs	Use as main Verb	Examples
To have	to express possession	I have a pet dog. Samaira has very long hair.
To do	to perform or complete an action	We have to do something to solve this problem
To be	to give information about the action to con?rm something about the subject	I am going to be a doctor. He is twenty-one years old.

Auxiliary Verbs	Use as helping Verb	Examples
To have	To form negative sentences	He does not want to go out on a trip.
To do	To form question sentences	Have I learnt from my mistake?
To be	To create emphatic forms	I do agree with you
To be	To form different tenses	I am eating a burger. – Continuous tenseI have eaten a burger. – perfect tense

Let's Reflect

Activity 5: Main Verbs and Auxiliary Verbs

Open any page of a book/newspaper/magazine that you read. Choose a paragraph from that page. Then write two sentences from that paragraph in which auxiliary verbs are used as main verbs and auxiliary verbs are used as helping verbs.

....

....

....

....

Activity 6: Auxiliary Verbs Exercises

Complete the sentences with auxiliary verbs from the choices given.

1. The children................ playing in the park in the morning. (is/was/are)
2. I .... not like swimming. (am/is/do)
3. Rishabh .... not want to for movie with his friend. (do/is/does)
4. Sara likes to................ a cup of coffee. (had/drink/have)
5. When .... you sleep last night? (do/did/have)
6. My mother .... going to bake a chocolate cake for my birthday. is/are/ has)
7. ....you know where my keys are? (do/did/is)
8. Manya is not going to market. She................ the headache. (has/is/had)
9. I................ already bought some snacks. (do/haVe/am)
10. My daughter................ the food for two hours.
    (is cooking/has cooking/has been cooking)

Let's Understand

|| HOW TO FORM NEGATIVE SENTENCES ||

For making negative form of a sentence-

- Add 'not' with the auxiliary verb.

  For example, He is not happy. Jay was not writing the letter.
- With the main verb, add do/does/did/ with 'not' to make it negative sentence. For example, I do not like cricket. He does not go to theatre.
- We use 'did not' to make negative sentences for actions happened in the past. For example, yesterday, she did not get up early in the morning.

Always remember when we use 'did not' in a sentence, we use first form of the verb because 'did' is already second form of verb 'do' and denotes past tense.

There is no use of using two past forms of verbs in a sentence. For example,

She did not corrected her mistake. ☒	She did not correct her mistake. ☑

Let's Assess

Activity 7: Make Negative Sentences

Complete the story with the correct form of verbs and add negative to these verbs also whenever required.

It was Sunday afternoon. Sebastian was sitting in his family's ice-cream parlour. Working there .... (be) Sebastian's ideas of an exciting Sunday morning. He had an essay as his assignment due on Monday, and of course, he.................. (start) writing it. He kept looking at the raindrops that rolled down the window besides him.

'It's high time you started your essay,' said Sebastian's father.

'Dad, it's too hard, I............. (write) an essay on "Reading is Fun¡". Said Sebastian.

'Oh, come on Sebastian, that.............. (sound) so hard!' said Sebastian's father.

'It is! When I..............(like) reading myself, how can I write an essay on "Reading is Fun'!' exclaimed Sebastian.

"Fine, Son! Go and write your essay¡" ordered Sebastian's father.

Sebastian thought he.............. (be) much of a choice. So he dragged himself to the room upstairs to do his essay.

He sat down to write but .... (write) more than the little, as his brain was empty. "How can reading be fun" he thought to himself.

Let's Understand

|| MODAL AUXILIARY VERBS ||

Modal verbs are used to express certain hypothetical conditions such as advice, likelihood, possibility, ability, permission, request, suggestion, obligation (duty).

Usage of Modal Auxiliary Verbs

Modal Auxiliary Verbs	Situations in which they can be used	Examples
Can	Ability to do something	I can jog for 3 kms nonstop in the morning.
Could	Possibility	Why didn't you tell me before? I could have picked you first.
Shall/Will	To make a suggestion With pronoun 'I' and 'We' – use "shall", and use "will" with other pronouns	It's too late, I shall go. I will be back tomorrow on time.
Should	Probability	I ordered this pizza so I should get the first slice.
Ought to	Probability– follow 'ought' with 'to'	I ought to go for a walk in the evening.
May/Might	Possibility	May I know what's the time right now? I am travelling to Jaipur next week so I might see you.
Will	To express future	I will do this for sure.
Would	To express opinion	Would you mind if I turn off the fan? I am feeling cold.

Let's Assess

Activity 8: Modal Auxiliary Verbs

Fill in the gaps using the correct modal auxiliary verbs:

1. I.................. call anyone for your help? (can/shall/will)
2. I.................. go to Sikkim in coming holidays. (might/can/could)
3. My mother.................. speak three different languages. (should/ought to/ can)
4. Last night, I had a headache, so I.................. not sleep. (should/could/can)
5. This restaurant serves delicious food, you.................. go once. (must/ should/ought to)
6. If you have an exam tomorrow you.................. sleep early. (can/shall/ should)
7. ....you take me out as I am hungry? (will/can/would)

SPEAKING SKILLS

|| HOW TO FRAME QUESTIONS ||

Let's Understand

For making question form

- With auxiliary verb: exchange the place of noun and verb. For example, Subject + Verb + object → Verb + subject + object

  I will give a call to her as well? → Will I give a call to her as well?
- With main verb: use do/does/did to make question form of sentence. For example, Does he want to go out on a trip?
- We use the forms of 'To do' with specific pronouns given in the table below.

Do	I, you, they, we
Does	he, she, it
Did	when you show that the action happened in past (use with all nouns and pronouns)

Let's Do

See this video by clicking the link given below to learn how you can do reservation or pre book the hotel before visiting any place.

https://www.youtube.com/watch?v=KY0K5f06adg

➢ **Do a role play activity with your friends for this video.**

Let's Understand

In the video above, there is a conversation between the hotel receptionist and the visitor who wants to reserve one room. The receptionist enquires about the details of the person and his choices to do the room reservation. Let's read what type of questions she asks.

(a) How may I help you?
(b) How many people is the booking for?
(c) What date will you be arriving?
(d) When will you be leaving?
(e) How much would that be?
(f) Does that include breakfast?
(g) Is there WIFI in the hotel?
(h) Would you prefer a room with a view of city or central park?
(i) Is there difference in price?
(j) May I take your full name?
(k) Will the room be ready by that time?

There are 3 types of questions words: auxiliary verb questions, modal verb questions, and wh- questions

Type of Question Words	Examples
Auxiliary verb questions	**Is** there WIFI in the hotel?
Modal verb questions	**Would** you prefer a room with a view of city or central park?
Wh- questions	**How** many people is the booking for? **What** date will you be arriving? **When** will you be leaving? **How** much would that be?

➢ Read the Table given below to learn how to use 'Wh-' words for asking different type of questions.

Question words	Uses	Examples
Whose	Possession	Whose book did you bring me? Whose birthday is today? Whose notebook did you borrow?
How much/how many	Quantity	How many books did you buy from the bookstore? How much money did your father give you?
Who	People	Who is your best friend?
Whom	People (possession)	With whom are you going to share your prize?
What	Information	What have you done to yourself?
When	Time	When did your father come home?
Where	Location	Where is my book?
Why	Reason	Why do I always stay at home?
Which	Choice	Which drink is your favourite?
How often	Frequency	How often do you go for a walk?
How	Manner	How did the thief enter into the house?

Let's Practise

Activity 9: Write Questions for given Sentences

With the help of the question words, write questions for these given sentences.

1. The train arrives at 8:15 am. ....
2. I wash my hair twice a week. ....
3. I prefer vanilla ice cream. ....
4. Oh! That's my neighbour's car. ....
5. I seldom read newspaper. ....
6. I spent ₹ 7500 on my birthday. ....
7. I got the first rank in English Olympiad with my mother's guidance and hard work. ....
8. I gave some money to my friend. ....
9. I have already revised my syllabus. ....
10. I am going to the college library to study. ....

Let's Apply

Activity 10: Ask five Types of Questions

Frame five types of question sentences for this given sentence using 'Wh-' words like why, what, when, where, etc. One example is done for you.

- Avik often goes to Cinema Hall to watch movies with his friends in the evening?

Example: When does Avik often goes to Cinema Hall to watch movies with his friends in the evening?

....

....

....

....

....

CONVERSATIONAL SKILLS

Let's Do

Read the conversation between Pranav and his friend over the phone. Look for the sentences that have been used to

- start the conversation between two friends,
- extend the conversation (development)
- end the conversation. (closure and farewell)

Pranav is 22 years-old and just given the exams for his last semester. Now he wants to go out on a trip but all his friends are busy with their families and no one has confirmed give. So he decided to call one of his school friends, Ankush.

Pranav: Hey brother, Long time how have you been?

Ankush: Good, just daily routine working for this company has taken a lot of time of my life but you tell me, how are you?

Pranav: I'm good, just done with the exams. By the way, which company are you working with?

Ankush: I am working for 'Policy Bazaar' as an Insurance Department Manager.

Pranav: Nice. Few days back, my dad was asking for getting our Car Insurance done, should I suggest him to get it done from 'Policy Bazaar'?

Ankush: Yeah, that will be more easy for you as this company doesn't charge anything as a commission.

Pranav: Also now I can rely as I will be having personal assistance from you as well, right?

Ankush: Since childhood you are still the same, haven't changed a bit.

Pranav: Yeah right, you know me but the reason I called you to know about your next weekend plans?.

Ankush: I haven't planned anything yet, nothing is there in planned yet.

Pranav: That's great ! Then I suggest you to take a break from your corporate life and let's travel together to Shimla, what do you say?

Ankush: That's sound exciting. Who else are there?

Pranav: Good question, currently I am just counting on you only as everyone else is quite dicy about their plans for the next weekend.

Ankush: Count me in then but why don't you ask Sumedha?

Pranav: Isn't she studying abroad?

Ankush: No, last time when I spoke to her, she mentioned that she has came back and now she is pursuing diploma in Fashion from 'Pearl Academy'.

Pranav: Then I will give a call to her as well, do ping me her number.

Ankush: Cool! Then let's pack our bags for next weekend and don't forget to book the place. I remember, last time, it was a real struggle in finding the good place so it's better if you pre book and do share the details.

Pranav: This time it won't happen as I have learnt from my mistake, don't worry I will keep you posted in couple of days.

Ankush: Ok, now I have to leave somewhere, will catch you soon.

Pranav: Alright see you, Bye.

Suggesting Tip: In a conversation, whether formal or informal, we should first acknowledge what we have heard and then express our point of view or answer whichhas been asked from the speaker. This kind of acknowledgment does not mean thatyou agree or approve speaker's statement. It gives confidence to the speaker that he isbeing heard or understood. In the given conversation above, you can see how these twofriends first acknowledge what is being heard and then express their thoughts or views.

Phrases that you can use for Starting and Ending a Conversation

Starting a conversation	Ending a conversation
Hey, Whatsup?	Alright, See you later
Hey, Where have you been?	Catch you soon
How 'sit going?	Sure, See you at the lunch
Good morning, How are you doing today?	Nice to meet you
Hey, How's life ?	Alright, I will text you the time
Hi ! How's everything	Have a great day ahead

Let's Assess

Activity 11: Complete the conversations

➢ **A :** Hi, So...?

B : Bro, it's a weekend. I might stay in the bed.

A : I know, but we cannot make this weekend boring, let's do something exciting!

B: All the excitement in my life has already been drained away due to hectic weekday.

➢ **A :** Hi,..?

B : Nothing much, just some household work.

A: I am planning on to going Pacific Mall in a while. Do you mind joining?

B: Well, even I wanted to buy a woolen jacket.

A: But winter is about to end.

B: That's fun fact that many brands might be selling jackets at the discounted prices.

A : Oh, yes! Why this idea didn't click me before.

- **Paras** : Hi Ankush!..?

  Ankush : Hi, Paras, nothing as such, just watching a web series. You tell me?

  Paras : ame..?

  Ankush : I am watching "Two and a Half Men" on Netflix.

  Paras : Ahea! One of my favourites, so our plan for the football match at 6 in the Central Park is still on?

  Ankush : Yes, obviously. How can I miss onto that?

  Paras : Great then I will pick you at 5:30pm.

WRITING SKILLS

Let's Do

Pranav has written about his experience of Shimla trip with his friends in his diary. Read his experience.

Vacations with friends are the best times of any year. Whenever my holidays start, I start wondering which place is going to be our destination this vacation. This time, after a long discussion I won the chance to decide the destination. We decided to plan a trip to my favourite destination, Shimla.

Shimla is the capital state of Himachal Pradesh and also a popular hill resort in India. One of my friends went to Shimla last year. She suggested me Shimla as one of the best places to visit.

We planned a long trip and had a proper schedule so that we do not miss any fun in the Hill Resort. First of all, we went to experience the most fun filled toy train ride which happens between Kalka and Shimla. After this, we visited a few temples through a short trekking. The trekking was a great experience that helped us to strengthen our friendship bond as we helped each other to complete the trekking.

We also had ultimate fun in a place called Kufri which is around 16 km from Shimla. This place has beautiful natural sceneries and we also enjoyed Yak riding there. One thing we missed in Shimla is the Ice Skating which is open prominently in December to February.

We also enjoyed an evening in the Lakkar Bazaar. This Bazaar is a famous wood market in Shimla that has a lot of wood items that includes beautiful articles like walking sticks and decorative articles. We bought a few precious wooden items for our home. Our trip to Shimla was an unforgettable experience. I wish we would visit this wonderful Hill Resort once again.

Let's Reflect

Activity 12: Reflection on your Memorable Trip

Now, it's your turn. You have to write about your one of the memorable trips in the space provided to you.

VOCABULARY

Let's Do

Read the Vocabulary words and their meaning related to Travel.

Luggage: Suitcases or other bags in which to pack personal belongings for travelling

To Commute: Travel some distance between home and place of work on a regular basis

Departure: The action of leaving, especially to start a journey

Fare: The money paid for a journey on public transport

See off: Go to the airport or station to say goodbye to someone

Check in: Arrive and register at a hotel or airport

To Pick up + from/at: Let someone get into your car and take them

To Drop off: To leave them

To take: to take a person from where they are right now to a distant location

Take off: When a plane departs or leaves the ground - the plane took off an hour late.

Let's Apply

Activity 13: Fill up the Blanks Using Travel Vocabulary

Fill in the gaps in the text with the vocabulary provided.

I was already late so I thought of travelling to the airport by the cab and not.................. by the Metro, my parents and I was carrying three luggage with myself, on the way I got a call from Indigo Airlines that I should be there at least prior an hour of .... for the security purpose so I told my cab driver to.................. to the airport as quick as possible and I am ready to give him tip as well apart from the .... and I finally made it on time after the security...................., flight on time. I was excited to visit Kerala and moreover excited to know that my college friends are arriving at the airport to.................................. One thing I have to do once I reach there is I have to find a decent hotel and.................. early so that I can get rid of my luggage.

Unit 2: Entertainment

INDEX

Learning Objectives

After reading this Unit, the students will be able to:

- uncover the life of a storyteller in a short extract taken from a popular book.
- comprehend the children animated film in English based on a classic text.
- make use of contractions while listening and speaking English.
- compose coherent and cohesive sentences in a paragraph on the topic familiar to them.
- frame sentences in context of right time and state of action (tenses).
- identify the contractions in a conversation.

READING SKILLS

Let's Do

Read the following article.

Read the introduction written by the great storyteller, Ruskin Bond, in one of his book.

Introduction from 'All-Time Favourites' by Ruskin Bond

A Storyteller's Life

I have been telling stories all my life, and that is a story in itself.

In the old days, a storyteller made a living by standing at the street corner and regaling children and grown-ups with the tales told from memory or inventions. His listeners threw him a few coins and went their way.

I do much the same thing, except that I use a pen to tell my stories and they get printed in books and go to a wider audience. A few coins come my way too, in the form of royalties from my publishers.

Recently, a reader, a young girl, wrote to me a kind letter and enclosed a hundred-rupee note, suggesting that I use it to enjoy a couple of fresh samosas. This was sweet of her, but don't do it again, friend, I have yet to arrive at the street corner like the storyteller of old.

Someone once asked me where I get the ideas for my stories. Well, if you like people and find them interesting, you won't run out of stories. If you like birds and animals and flowers and trees and the world around you, you won't run out of ideas. Stories and ideas for them are swirling around you if you keep your eyes and ears open.

Many of my favourite stories are in this collection. I have added a few ones, written in recent months. I hope you will enjoy them. And while you are busy leafing through this book, dear reader, I will take off to the bazaar in search of a hot, fresh samosa.

Let's Assess

Activity 1: Comprehension Questions

Based on your reading, answer the following questions.

1. Which story is the writer talking about in the beginning of the passage?

Ans....

....

....

2. What differences does the writer highlight between the storyteller in old days and himself ?

Ans....

....

....

3. What did the writer request the young girl for? And why?

Ans....

....

....

4. Where does the writer get the ideas for his stories?

Ans....

....

....

5. What does the writer want to say with this line, "and while you are busy leafing through this book, dear reader, I will take off to the bazaar in search of a hot, fresh samosa."

Ans....

....

....

6. Who is a storyteller? Do you have someone in your family who is a storyteller? Write something about him/ her?

Ans....

....

....

Let's Reflect

Vocabulary Words

Words	**What you think**	**What Dictionary says**
Regaling	....	....
Invention	....	....
Except	....	....
Royalties	....	....
Enclosed	....	....
Leafing	....	....

Let's Understand

Many of you might be very confused about tenses. Let's understand what the tenses exactly are.

Cambridge English Dictionary says: Tenses are the form of verbs which shows the time at which the action happened. In other words, tenses tell you the time when the action happened. There can be only 3 times:

Present (today) Past (yesterday) Future (tomorrow)

Let's Think

Activity 2: Identification of Present, Past, and Future tense

You have read the passage under Reading Skills. Now on the basis of your understanding, pick out and write 2 sentenceswhich indicate the present, past, and future actions.

Present: ....

....

Past: ....

....

Future: ....

....

GRAMMAR SKILLS

‖ TENSES ‖

Let's Understand

You have already learnt tenses in your secondary classes. Read the table given below to recall the types of tenses and their examples.

Type of Tenses	Examples
Present simple	Every day I teach English.
Present continuous	Now I'm teachingEnglish.
Past simple	Yesterday, I taught English.
Past continuous	Yesterday at 7 am, I was teaching English.
Future simple	Tomorrow, I am going to teach English.
Future continuous	Tomorrow at 7 am, I will be teaching English.
Future perfect	By the end of this module, I will have taught English to all of you.
Present perfect	Since August, I have taught English on online mode many times.
Present perfect continuous tense	I have been teaching English on online mode for 6 months.
Past perfect	Before August, I had never taught English on online mode.
Past Perfect Continuous tense	I had been teaching English for 2 hours before he called.
Future Perfect Continuous Tense	I will have been teaching English for 2 hours by the time he calls.

There are 4 aspects of each tense:
PRESENT, PAST, FUTURE

Aspectsof Tenses	Situationsin which these are used	Form of Tense
Simple	• Single action • Habit or repeated action	**Present:** Main verb +' s/es' **Past:** Main verb + 'ed' **Future:** 'will' + main verb
Continuous (Progressive)	• Ongoing or incomplete action	To be + main verb + ing
Perfect	• Completed action and • Connects two points in time – something happened before something else happened	To have + main verb +' ed' or irregular
Perfect continuous	• Connects two points in time (like Perfect) and expresses that an action is incomplete (like continuous)	To have + been + main verb + ing

Let's Reflect

➤ Timeline to Understand 4 aspects of the tenses:

Simple Tense:

Talking about a point in time

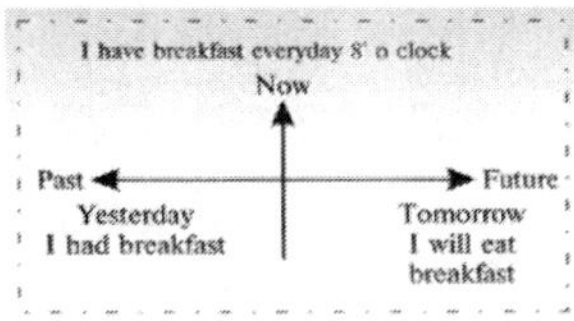

Continuous Tense:

Talking about a length of time

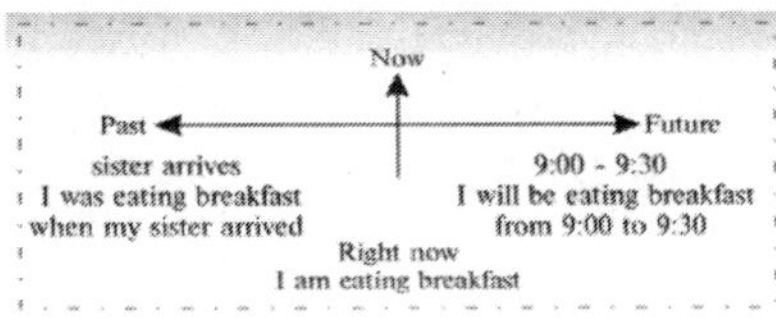

Perfect Tense:

Talking about a point in time before another point in time

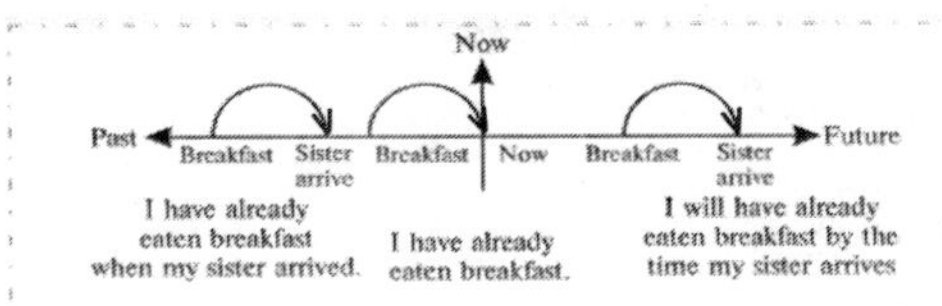

Perfect Continuous Tense:

Talking about a length of time up to a point in time.

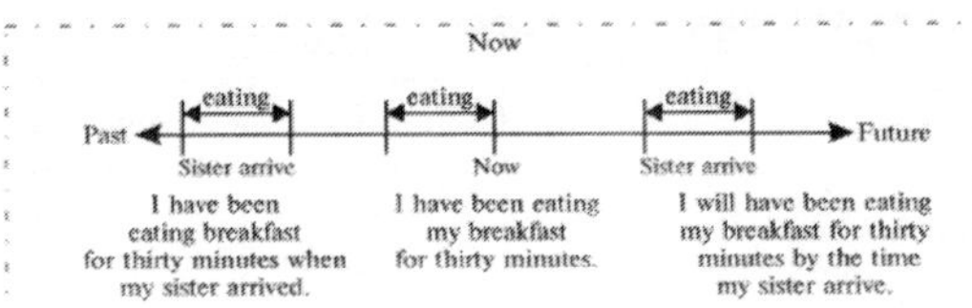

Let's Think

Activity 3: Things you did and things you do

I went for a walk this morning or yesterday. In fact, I go for a walk every morning. Can you name some things you did this morning and things you do every morning?

....

....

....

....

Let's Apply

Read these 3 stories given below in the table 1, 2, and 3 to have more ideas about all types of tenses. Table 1 has story in which all the 4 types of Present tenses has been used.

In Table 2, tenses for future have been used to create that story. In story given in Table 3, tenses related to past tenses have been used.

Table 1: Present Tense

<table>
<tr><td rowspan="4">**Preset Tense**</td><td>Simple Present – action or state happens in the present</td><td>Who is she? Where is she? What does he do?</td><td rowspan="4">She is Mishthi. She is 8 years-old girl. She likes painting and dancing. She enjoys painting more than dancing. Now she is sitting in her room, she is doing painting. Aadit is sitting next to her and helping her. She has just finished her homework and started doing painting. She has not completed the painting yet. Aadit does not like painting but still he is helping her. Mishthi has been doing painting since she was small. Lately Mishthi has been learning new painting styles from her teacher. From then she has been practicing this art 2 hours everyday.</td></tr>
<tr><td>Present Continuous – the action or state is in progress in the present</td><td>What is she doing at the moment?</td></tr>
<tr><td>Present Perfect – action or state was complete just before the present</td><td>What has she done? What has happened?</td></tr>
<tr><td>Present PerfectContinuous – action or state started in the past and still continue until the present.</td><td>What has she been doing for/since.</td></tr>
</table>

Table 2: Future Tense

<table>
<tr><td rowspan="4">**Future Tense**</td><td>Simple Future – action or state that will happen in the future</td><td>Who is she? What will she do? What is going to happen?</td><td rowspan="4">On Saturday, Mishthi's father birthday will be there. Mishthi with her brother, Aadit is planning to have a surprise birthday party for him. Mishthi is going to bake a chocolate cake. Her father will love her cake! The party will be starting at 8 o'clock on Saturday night. Both the children will be preparing all day before the party starts. By the time, their father reaches home; they will have □nished all the arrangements for the party. They will have baked the cake and decorated the house. Both will have working hard for the last □fteen days by the time party starts on Saturday. This weekend, all will be having so much fun!</td></tr>
<tr><td>Future Continuous – action or state will be in progress at some time in the future</td><td>What will she be doing? What will be happening?</td></tr>
<tr><td>Future Perfect – action or state will be complete before sometime in the future</td><td>What will she have done? What will have happened?</td></tr>
<tr><td>Future Perfect Continuous – ac on or state started will con nue un l some point in the future</td><td>What will they have been doing?</td></tr>
</table>

Table 3: Past Tense

<table>
<tr><td rowspan="4">**Past Tense**</td><td>Simple Past – action or state happened in the present</td><td>Who was she? Where did she go? What happened?</td><td rowspan="4">Last week, Mishthi baked a cake for her father on his birthday. First, she mixed all the ingredients in a big bowl and poured the batter into a baking pan. Then she put the pan in the oven and baked the cake for 20 minutes. Mishthi had never baked a cake before that day. When Mishthi was baking the cake, Aadit was decorating the house for the party. When they were doing all the preparations, the phone rang. Her father was calling to say that he was coming home in an hour. Both children had never excited so much before! They had done all the preparation by themselves. When they had been getting ready for the party they heard the voice of their father's car. Their father entered into the house, carrying two gifts for his children. The children hugged their father and told him that they had been doing all the preparation for his surprise birthday party for about 2 weeks.</td></tr>
<tr><td>Past Continuous – action or state was in progress in the past</td><td>What was she doing at some point of time in the past?</td></tr>
<tr><td>Past Perfect – action or state was complete before sometime in the past</td><td>What had she done? What happened?</td></tr>
<tr><td>Past Perfect Continuous – action or state started in the past and continue until some point in the past.</td><td>What has she been doing for/since.</td></tr>
</table>

Let's Assess

Activity 4: Write sentences, using the tenses given.

1. I – write – a letter (present perfect continuous)

   ....

2. My dad – go – the office – next Monday (present continuous)

   ....

3. They – have – their lunch. (past perfect simple)

   ....

4. We – can – go – upstairs through elevator (past simple)

   ....

5. What – you – think – of yourself? (present simple)

   ....

6. My friends – play – the whole evening (present perfect continuous)

   ....

7. I – talk – over – the phone (past continuous)

   ....

8. My sister – never – tell – a lie (present simple)

   ....

9. I – wander – in the Mall - two hours (past perfect continuous)

   ....

10. When – she – get – admission – in the college? (present continuous)

    ....

11. Riya – cannot – speak – after the accident (past simple)

    ....

12. I – never – be – to India (present perfect simple)

    ....

13. I – think – I – go to evening walk – now (future)

    ....

14. He – not have – the class – yesterday (past simple)

    ....

15. My mother – work – as a professor (present simple)

    ....

Let's Assess

Activity 5: Complete the Story

Water has been spilled over this story and some words have been erased. Now complete this story of Damru and Cynthia Fox. You have to fill the correct tenses of the verbs given below, ordered with the corresponding numbers.

1. Take;	2. Return;	3. Be;	4. Be;	5. Can;
6. Tear	7. Handle;	8. Return;	9. be;	10. Tear;
11. Arrange;	12. Tell;	13. Be;	14. Say;	15. rob

Activity 6: Complete the newspaper article

Complete the newspaper article with correct form of verbs using the verbs given in the bracket.

In coming November, UK and Italy .... (co-host) a global climate conference called COP26. One of the goals of the meet is to persuade all countries to work towards net emission of greenhouse gases caused by human activity to zero by 2050. A pathway to the goal up for discussion.................................... (revolve) around ways to curtail deforestation. A global summit in 2021 which plans to discuss deforestation ....(highlight) how far ahead of its time was the Chipko movement, spearheaded by Sunderlal Bahuguna who .... (pass) away last week.

Chipko .... (be) a product of the restless 1970s, though the seeds were sown earlier. It's arguably the most impactful environment movement India .... (witness) in recent memory. What .... (make) it unique is that call to action was not top down, catalysed by complex science. It was a grassroots movement in Uttarakhand where the forest...............................(become) the focal point of both environment and livelihood issues. If Bahuguna and his associate Chandi Prasad Bhatt were the faces of the movement that began in March 1973, its durability and impact came from villagers in the Himalayas, particularly women. Lived experience of villagers.............................. (be) the motive force of the Chipko movement.

LISTENING SKILLS

Let's Do **https://youtu.be/uu7gNBZu5Ps**

Activity 2 : Complete the sentences

A YouTube link is given above. Click the link to watch a clipping about the man cub Mowgli from the story The Jungle Book by Rudyard Kipling. After listening, complet the sentences given below.

- Baloo thought it was the .... way to cross the river.
- The baby deer was in danger because ....
- Mowgli suggested the baby deer that they ....
- Father Deer took .... as Kala and warned him to stay back from him.
- When Kala caught Chuchip and Mowgli for the first time, Mowgli made fool of Kala by ....
- Baloo found Mowgli's .... over the stone lying in the river.
- When Chuchip was starving, he ate some fruits from a tree and because of that...
- When Chichup was fighting with Kala alone, Mowgli encouraged him ....
- In the end, Baloo advised Chuchip to ....

WRITING SKILLS

Writing is a process. Before writing anything, first think about it and read about that topic from various sources like books, magazines or you can google it also. Then jot down all the important points in the form of list. Next step, order them as you want them to write. An example is given for you in which all important point or ideas on Diwali are present through a mindmap. A mindmap is an organised display of information which can be easily converted into draft of the writing. The mindmap also helps to make the hierarchical (chose the order of the ideas in writing) relationships of ideas.

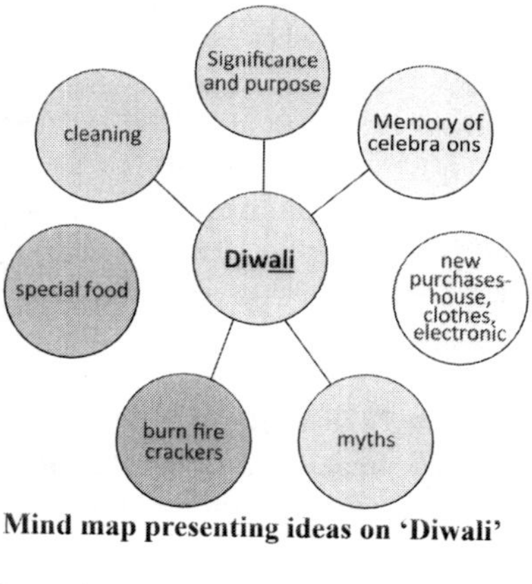

Mind map presenting ideas on 'Diwali'

This step makes students aware that there is particular way to express their ideas. Their ideas should be presented in the connected and logical sentences in a paragraph. Each paragraph in their writing conveys their messages successfully and writing should be reader friendly. The logical development of different ideas and ordering of arguments in each paragraph makes the writing coherence.

When you write any article, essay, blog, document, description, letter, report writing, cleaning etc. other than correct format, one of main mandatory requirement in your writing is that readers can understand the content of yourwriting or it should make sense for them. The sentences and paragraphs in your writing should have fundamental flow and follow logical transition.

Cohesion is the technique that connects ideas, sentences, and paragraphs with the variety of tools called cohesive tools. **Coherence** is the quality of the content of being logical or unified whole. With cohesion and coherence, you can have good and effective piece of writing.

When you write a paragraph, it should be both cohesive and coherent. A paragraph is cohesive if the parts in it are linked together. A paragraph is coherent if it makes sense. Cohesion is unity at the sentence level and coherence is unity at paragraph level.

‖ COHESION: SENTENCE DEVELOPMENT ‖

Let's Understand

In a paragraph, the first sentence always provides you some information about a topic. The topic in that sentence is called 'theme' which is familiar to the reader and other is 'new information' added with the theme. In a sentence, it is important to choose the 'theme' and 'the new information'. This 'new information' further leads to development of the topic in the following sentences. For Example,

Dr A P J Abdul Kalam was the president of India from July 2002 to July 2007. He was a famous space scientist. His statue has been put up in Railway Depot in Karnataka. He is also called 'Missile Man'.

In this example,

'Dr A P J Abdul Kalam' topic of the sentence or theme

'president of India from July 2002 to July 2007' is new information added with theme.

Now in this paragraph, sentences follow to first sentence must be connected with the theme mentioned in the first sentence. In the above example,

'Dr A P J Abdul Kalam' - 'theme' is there in the second, third, fourth sentences through the words 'he' and 'his' and these sentences are adding some 'new information' to the theme of the paragraph.

In this way, we can develop sentences and make connections between them. This connection in the sentences is called cohesion. Cohesion is the act of connecting the parts of the sentences linked together.

Let's Assess

Activity 8: Identify the theme with new information

Some sentences are given below. Read the sentences and encircle the 'theme' and underline the 'new information'.

The government has made it mandatory for automakers to provide three-point seat belts for all the front-facing passengers in a car. The norm will also be applicable for the middle seat in the rear row of a car, Union minister said. He did not mention the date from which the new requirement will come into force. Last month, the ministry said it will make it mandatory for carmakers to provide a minimum of six airbags in motor vehicles that can carry up to eight passengers for enhanced safety of passengers.

DEVELOP AN IDEA THROUGH CONNECTED SENTENCES IN A PARAGRAPH: COHERENCE

Let's Understand

In a paragraph, you can develop an idea through connected sentences. You can introduce the 'theme' in the first sentence and the 'new information' in the forthcoming sentences in three patterns and further develops the whole paragraph.

In the given patterns, 'A' is the 'theme' and 'B' and 'C' is the 'new information'. Let's learn through some examples.

1. **AB : BC**
   - Laughing and smiling encourages the release of **serotonin. Serotonin** has any positive benefits, one of which is boosting the immune system.
   - Freedom and power bring **responsibility. The responsibility** rests upon this assembly, a sovereign body representing the people of India.
2. **AB : AC**
   - The animals we keep as pets are totally **dependent on us**. They must be loved and kept with dignity like we would keep our brothers and sisters.
   - Exports means **selling things to people outside the country in which it is made.** Export helps in the development of the nation as it brings money into the country. Exports of India's organic farm products *rose 51 per cent in 2020-21.*
3. **AB : CA**
   - A no-fly zone is a territory or area established by **a military power over which certain aircrafts are not permitted to fly.** Tibet is a region in Asia which is a natural no-fly zone.
   - We often look into a mirror to see how **we're looking**. Most animals cannot even recognize themselves in the mirror. But *Bottlenose Dolphins can recognize* themselves in the mirror.

Let's Do

Activity 9 : Develop a Paragraph

A sentence is given below. Complete the paragraph by developing the ideas given in the first sentence. For this, choose the structure that best links the new information to the known information for the forthcoming new sentences in that paragraph.

Source:

https://www.linkedin.com/pulse/technology-future-entertainment-sanjiv goyal/?trk=articles_directory

➢ In the last decade or two, smart phones, advanced sound systems, high-speed computers, and technologies such as artificial intelligence and mixed reality have transformed the media and entertainment industries. (a) ....
....
....

(b) ....
....

(c) ....
....

(d) ....
....

(a) (i) Social media, digital advertising, enhanced access to the Internet, and various devices have shaped media trends.

(ii) Access to the Internet has enhanced for the people and that has shaped the media trends.

(b) (i) Digital content consumption has increased due to COVID 19 pandemic happened last year.

(ii) Last year the COVID 19 pandemic increased digital content consumption more than ever before.

(c) (i) According to the Social Media Examiner, Live Video streams captivated viewers and marketers alike, with the adoption rate in 2018 at 35 percent over the 28 percent in 2017.

(ii) The adoption rate has increased with the adoption rate in 2018 at 35 percent over the 28 percent in 2017 as Live Video streams captivated viewers and marketers alike, according to the Social Media Examiner.

(d) (i) These trends are unlikely to change regarding the future of media because of innovation which is the new norm.

(ii) Innovation is the new norm in the media sector, and these trends are unlikely to change regarding the future of media concepts.

‖ COHESIVE DEVICES ‖

Let's Understand

Read this paragraph and look at the highlighted words.

In recent years, WhatsApp has brought in a flurry of new updates and features to make their platform more secure and user-friendly. **However,** the recent decision to give the group admin the power to delete messages seems to be a bit far-fetched. **It** is extremely tedious to keep track of conversations **and** have a concrete record of them, **especially when** any person can be anonymous and potentially dangerous on an online platform. Yes, but extending the time limit is a good move.

These highlighted words are called Cohesive Devices – these are the words used to indicate the relationship or connection among the sentences in a paragraph. There are many cohesive tools through which you can connect the parts of the sentences with each other. In this unit, we will cover only two cohesion tools:

- Cohesion through connectors
- Cohesion through references

Connect Sentences with Connectors (linking words)

Let's Understand

We can use these linking words to give connection in parts of sentences so that a logical flow of idea can be maintained. On the basis of the ideas the sentences are representing, they can be connected using different linking words. A list is given below to show that how different connectors are used for connecting different ideas:

Two sentences having	Connectors used to connect
Similar ideas	in addition, also, and, furthermore, too, moreover, in the same way, just as ... so too, likewise, similarly
Contrasting ideas	but, however, in spite of, on the one hand ... on the other hand, nevertheless, nonetheless, instead, notwithstanding, in contrast, on the contrary, still, yet
Giving examples	for example, for instance, namely, such as, to illustrate
Giving results	So, therefore, as a result, thus, because
Sequencing	first, second, third, ... next, then, finally
Additional Support or Evidence	additionally, again, also, and, as well, besides, equally important, further, furthermore, in addition, moreover, then
Giving conclusion	finally, in a word, in brief, briefly, in conclusion, in the end, in the final analysis, onthe whole, thus, to conclude, to summarize, in sum, to sum up, in summary
Telling Time	after, afterward, at last, before, currently, during, earlier, immediately, later, meanwhile, now, recently, simultaneously, subsequently, then, since
Telling position/place	above, adjacent, below, beyond, here, in front, in back, nearby, there

Let's Reflect

Two examples are given below for learning the right use of connectors as cohesive device.

Example 1,

Read this newspaper report and look for the highlighted words. These highlighted words are connector used to connect the sentence with the preceding one and helps to create cohesion in the whole paragraph.

The parade on January 26, 2022 begins with the arrival of the President. ***First,*** *the cavalier bodyguards of the President salute the National Flag.* ***During*** *this time, the National Anthem is played and 21 Guns Salute is given.* ***But*** *do you know that firing is not done with 21 canons?* ***Instead,*** *7-canons of the Indian Army, known as '25-Ponders' are used for firing in 3 rounds.*

First	Used to tell the sequence of a process
During	Tell the time mentioned in the previous sentence
And	Addition of similar ideas that happened at that time
Instead, But	Connect two Contrasting ideas

Example 2,

Plants and flowers are the most beautiful creation of nature. ***So,*** *gifting a potted plant is a nice option for many special occasions.* ***While*** *choosing a plant to give, pick one in a beautiful* ***and*** *attractive pot* ***so that*** *can be used for home embellishment. You can also plant an old pot, plant a herb and gift it to someone.*

So	Telling the result of something that mentioned in previous sentence
While	Tell the time
And	And similar ideas
So that	Telling the reason of something mentioned in previous sentence

Let's Apply

Activity 10: Linking Words

Look at the sentences below and then choose the best linking word to complete the sentences.

- Scientist believe that following a low-glycemic diet acne reduce acne .... this diet eliminates spikes in your blood sugar.
- May 20 is regarded as the birthday of jeans, ... it was the day when Levi Strauss patented his idea.
- Multitasking can drain your energy .... lower your productivity.
- Harshal Patel was the joint highest wicket-taker in a single season of IPL. .... late in his career, he is slowly getting the recognition he deserves.
- Our teachers or gurus are held in great reverence ...., teaching is considered to be one of the noblest professions.

‖ CONNECT SENTENCES USING REFERENCE ‖

Let's Understand

Reference are the pronouns used to create cohesion in the sentences. Here are the types of references.

Personal Pronoun	Demonstrative Pronoun		Comparatives
I, me, she, you, we, my, mine, his, hers, it, its, their, theirs	Denotes near	Denotes far	Another, other, similar, better, different
	This, these, here	That, those, there	

Let's Reflect

Example

- Bunny had a very special birthday **this** week, and **she** was very excited about **it**. What was special about **her** birthday was that the date of **it** read the same forward and backwards – 22-02-2022. **Such** numbers are very rare, coming as **they** do every once in a long while. The next such numbers is going to be February 03, 2030. **These** types of numbers are called palindromes, a word derived from the Greek 'to run back'. Bunny doesn't believe in numerology but she was still pleased as punch at receiving a palindrome as a surprise birthday present. Greek 'to run back'. Bunny doesn't believe in numerology but **she** was still pleased as punch at receiving a palindrome as a surprise birthday present.

The highlighted words in the above paragraph are called **reference words**. These reference words are used to refer the noun in the preceding sentence.

Reference can be Forward and Backwards

- **Forward reference:** the reference is used in the first sentence and is referring the noun mentioned in the next sentence, not in the previous sentence. For example, Essential for **their** social, emotional, creative, and cognitive well-being, play helps teach children self- regulation, boundary-setting and decision making.
- You have to read further into the complete sentence to get the understanding of what 'their' refers to.
- **Backward reference:** the reference is used in the second sentence for the noun mentioned in the previous sentence. For example,

  Coconut oil is a popular skincare ingredient worldwide and many people also use **it** as oil-based makeup remover, under eye moisturizer and even as a night cream.'
- It' is called Backward Reference, which refers to the noun 'coconut oil' in the first sentence.

Let's Apply

Activity 11: Back References

Look at the extract from a story below and find as many back references as you can.

Although I was only eight, I could read quite well. Miss Kellner produced a book that she had loved as a girl – Black Beauty, the story of a horse and I read to her in my shrill, unformed voice. Presently, she fell asleep, but I kept on reading – first out loud, then to myself – the story enthralled me, and when she woke up, she rewarded me with a chocolate.

Activity 12: Forward References

Complete the sentences using pronoun as forward reference:

1. If you need ...., there are fruits in the refrigerator.
2. Although .... loves all sorts of activities, watching cartoons and playing football was Aryan's favourites.
3. It's true that .... are scary, though snakes are an integral part of our ecosystem.
4. Although I phone .... every week, my parents still complains that I don't keep in touch with them often.
5. ....was lying on the table and you were looking for your book everywhere in the house.

Activity 13: Read a cohesive and coherent paragraph

Here, a sample of a cohesive and coherent paragraph is given. Read it to get the more clarity.

ROLE OF ENTERTAINMENT IN MODERN LIFE

People are still able to find time for entertainment despite the fact that modern life has made them highly busy in their day-to-day lives. There are many ways through people can entertain themselves like playing a sport, reading books, travelling, listening music, watching TV, etc. With the development of numerous sorts of multimedia devices, the enjoyment of video and audio has increased. One of the most popular leisure and amusement activities today is music. With the aid of music, stressed people can unwind their stress and tension in today's fast-paced environment.

A person who is restless or exhausted may find solace in music to lift their spirits. Nowadays, we have a variety of small, portable multi-media audio players, including the iPod, MP4 and MP3. Electronic devices are always being improved in the modern era to make them more fun and convenient.

Let's Think and Apply

Activity 14: Let's Compose a Paragraph

Compose a paragraph on 'Smoking and Health' using sentences the given sentence beginning with Cohesive words. An example is done for you.

Smoking and Health	Smoking and Health
It's important that	It's important that we must take into account the dangers of smoking for our health.
For example, ...	For example, smoking can lead to blood flow issues, gum disease, and cancer.
However, ...	However, in movies, smoking looks attractive because my favorite actor smokes while he fights villains.
Nevertheless, ...	Nevertheless, those heroes might one day end up in the hospital from smoking.
In conclusion, ...	In conclusion, we need to find ways to quit smoking.

Source: David Courtney, Vietnam, Activities to Activate and maintain a communicative classroom, americanenglish. state.gov/English-teaching-forum.

Now, compose a paragraph on 'Advancement of Technology' using the given sentences beginning with Cohesive words.

ADVANCEMENT OF TECHNOLOGY

It's important that ....

....

For example, ...

....

However, ...

....

Nevertheless, ...

....

In conclusion, ...

....

‖ VOCABULARY BOX CONTRACTIONS ‖

Let's Understand

In English language, we often "contract" or shorten words. For example, we may say *"You're"* instead of *"You are"*. We insert an apostrophe *(')* in place of the missing letter or letters in writing. Here are some more example sentences:

- She will call you. – She'll call you.
- Who is there in the car? – Who's there in the car?
- I have been reading the book since morning. - I've been reading the book since morning.

Contractions are not used in written English. They are commonly used in spoken English. If you want to use contractions in written English, use only informal situations, not in formal. Here is the list of some contractions for positive verbs and the contractions for verb with 'not'.

Positive Contracted Forms	Negative Contracted Forms	Other Contracted Forms
He is – he's	Should not –shouldn't	What is – what's
She is – she's	Was not – wasn't	Who is – who's
He will –he'll	Are not – aren't	Who will – who'll
He would- he'd	Can not- can't	What will – what'll
Here is - here's	Could not – couldn't	When is – when's
She has – she's	Did not- didn't	Where is – where's
She will – she'll	Do not – don't	Who would – who'd
She would – she'd	Does not – doesn't	That is – that's
We are – we're	Had not – hadn't	There is – there's
We have – we've	Have not - haven't	There will – there'll
We will – we'll	Will not – won't	They are – they're
We would – we'd	Ain't – is not/ are not/am not /	They have – they've
I am' I'm	have not/ has not	How is - how's
I have – I've	Were not – weren't	
I will – I'll	Is not – isn't	
I had – I'd	It is – it's	
I would – I'd	Is not – isn't	
You are – you're	It has – it's	
You will – you'll	It will – it'll	
You would – you'd	Must not – mustn't	
You had – you'd		

Let's Do

See these videos to learn the correct pronunciations of these contractions:

https://www.youtube.com/watch?v=AFoG4hmcqZQ - for positive contractions
https://www.youtube.com/watch?v=mdvRis4_79Q - for negative contractions

Let's Assess

Activity 15: Contraction Exercise

Listen to this audio and complete the paragraph by filling the contractions.

h ps://anchor.fm/payal56/episodes/Unit-2-Entertainment---Activity-12-e1gpv0c

It was Joe who finally said, "............................stop being pirates now...................... so lonely here and I really miss my home." Tom tried to cheer him up by telling him how wonderful the fishing was on the island. "I .... care about fishing," cried Joe. "I want to go home." "But Joe, this is the best place for fishing. And think of all the fun .... having!"

Tom tried to convince Joe. "And .... sure there've been pirates here before.. you feel if we found a whole chest of treasures?"

Joe was still sad. Tom tried cheering him up by telling about the lovely swimming here, which they .... have anywhere else, but.. succeed in raising his spirits.

CONVERSATIONAL SKILLS

Let's Do

A dialogue for booking movie tickets

Radhika : I'm in mood to watch a movie at the theatre. Let me know who's up?

Aman : Yes, sure. Which movie?

Sumit : Yes, but I'm more excited about the Nacho and soda.

Radhika : Don't worry Sumit, I'll add nachos while booking the tickets online.

Rajni : I've tight schedule this week. But, somehow I'll arrange.

Radhika : The movie I'm talking about is 'The Life of Pi". If everybody is comfortable, I don't mind to plan it for Weekend.

Aman : I've heard good reviews about this movie.

Sumit : So sweet of you, Radhika. Then the dinner is on me.

Rajni : I've read there is 50% occupancy allowed in the theaters, so let's reserve our seats (hold our seats) as early as possible.

Radhika : So I'm booking the tickets and I don't expect last minute cancellation from anyone.

Aman : If possible, please reserve corner seats.

Radhika : Sure, I'll look into that.

Activity 16: Role Play

Look for the contractions used in the above conversation and do the practice of speaking these contractions while practicing these dialogues in the conversation.

Activity 17: Fun Time

Read these some ways to play prank on your friends and family members and share their reactions in the class.

Prank Time!

This April Fools' Day, prank your family members and friends.

Freeze Screens

- Take a screenshot of your friend's smartphone and turn the image into their screen saver
- Let them freak out for a few minutes as they think their screen is frozen before you come in to save the day.

Ice-cream swap

- Call your friends over and offer them ice-cream
- Instead of using ice-cream, use potato mash mixed with edible food colours
- Pour chocolate syrup over it and serve. Wait for their reactions as they gobble onto a big bite!

Shampoo Block

- Unscrew the cap of the shampoo bottle
- Cover the top of the bottle with a transparent plastic wrap or cling wrap
- Screw the cap back. Your sibling will try hard to get some shampoo out but won't be able to.

Can't Drink

- Put some gelatin in a glass of milk and keep it in the refrigerator.
- Ask your mom/dad to pour milk for you in your cereal bowl.
- Wait until they try pouring it but it doesn't pour out of the glass.

14

CHAMPAK

Unit 3 : Health and Food

INDEX

Learning Objectives

After reading this unit, the students will be able to:

- justify their decision of buying any packaged item on the basis of newspaper article
- follow detailed directions or simple technical information such as operating instructions for everyday equipment.
- participate in a conversation while placing an order to a restaurant.
- compose formal and informal emails.
- communicate clearly using imperative sentences and causative verbs.
- give a presentation using prescribed phrases or sentences on any familiar topic.
- solve crossword for the vocabulary related to food.

READING SKILLS

Let's Do

Read the following article from the newspaper.

Read Between Food Labels

We all know food is medicine. The bigger question, rather concern is the quality of food. What kind of food is genuinely pure, honest and healthy, for it to be able to work as medicine? Market shelves today are filled with a variety of food which we think is healthy; but have you ever stopped for a bit and checked if it's really healthy? There are lot of products in the market that make their way easily to the health food/diet food section but in reality, they are loaded with sugar, salt, trans fats, artificial colours, flavour enhancers, MSG or pesticides.

Our endeavour should be to find the right quality and source of food. These clues that can help you read through deceptive food labels.

1. **Don't be fooled by the big letters on the front package.** Flip the packet and look for the small letters under nutritional labels and ingredient list. For example, kids' snacks like cereal biscuits are attractively packed and marketed as good food for the brain, bones, but when you look at the nutritional label and check the product compositions, you'll know the truth of how many chemical and artificial ingredients have gone inside the product.
2. **Know the hierarchy of the ingredients** mentioned under the composition. For example, if the foremost ingredient is sugar, the product is made up mostly of sugar regardless of the claims the product makes like "less sugar", "suitable for diabetics" and more.
3. **Avoid foods that contain the following:** Partially hydrogenated oil, artificial flavours and colours transfats, high salt content, high fructose corn syrup, mono sodium glutamate and artificial sweeteners. A lot of the products use different names for these to confuse consumers, but one has to be aware of these gimmicks.
4. **Avoid foods with a long in gradient list.** There is a high possibility that more than half the ingredients would contain chemicals and aren't natural. Use the simple rule of thumb–avoid food with ingredients you can't even pronounce fluently.
5. **Fibre is your fiend!** Beware of whole grain imposters. When buying breads, cereals, granola bats, crackers and pasta, choose product with at least 2 gm of fibers per serving on the label. Know the fact that wheat flour often labelled on products

is actually maida or refined wheat flour. It's going to be actual wheat flour only if the label mentions it as whole wheat flour.

6. **Check the servings:** At the top of the nutrition facts label, you will find the total number of servings in the container and the size of each serving. The serving size on the label is based on the amount of food that people naturally eat at one time and is not a recommendation of how much to eat. Make sure not to go beyond the nutrition label it often has an explanation of nutrients present per serving and per 100 gm. It is advisable to check that in detail before buying. For instance, a protein bar may look healthy, but could also have too much sugar per serving size.
7. **Lastly, the disguises of sugar:** Irrespective of how they sound, these are all sugar. Sucrose, maltose, dextrose, fructose, glucose, galactose, lactose, high fructose corn syrup, glucose solids, cane juice, dextrin, maltodextrin, dextran, barley malt, beet sugar, corn syrup, caramel, carob syrup, brown sugar malt syrup, diatase, diatastic malt, fruit juice, fruit juice concentrate, dehydrated fruit juice, fruit juice crystals, golden syrup, turbinado, sorghum syrup, refiner's syrup and ethyl maltol.

   Giving up on the food you like is not the solution, all you need to do is to make the right picks and choice.

Let's Assess

Activity 1: Comprehension Questions

After reading the article, answer the questions given below:

1. What cautionary advice is given in the above article for having genuinely good and healthy food?

Ans. ....

....

2. Why is it important for kids to learn the skill of reading label?

Ans. ....

....

3. Why is it advisable to check the ingredient list before buying any food packet?

Ans. ....

....

4. Take any food packet brought in your house. Check its nutritional and ingredients list. On the basis of what you have read in the article, what would you decide for that food packet? Was the decision of buying that food packet right or wrong decision and why?

Ans. ....

....

5. Choose another title for the article. Also mention why you have chosen that title.

Ans. ....

....

6. Match the words from the above article with their meaning:

(a) Endeavour	most prominent in importance or position
(b) Deceptive	a thing that enhances something
(c) Enhancer	deceive

(d) Gimmicks — a person pretends to be someone else in order to deceive others

(e) Foremost — an attempt to achieve something

(f) Imposter — a trick intended to attract attention

(g) Disguise — misleading

LISTENING SKILLS

Let's Do

A link is given below. By clicking on that link, listen the audio-visual Induction Operating Guide on how to use an Induction cook top.

Follow Detailed Instructions

https://youtu.be/UbypqSoXs2M

Activity 2: True or False

After hearing the audio, mark whether the given statements are true or false. If the statement is false, then you need to write the true statement for it in the space provided to you.

(a) This cooktop has elegant design and can be operated through hard touch buttons.

Ans. ....

....

(b) You can adjust the power and temperature for manually operating mode.

Ans. ....

....

(c) The timer function sets the timer where the appliance has to start the cooking.

Ans. ....

....

(d) The power saver technology monitors the time for the cooking and adjusts the temperature level based on its size.

Ans. ....

....

(e) The dual heat sensor prevents overheating and saves power.

Ans. ....

....

(f) The cooking surface is elevated and hard and hence cleaning is hassle free and ecofriendly as compared to LPG.

Ans. ....

....

GRAMMATICAL SKILLS

Let's Understand

‖ IMPERATIVE SENTENCES ‖

The instructions for how to cook 'maggi' are given on the packet. Read these instructions. Look carefully how these sentences are structured.

These sentences start directly from the verb. They do not have a subject. These kinds of sentences are called imperative sentences. Imperative sentence is a sentence used to give a direct command, request, invitation, warning, or instructions.

For example, Many times, instructions on the label of the cleaning products are written in imperative sentences. Here, is the glimpse of the label on a cleaning product.

These are warnings written on a cleaning product.

Let us read more examples for imperative sentences which we use in our daily routine:

• Wait for me • Stop talking • Enjoy your food • Get out of my way! • Go left

There are two types of imperative sentences:

1. **Positive Imperative Sentences:** These imperative sentences are used to motivate or force someone to do something. These sentences do not have a subject and start with the base form of the verb. For example,
   (a) Come back to your position.
   (b) Have a seat.
   (c) Finish your breakfast.
   (d) Pull/Push (written on door)
2. **Negative Imperative Sentences:** These imperative sentences are used to stop someone to do something.

   We start the sentence with 'don't' and followed by the base form of the verb.

   For example,
   (a) Do not throw litter here.
   (b) Do not disturb.
   (c) Don't shout.

Let's Assess

Activity 3: Complete the poster

Provide the suitable verbs to make these affirmative or negative imperative sentences complete.

1. .... a mask.
2. .... your hands frequently.
3. Cough etiquette – .... with sleeves or elbow.
4. ...., ... eyes, nose or mouth with unwashed hands.
5. ...., ... with sick people.
6. .... and ....

‖ IMPERATIVE SENTENCES WITH 'LET' ‖

Let's Understand

Read these sentences which are starting with 'Let' used by all of us in daily routine:

- Let me see
- Let me try it.
- Let me look into the matter.
- Let's go for shopping

Imperative sentences with 'Let' are used to make suggestions and invitations.

For example,

- Let's have a dinner together. (invitation)
- Let him relax and then talk to him. (suggestion)

Form of the sentence: Let + object + basic form of verb

We can use 'let' with negative imperative sentences. Add 'don't before 'let' in the sentence. For example,

- Don't let her cross the road alone.
- Don't let them enter into the room.
- Don't let children play with matchsticks.

Let's Apply

Activity 4: Use of Imperative Sentences

1. Make imperative sentences with 'Don't'.

(a) Driving/talk/while

....

(b) And/Smoke/drink

....

(c) Food/eat/junk

....

(d) The/feed/animals/zoo/in/the

....

(e) About/worry/it

....

2. Give your advices for what a person should do in the following pictures using imperative sentences.

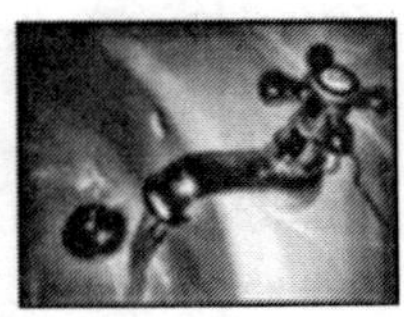

(a) ....

(b) ....

(c) ....

3. Complete the dialogues using let/let's

(a) An old lady is not able to carry her heavy shopping bag and a person is offering his help.

Person: ....

(b) A father is suggesting playing carom to his children.

Father: ....

(c) A friend is inviting her friend to go for shopping with her.

Father: ....

(d) An elder brother is inviting his brother to come with him to buy a book from the bookstore.

....

CONVERSATIONAL SKILLS

Let's Do

Read this conversation given below and learn how to place an order to a restaurant.

Company Representative (CR):	Thank you for calling Dominos. My name is Siddharata. How may I help you!
Radhika :	I would like to place an order.

CR : Yes mam, please tell me what you would like to order from us.

Radhika : Please note; 1 country special, 1 double chesse margherita. And also tell me are you serving hot choco lava cake as well?

CR : Yes mam, but we are running short of country special; but yes chocolava will surely be delivered.

Radhika : Oh no! Apart from country special what else you would suggest?

CR : Yes, you can surely go for Farm House Pizza in case you prefer mushroom.

Radhika : Thank you for your suggestion. I would love that. Please add on.

CR : Then anything else that you would like to add on?

Radhika : No, I think I am good to go with this.

CR : So your order is 1 double chesse margherita, 1 hot choco lava cake, 1 Farm House Pizza.

Radhika : Right.

CR : Your order no is x x x x x x. And it will be delivered shortly to your address which has already sync from your mobile number.

Radhika : Thank you.

CR : Thank you for placing an order to Dominos.

When you ask someone or request someone for something we use 'would like'. It is the polite way of requesting and asking something.
Its contracted form is 'd like'.

In a restaurant, you can order food and get your order in four different ways:

- "for pick-up" - order placed on phone but you will pick up from the restaurant.
- "to go"-place an order in the restaurant and take the packed food and eat somewhere else.
- "to dine in" - to have dinner at the restaurant.
- "for delivery" - order food on the phone and get your order delivered at your doorstep.

Let's Practise

Activity 4: let's have some conversations

Now read some conversations to learn the above vocabulary words. Complete the incomplete dialogues in the conversations.

1. **Customer :** Hello, I'd like to order food for pick-up.

   Manager : Sure, sir. What would you like to order?

   Customer : Let me get 1 Dal Makhani, I mix veg, I pineapple raita, and 3 Butter naan.

   Manager : Ok sir. Anything else you would like to add.

   Customer : Nothing. Thank you so much. When can you have our order ready?

   Manager : You can pick it up in 30 minutes. We will have your food ready at the "pick-up" counter. Now can I have your credit?

2. **Customer :** Hello, I'd like to order some food to go.
 Manager : Sure, sir. What would you like to order?
 Customer : ....
 Customer : How long will it take?
 Manager : It will get ready in 15 minutes. When your order will be ready, your order no. 545 will be displayed on the screen. You can pick up your order.
 Customer : Ok, I am waiting.
3. **Customer :** Hello, I'd like to order an order for delivery.
 Manager : Sure, sir. What would you like to order?
 Customer : ....
4. **Customer :** (going inside the restaurant and ask the manager): Is it possible to dine in tonight?
 Manager : Sure, sir. We are giving two options for seating: one is on the terrace and other inside this hall. Where would you like to dine in?
 Customer : I would like to enjoy on terrace.
 Manager : Ok sir. Tonight, we are providing live singing there at the terrace. I hope you will enjoy it.
 Customer : ....

Activity 6: Role Play

Create a conversation with your partner using the phrase 'would like' and the new vocabulary that you have learnt. Prepare to role-play it in the class.

WRITING SKILLS

Let's Understand

You have bought a microwave oven for your house. You have set it in the operational mode after following all the instructions given in the 'Instruction Manual'. But it is not working properly. You have also telephoned the Service Manager, complaining him about this problem but satisfactory response was not given. Now you are writing an email to the company, complaining about the problem that you are facing with microwave and not getting the satisfactory response from the Service Manager.

When you say an email address:

- Remember that @ is pronounced 'at' and '.' is pronounced 'dot'.
  Eg: payalmittal111@rediffmail.com is pronounced as payal mittal triple 1 at rediffmail dot com
- **Payal.mittal@rediffmail.com** is pronounced as payal dot mittal at rediffmail dot com
- **Payal_mittal@rediffmail.com** is pronounced as payal underscore mittal at rediffmail dot com
- Note that it is not necessary to use capital P and M in Payal Mittal's email address. People sometimes write email addresses with capital initial letters **(Payal.Mittal111@rediffmail.com).** Sometimes it is all in capitals **(PAYALMITTAL111@REDIFFAMIL.COM).** However, most people write email addresses without capital letters **(payalmittal111@rediffmail.com).**

WRITING AN EMAIL

When you are writing an email first decide whether you are writing an informal email or formal email.

Formal email: We write formal emails when we do not know the reader very well and we want to be polite. Office emails or emails written to any officials come under formal emails. Examples are an email to a customer, a job application, an email to your manager, a complaint to a shop, an email form one company to another company.

Informal email: We write informal emails when we know the reader well and we are very friendly to him/her. Social emails or emails written to friends, parents, or relatives come under informal emails. Examples are a birthday greeting to a friend, an email to a colleague who is also a good friend, a social invitation to a friend at your house.

Phrases for starting and ending an email

	Formal	Informal
Starting phrases	➢ Dear Mr Gupta, (if you know the name) ➢ Dear Sir/Madam,	➢ Hi Sameer, ➢ Hi there Sameer ➢ Morning/afternoon/Evening Sameer
Ending phrases	Yours sincerely, Yours faithfully, Yours truly	Rgds Cheers Bye for now See you soon

We write a comma after the opening phrase. We start a new line after the name of the person we're writing to. We also write a comma after the closing phrase. We start a new line to write our name at the end.

Organising your writing an Email into paragraphs

Let's learn how to write the content of an email into different paragraphs. What you write in which paragraph has been given in details in the given table.

Informal Email	Formal Email
Opening phrase Greeting – paragraph 1 Reason for writing - paragraph 2 Request - paragraph 3 Other news - paragraph 4 Look forward to - paragraph 5 Ending phrase	Opening Phrase Reason for writing – paragraph 1 Explain what happened previously (if required), State the conditions – paragraph 2 Action needed – paragraph 3 Ending phrase

Let's Reflect

Format of writing an Email

Now with the understanding, let's read the sample email (both formal and informal)

Informal Email	Formal Email
Hello Sameer, How is life? It has been a year that I haven't met you. How are uncle and aunt? I'm writing to share good news. I have cleared the MBA entrance for admission in ITM- Mumbai with good score. My whole family and I are very excited for this. Now I am waiting for the interview call from the institute. You told me once that you also had an interview of same kind and cleared it. Could you let me know what kind of preparation I need to do to clear this interview? By the way, we are coming next month at your place. It's going to be fun as Christmas vacation is also there at that time. Anyway, I look forward to hearing from you soon. Give my greetings to the whole family. Regards Aman	Dear sir or madam, I am writing to let you know that, one week ago, I bought a Microwave Oven from one of you dealers at West Punjabi Bagh. So as your customer, I am not satisfied with the Microwave as well as its after-sales service. Now the Microwave is not working as it claimed to be. The food in the oven is still cold after heated even for 5 minutes. It seemed to be something wrong with it. Then I telephoned customer care and registered a complaint for it. They told me that your engineer would visit in next 48 hours. But surprisingly, until now, it has been three days that no engineer has visited yet. If possible, I would like you to refund the amount that I paid for it. As I could not go on with your poor service, I don't want to get a new one instead. I have attached the bill receipt and the complaint number of the Microwave. Looking forwards to your reply! Yours sincerely, Aman

Activity 7: Writing an Email

Write an email to your friend telling her about your favourite food item and share the recipe for the same.

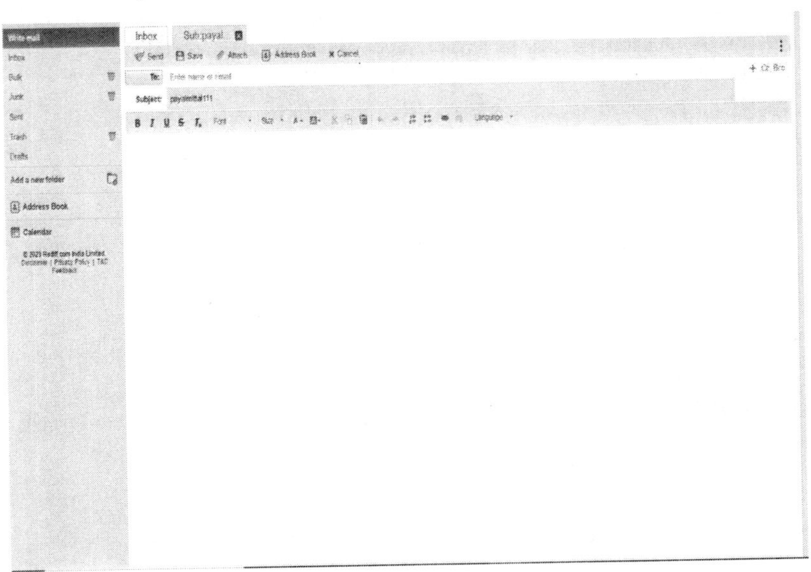

GRAMMATICAL SKILLS

Let's Understand

CAUSATIVE VERBS

Read these sentences:

1. I had my haircut.
2. Mr Mehta is having his room painted.
3. My brother got her car repaired.
4. The teacher made the children do the homework on their own.
5. Please don't let those stray dogs enter into the main street.
6. My mother will help me to complete my project.

In all these sentences, the subject is not doing the work. Some other person is doing his/her work. Some other person is responsible to do that task for you. In the above examples,

1. I **had** my haircut. - Someone has done your haircut. You didn't cut your hair yourself.
2. Mr Mehta is **having** his house painted. – he is not painting his room.
   He has someone who will paint his room.
3. My brother **got** her car repaired. – My brother did not repair his car himself; he has someone who repaired his car.
4. The teacher **made** the children do the homework on their own. – he teacher did not do the homework; she made the children to do their work.
5. Please don't **let** those stray dogs enter into the main street. – You are not doing this task; asking someone else to not allow the stray dogs enter.
6. My mother will **help** me to complete my project. – Mother is not completing the project; she is just assisting her child in doing so.

When you have someone to do your work or persuade/force/assist you to do some work, you use verbs 'have', 'get', 'make', 'let', and 'help' to indicate this. These verbs are called **causative verbs**. These causative verbs are highlighted in the above examples.

Use of Causative Verbs, their Structure, with Examples

Verbs	Structure	Examples
Have – some other person is doing a task for you	Subject + have + object + past participle (V3)	Riya loves having her photo taken. My brother never has his room cleaned.
Have – where you are mentioning the name of the person who is dong that task for you.	Subject + have + person + infinitive (to + V1)	I'll have my assistance to contact you. You have your sister to help you in painting.
Get – to persuade someone to do something	Subject + get + person + infinitive (to + V1)	I got my best friend to accompany me for the party. I got the Manager to arrange an extra bed in our room.

Make – force someone to do something	Subject + make + person + infinitive (to + V1)	The teacher made the students to submit the assignment by tomorrow.
Let – to allow someone to do something	Subject + let + person + infinitive (to + V1)	My parents let me to attend my friend's brother marriage. I let my maid to rest for sometime as she was very tired.
Help – to assist someone	Subject + help + person + infinitive (to + V1)	I helped my friend to shift to other apartment. My brother helped me to crack this interview.

Let's Apply

Activity 8: Using Causative Verbs

Unjumble the jumbled sentences using causative verbs. (have/get/make/let/help)

1. My/every month/I/hair cut/have

   ....

2. The/roof/two years ago/had/they/replaced

   ....

3. Cleaned/the hotel/the windows/has/regularly

   ....

4. My/always/mother/my room/me/makes/to clean

   ....

5. 2 hours/I/can/you/get/to/in that location

   ....

6. My brother/in one day/to/write/me/the whole essay/made

   ....

7. Wear/my/got/mother/a family function/a saree/me/to/in

   ....

8. Need/get/to resolved/this issue/I

   ....

9. Father/helped/to/learn/My/me/driving

   ....

10. Raghav/the police/helped/the thief/to/catch

    ....

11. a school trip/did/my parents/not/me/let/go/on

    ....

PRESENTATION SKILLS

Let's Understand

‖ HOW TO GIVE PRESENTATION ‖

A presentation is a communication tool in which a person or a group of people explains their idea, proposal, system, process, past performance, or any other topic. The person who does the explaining is called the presenter.

For a non-native people, it is difficult to give presentation in English. So let's get familiar with phrases and sentences that you can use for making your presentation impressive and effective. These sentences and phrases will help you to make connections with the audience as it is important to make any presentation successful.

- **First of all, you have to welcome and greet the audience.**
  - Hello everyone. First of all, I'd like to thank the organizer of this presentation for inviting me here.
  - Good morning everyone and welcome to my presentation. I'd like to thank you all for coming here.
  - Good morning, ladies and gentlemen! It's honour for me to present in front of you.
  - Hello everyone. I would like to give you warm welcome.

- **Introducing yourself – your name, position,**
  - Let me start with my brief introduction. I'm Payal Walia from University of Delhi, India.
  - Let me introduce myself. I am Payal Walia, a PhD student of Education at G D Goenka University in Haryana.

- **About the title/topic**
  - I would like to start by ....
  - I'm here today to present ....
  - What I'd like to present to you today is ....
  - The purpose/aim of my presentation is ....

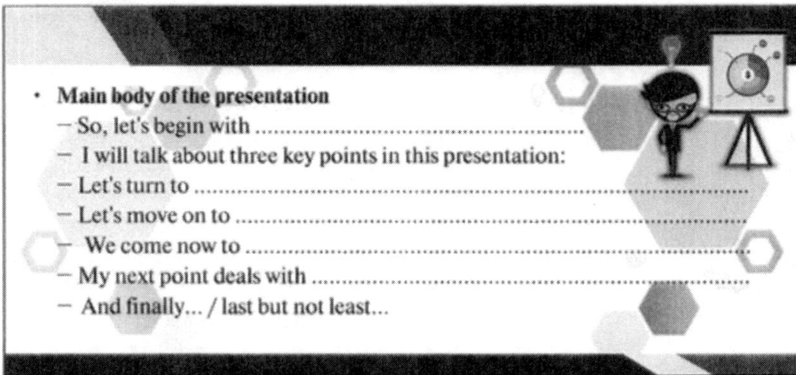
• Main body of the presentation
– So, let's begin with ....
– I will talk about three key points in this presentation:
– Let's turn to ....
– Let's move on to ....
– We come now to ....
– My next point deals with ....
– And finally... / last but not least...

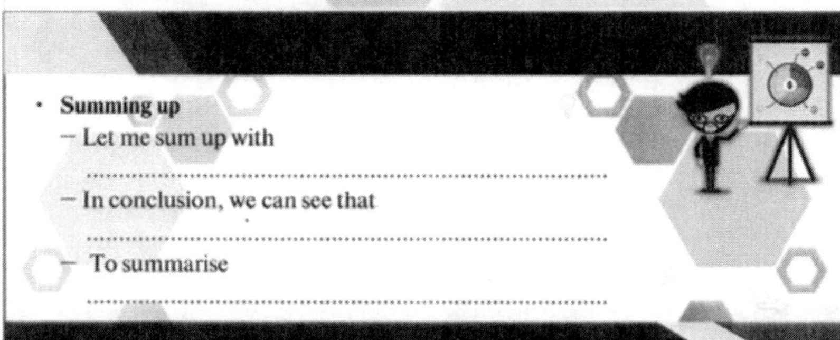
• Summing up
– Let me sum up with
....
– In conclusion, we can see that
....
– To summarise
....

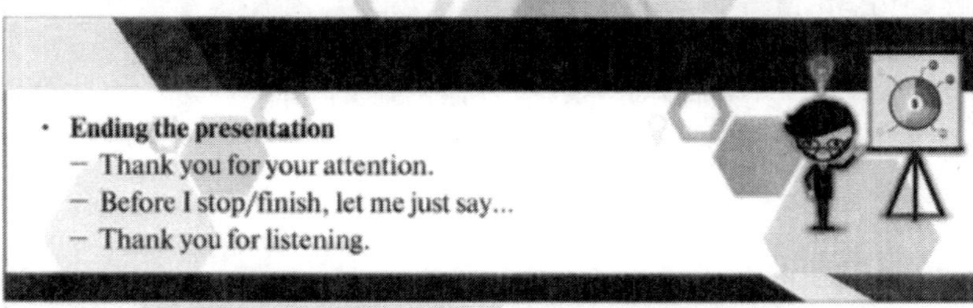
• Ending the presentation
– Thank you for your attention.
– Before I stop/finish, let me just say...
– Thank you for listening.

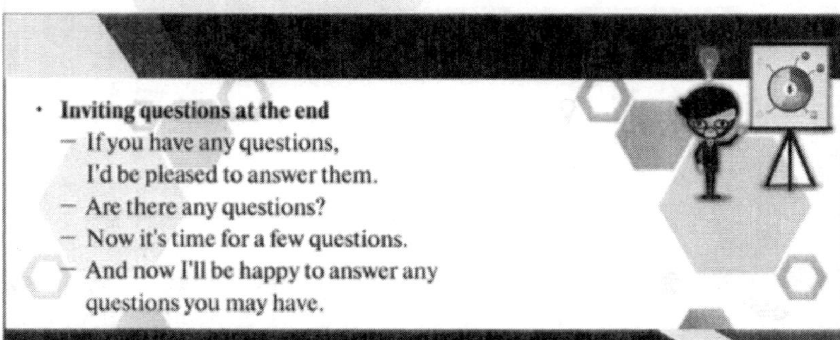
• Inviting questions at the end
– If you have any questions,
I'd be pleased to answer them.
– Are there any questions?
– Now it's time for a few questions.
– And now I'll be happy to answer any
questions you may have.

Let's Assess

Activity 9: Giving a Presentation

Make a presentation with your partner using these sentences. In your presentation, you can talk on any topic or describe or show the features of any object

Activity 10: Solve the Crossword

Find out the words related to food whose meanings are given here. Also search all words in the crossword puzzle.

Across	Down
1. food served before the main course	6. (phrasal verb) have a meal in a restaurant
2. distinctive, typically pleasant smell	7. food that is salty or spicy rather than sweet
3. the state of being fat or overweight	8. an extra amount added to a restaurant bill that's meant to be given to staff for their service
4. shellfish and sea fish serves as food	9. mild-tasting food
5. a country's or region's style of cooking	10. the sweet course eaten at the end of a meal

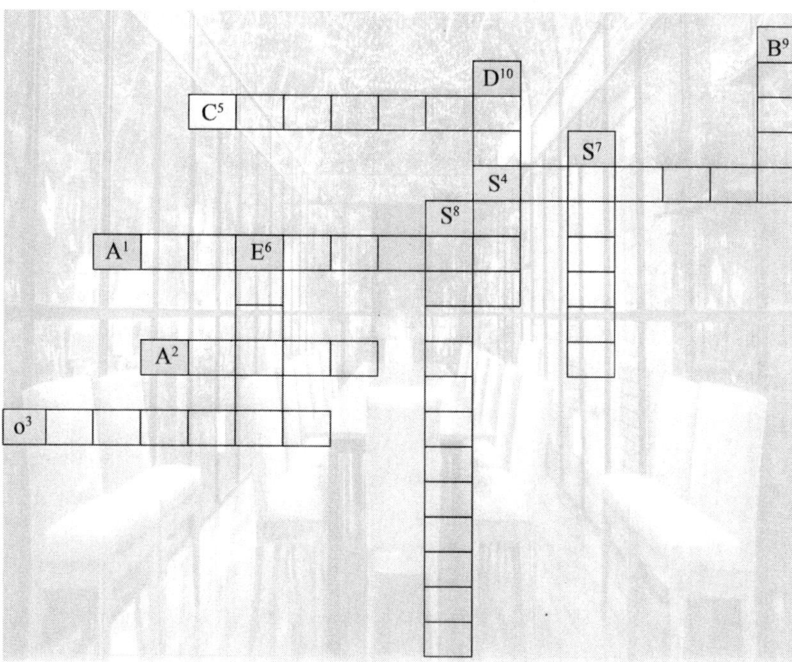

Unit 4 : Technology

INDEX

Learning Objectives

After reading this unit, the students will be able to:

- outline the important points and its sub points in the article published in e newspaper
- recall the information listened through a episode broadcasted on a Radio channel
- participate in a conversation where someone asks you some short questions
- design a work report and a newspaper report
- distinguish the use and structure of active and passive forms of sentences
- restructure the sentences using common phrasal verbs while listening and speaking

READING SKILLS

Let's Do

Read the article from the e-newspaper.

WhatsApp takes on Google, Paytm, Flipkart...

Source:

http://timesofindia.indiatimes.com/articleshow/89114484.cms?utm_source=contentofinterest&utm_medium=text&utm_campaign=cppst

TIMESOFINDIA.COM | Updated: Jan 25, 2022, 15:34 IST

WhatsApp takes on Google, Paytem, Flipkart and others with this new feature

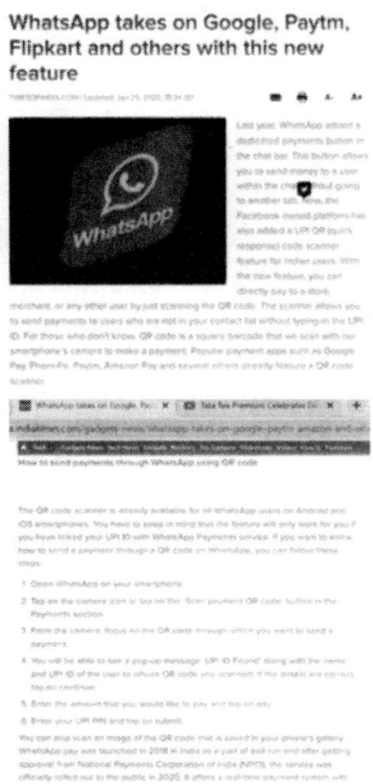
WhatsApp takes on Google, Paytm, Flipkart and others with this new feature

Last year, whatsApp added a dedicated payments button in the chat bar. This button allows you to send money to a user within the chat without going to another tab. Now, the facebook owned platform has also added a UPI QR (quick response) code scanner feature for Indian users. With the new feature, you can directly pay to a store, merchant, or any other user by just scanning the QR code. The scanner allows you to send payments to users who are not in your contact list without typing in the UPI ID. For those who don't know QR code is a square barcode that we scan with our Smartphone's camera to make a payment. Popular payment apps such as Goggle Pay, Phonepay, Paytm, Amazon Pay and several others already feature a QR code scanner

How to send payment through WhatsApp using QR code

The QR code scanner is already available for all WhatsApp users on Android and IOS smart phones. You have to keep in mind that the feature will only work for you if you have linked your UPI ID with WhatsApp Payments service. If you want to know how to send a payment through a QR code on WhatsApp you can follow these steps.

1. Open WhatsApp on your smartphone.
2. Tap on the camera icon or tap on the 'Scan payment QR code' button in the Payments section.
3. From the camera, focus on the QR code through which you want to send payment.
4. You will be able to see a pop-up message 'UPI ID found' along with the name and UPI ID of the user to whose QR code you scanned. If the details are correct, tap on continue.
5. Enter the amount that you would like to pay and tap on pay.
6. Enter your UPI PIN and tap on submit.

You can also scan an image of the QR code that is saved in your phone's gallery. WhatsApp pay was launched in 2018 in India as a part of trail run and after getting approval from National Payments Corporation of India (NPCI), the service was officially rolled out to the public in 2020. It offers a real-time payment system with over 227 banks and is live for all users across the country.

Let's Assess

Activity 1: Comprehension Questions

(a) After reading the article in e newspaper, complete the questions with the words in the box.

• When • Where • Which • Who • What • How

1. .... added a dedicated payments button in the chat bar?
2. .... can you do with this new added feature?
3. .... others popular payment apps have already this feature?
4. .... can this feature of real-time payments in Whatsapp using QR code be used in your Android phone?
5 .... did WhatsApp officially start this real-time payment service for the public in 2020?
6 .... is the scanned image of the QR code saved in Android phones?

(b) Now write the answers of the above questions.

....

....

....

....

....

....

....

....

© Match these phrasal verbs related to technology with their meanings.

1.	Add on	printed pages obtained from computer's pages
2.	Back up	stop working as its parts have become stuck
3.	Freeze up	act of making the program ready for execution
4.	Log in	feature turning off a computer
5.	Log out	an increase in speed
6.	Print out	stop using a computer or website by clicking on an instruction
7.	Setup	make a spare copy of data or a disk
8.	Shut down	a software added to computer system to give extra
9.	Speed up	to make the image smaller
10.	Zoom in	a software or equipment that can be connected to computer to give it an extra use
11.	Zoom out	to make the image larger
12.	Plug in	to connect to a computer system by putting in a particular set of letters and numbers

GRAMMAR SKILLS

Let's Understand

‖ ACTIVE AND PASSIVE FORMS ‖

Read the sentences in two pictures.

Picture 1

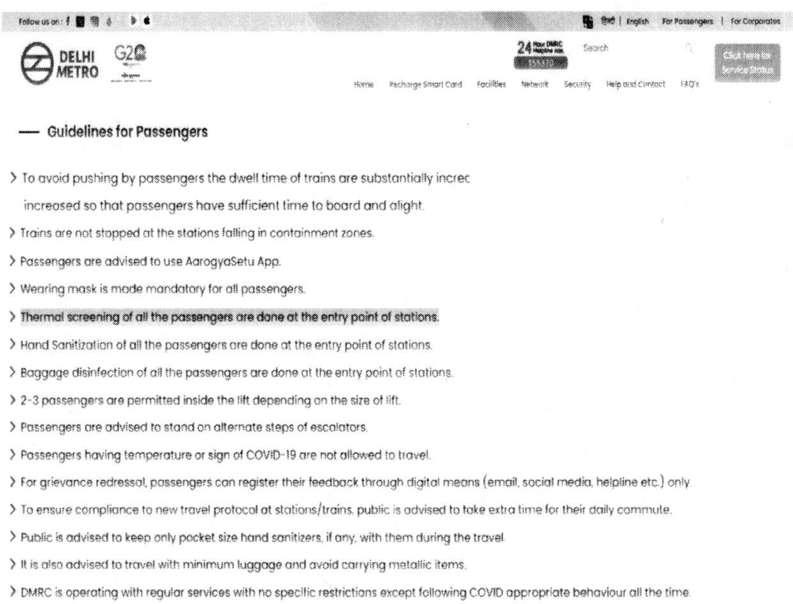
Follow us on :
English | For Passengers | For Corporates
DELHI METRO
Search
Home | Recharge Smart Card | Facilities | Network | Security | Help and Contact | FAQ's

— Guidelines for Passengers

> To avoid pushing by passengers the dwell time of trains are substantially increc increased so that passengers have sufficient time to board and alight.
> Trains are not stopped at the stations falling in containment zones.
> Passengers are advised to use AarogyaSetu App.
> Wearing mask is made mandatory for all passengers.
> Thermal screening of all the passengers are done at the entry point of stations.
> Hand Sanitization of all the passengers are done at the entry point of stations.
> Baggage disinfection of all the passengers are done at the entry point of stations.
> 2-3 passengers are permitted inside the lift depending on the size of lift.
> Passengers are advised to stand on alternate steps of escalators.
> Passengers having temperature or sign of COVID-19 are not allowed to travel.
> For grievance redressal, passengers can register their feedback through digital means (email, social media, helpline etc.) only.
> To ensure compliance to new travel protocol at stations/trains, public is advised to take extra time for their daily commute.
> Public is advised to keep only pocket size hand sanitizers, if any, with them during the travel.
> It is also advised to travel with minimum luggage and avoid carrying metallic items.
> DMRC is operating with regular services with no specific restrictions except following COVID appropriate behaviour all the time.

The first picture shows the guidelines for the passengers commuting in Metro Rail and the Second picture shows the tagline of 'Raymond' Company.

For example, 2-3 passengers are permitted in the lift.

The perfect fit is not found.

All these sentences are written in passive form. We use passive form when

- We do not know who does something. For example, "The cat was rescued."
- It is not important or not necessary to say who does it. For example, "The test was administered." (It is not important who administered the test)
- Action is important than the person who did it.
- The one performing the action is obvious. For example, "Financial Budget was released." (it could be only be released by government.)

Picture 2

To make it more clear, let's see another example from Picture 1,

- People are advised to use Aarogaya Setu/app – in this sentence, action of using Aarogaya Setu app is important and the people to whom this guideline is directed; not the person who released this guideline.

In active form of sentence, the subject who does the work is important and it is active so the sentence starts from the subject. For example, the government has asked to use the Aarogaya Setu App.	In Passive voice, the 'subject' and 'object' flip-flop. The subject becomes passive and the object becomes active so the passive sentence starts from 'object'.

Passive voice requires double verbs – action verb and helping verb:

- "to be" verb – is, are, am, was, were, being, has, had
- Past participle of verb – V3 form of verb (action words)

Let's Apply

Now, let's check the active and passive form in all tenses through an example:

Structure of Active form	Structure of Passive form	Tenses
Subject + Verb + Object	Object + to be verb + main verb	
Tom cleans the house.	The house is cleaned.	Present Simple Tense
Tom is cleaning the house.	The house is being cleaned.	Present Continuous Tense
Tom cleaned the house.	The house was cleaned.	Past Simple Tense
Tom was cleaning the house.	The house was being cleaned.	Past Continuous Tense
Tom will clean the house.	The house will be cleaned.	Future Simple Tense
Tom has cleaned the house.	The house has been cleaned.	Present Perfect Tense
Tom had cleaned the house.	The house had been cleaned.	Past Perfect Tense

- In passive form, if we want to tell who does the action, we use 'by + Subject' at the end of the sentence. For example, The house is cleaned by Tom.
- If pronouns like 'I', 'You', 'They', 'We', 'He', 'She' are used in active form then in passive form, they are changed into 'me', 'you', 'them', 'us', 'him', 'her'. For example,

  I cleaned the house. → The house was cleaned by **me.**

  He cleaned the house. → The house was cleaned by **him.**

Let's Apply

Activity 2: News report

Look for a news story in a newspaper or any news website that have used the passive form of sentences in writing news. Underline the passive sentences in that news story and write them in the space provided. Also write the reason why the passive form is used there.

....

....

....

....

....

....

....

....

Let's Apply

Activity 3: Change into Passive Form

Change the sentences into passive form.

1. I completed the project yesterday.

   ....

2. The painters are paining the house.

   ....

3. May God bless you with good health!

   ....

4. He was wearing a black shirt.

   ....

5. Who wrote this essay?

   ....

Let's Apply

Activity 4: Change into Active Form

Change the sentences into active form. Add subject wherever required.

1. The issue was not resolved by me.

   ....

2. The room was cleaned last week (by someone).

   ....

3. We had been given the wrong question paper.

   ....

4. New Policy will be released next week.

   ....

5. He has been told to come early in the office.

   ....

VOCABULARY BOX

Let's Do

‖ TELEPHONE PHRASAL VERBS ‖

Some phrasal verbs are given which we use in our daily conversation over the phone. Let's learn them with their meaning.

Cut off – to interrupt a telephone conversation
Get through – to succeed in speaking to somebody on the telephone
Hang on – to wait for a short time
Hang up – to end a telephone conversation and put the phone down
Call back – to telephone somebody again or in return
Pick up – to answer a telephone call
Put through – to connect by telephone
Speak up – to speak louder
Break up – to become inaudible over the telephone
Hold on – to wait for a short time

Let's Reflect

Activity 5: Phrasal Verbs

Insert the correct phrasal verb in the space provided. Choose from the above phrasal verbs.

- I was just talking to Ridhi. We were .... in the middle of our conversation and due to .... of her voice and I could not hear her anymore.
- I can't .... the doctor. His number is constantly busy.
- **Mita:** Hello, Can I speak to Rashi, I am her friend, Mita.
  Rahul: Ok, ... I'll see if she's here.
- To make a purchase, simply ....the phone and give a missed call on given the toll-free number here any time. Our executives will ....in 24 hours.
- **Client:** May I speak to Mr Mehta. I am Ravi from Tata Sales.
  Receptionist: Ok. Please .... I'll .... you .... to Mr Mehta.
- You need to .... because I am in the market.

‖ PHRASAL VERBS ‖

- Phrasal verbs are two or more words that together act as a completely new word, with a meaning separate from the original words. For example, 'Kick off' means to 'start' which is very different from the meaning of 'Kick' and 'off'.

Read these single verbs whose similar phrasal verbs are given:

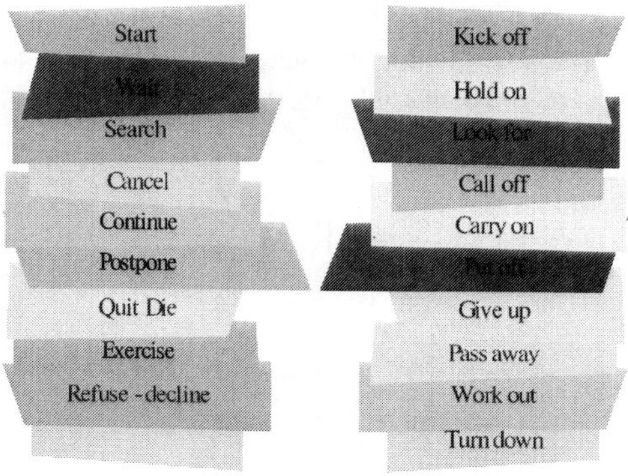

Form	Meaning	Use
Most Phrasal verbs are the combination of two words – a word + a preposition or adverb. For example, *look into,* in which *look* is a verb and *into* is a particle. It gives new meaning to the word *look into* which means "investigate something". Many phrasal verbs can be formed by the combination of three parts: verb + particle + preposition. For example, *come up with* as in *She has come up with great scheme.* In many phrasal verbs, particle can be separated by adding the object in between them. For example, *Sarita looked the word up in the dictionary. He took his friends out for lunch.*	Some phrasal verbs have direct literal meaning. For example, *hang up-* it is not difficult to figure out its meaning in the given sentence – *She hangs up the picture on the wall.* Some phrasal verbs are figurative phrasal verbs. They have a different meaning from the original verb. For example, *set off* - if you know the meaning of the verb *set* and the particle *off,* it is of no use. The phrasal verb *set off* has other meaning "begin a journey" as in *they set off together in a small car.* Depending on the context, Some phrasal verbs have more than one meaning. For example, *go through* means "undergo a difficult period, as in *As I lost my job I am going through a tough time,* or "examine something" as in *Please go through these answers carefully.*	Phrasal verbs are used in informal conversations and informal writings. For example, Last week I *came down* with flu. But luckily I soon *got over it.*

Let's Practise

Activity 6: Complete the Phrasal Verb Chart

Complete each Phrasal verb by adding verb and preposition. For example, for the combination *go* and *on*, you could fill in (*go on*) and you have to write its meaning also.

	On	In	Off	Up	Down
Go					
Turn					
Put					

Activity 7: Phrasal Verbs with 'take', 'go', 'come', 'get'

Complete each sentence with the verb in the box and a preposition to make a phrasal verb. Write the phrasal verb in its correct form. There are words at the end of the sentence that describe the meaning of that phrasal verb.

Take →	On	Off	Over	Up

1. The plane wil .... sharp at 7:00 pm. (leave the ground and fly)
2. My friend is going to..Classical dance in her free time. (start to learn)
3. The MTN Company is ....New employees. (recruiting)
4. Usually the small industries are ....By the big multinationals. (taken control of)

Go →	On	Off	Through	Down

1. A bomb .... In a market. (exploded)
2. I can't take my online class as the internet has .... (stopped working temporarily)
3. Sorry for interrupting. Please you .... with your speech. (continue)
4. Please .... this report carefully to make sure that it is error free. (look carefully at)

Come →	Over	Up	Across	Out

1. I reached late in the function because something .... at the last minute. (happened)
2. My friend is .... this weekend to spend some time with me. (visit me)
3. from your hiding place. (appeared)
4. I .... my old friend in a shopping mall yesterday. (met)

Get →	Over	In	By	Through

1. Last month my grandmother passed away, but now I am .... (recover from)
2. What time does the plane ....? (arrive)
3. My younger sister cannot .... anything without me. (manage)
4. I tried to call her many times but I was not able to .... (make contact)

Let's Practise

Activity 7: Phrasal Verb

Think of other phrasal verbs with the verbs take, go, some, and get. Then write down their meaning and use them in sentences.

1. Verb: take Preposition: .... Phrasal verb: ....
   Meaning of the phrasal verb: ....
   Sentence: ....
2. Verb: go Preposition: .... Phrasal verb: ....
   Meaning of the phrasal verb: ....
   Sentence: ....
3. Verb: come Preposition: .... Phrasal verb: ....
   Meaning of the phrasal verb: ....
   Sentence: ....
4. Verb: get Preposition: .... Phrasal verb: ....
   Meaning of the phrasal verb: ....
   Sentence: ....

LISTENING SKILL

Let's Do

A link for a radio episode is given below in which AIR (All India Radio) is celebrating the "The Journey of Freedom Movement" where it brings you a glimpse of struggle of freedom fighters every day in its episodes. In this particular episode, they are introducing two freedom fighters, Jai Narayan Vyas from Rajasthan and Sankaran Kutty Pottekkat from Kerala.

https://t.co/fIuxTXyTfR

Let's Assess

Activity 9: Complete the paragraphs

After listening the episode, fill up the blanks to complete their biographies.

Jai Narayan Vyas

Jai Narayan Vyas was a prominent leader in Jodhpur during the freedom struggle. He was born in princely state of .... in 1899 and died on .... He started Marwar Hitkari Sabha to fight against both

.... which also received the support of the Maharaja of Jodhpur. However, he also got involved in freedom movements led by the Congress party which were not sympathetic to the Maharaja and resulted .... He returned to his hometown and in 1941 became .... of the Jodhpur Muncipilaity. Jai Narayan was imprisoned 5 times including for a period of two years .... for his involvement in the Jodhpur Praja Mandal, the Youth League, and the Marwar Lok Parishad. Vyas was elected to the Constituent Assembly from Jodhpur and put forth his views on the issues of .... and the drawing up of state boundaries. After independence, Vyas became the .... of the princely state of Jodhpur in March 1948. He also headed the Rajputana Pradesh Congress Committee until 1949. Later .... of the independent state of Rajasthan, a position he held twice between .... .We salute the great nationalist!

Sankaran Kutty Pottekkat

We also remember famous .... writer Sankaran Kutty Pottekkat. He was born on 14 March 1913 in Calicut. He was involved with the activities of the .... and attended the Tripuri Session of 1939 for which he resigned from his teaching job as the school authorities did not allow leave for absence. He was involved in the.............................. and worked alongside freedom fighters like Matimarjr. In 1962, Pottekkat won the parliamentary elections from Pillideri, Kerala.

Pottekkat was a writer of strong social commitment and ideals possessing on individualistic vision. Pottekkat made his mark in literature with a few short stories in the 1930s. His first story 'Rajaneethi' was published in..............................'Makan er Konna Madyem' and 'Hindu Muslim Maithri' were some of his notable works. Pottekkat won the .... award in 1961 for the novel 'Oru Theruvinte Katha'- The story of a Street' and the Jnanpith

Award in 1980 for the novel 'Oru Desathinte Katha – the Story of the Local'. His works have been translated into

English, Itlaian, Russian, German, and Czech besides all major Indian languages. He dies on ....We salute the Great Indians!

WRITING SKILLS

Let's Understand

‖ REPORT WRITING ‖

Oxford Dictionary defines report as "to give people information about something that you have heard, seen, done, etc."

- When this report publishes in a newspaper, it is called **newspaper report writing.**
- In any organization, when you specify the progress of a project you are working on, it is called **work report writing.** For example, report writing about a school event, about sales target achievement of your sale steam, etc.

‖ WORK REPORT WRITING ‖

Every organization has different requirements on how you should submit the report. But there is standard report writing format that we should follow:

- Introduction

- Body with headings and subheadings
- Conclusion
- Summary

Introduction: Start with the aim of writing this report and say where the information comes from. For example,

This report aims to describe the problems faced by teachers in the College Staff Room and discuss the implementations that can be done to resolve those issues. The meeting with teachers was held on Saturday, 12 August, which was attended by 20 teachers out of 30 and discussed their problems.

Body: Use subheadings to make the layout clear. Give each problem or issue a separate heading or section.

Issue 1: No Electric PowerPoint to charge their Phones.

Many teachers complained that there is no electric power point through they can charge their mobile phones. Concerns were raised about switching off the mobile phones during college timings and not able to communicate students about reshuffling of classes, its timings, and rooms. A power extension or installing more power points was suggested as possible solutions. However, installation cannot be carried out during teaching hours.

Issue 2: Arrangement for cold drinking water in summers.

It was noted that teachers do not have the facility of having cold water during summers as there is not water cooling machine in the staff room. Many teachers have to take the classes till late in afternoon. At the time, the dire need of cold water is there. Only the installation of water cooling machine was proposed as s solution for this issue.

Conclusion and Recommendations:

Taking the factors mentioned into account, the extension would be best immediate solution and during mid-semester break in March, the college could install ore power points in the staff room.

For installation of water cooling machine, the kitchen would be best place as it also has some spare space where it could be installed. This work can take place immediately and should be a priority.

Tips for effective Report Writing:

Write only brief introduction as the person reading the report has asked you to write it and is well aware about the topic.

- Use an impersonal and formal style.
- Use the passive voice to give emphasis on the work and issues not on the individual or people. For example,

  Concerns were raised about.......................... It was noted that ....
- Use objective language for recommendations and conclusions: would be the best .... the college could consider .... is recommended ....

Let's Assess

Activity 10: Work Report Writing

You are in-charge of a project in which your school has organised a 'Best Out of Waste' Competition for the students of Class 6-8. You have to report to the Principal about this event in form of writing.

....

....

....

....

....

....

....

....

....

....

....

....

....

....

‖ NEWSPAPER REPORT ‖

Let's understand

Newspaper Report is formal documentation of an event, accident, a person, etc. with details and insights in the organised form to be published in a newspaper.

Format of Newspaper Report

- **Headline** – a short, clear title represents what the news story is about. It captures the reader's attention. Keep these rules in mind while writing a heading for a newspaper report:
  - Omit the articles (a, an, the)
  - Omit unnecessary adjectives, pronouns
  - Use the present simple tense for the recent event
  - For the past event, use passive form and omit the verb 'to be'
- **Byline** – contains the name of the person who is writing the report and his/her designation.
- **Date and place of reporting.**
- **Opening paragraph** – Overview of the event.
- **Main Body** – describes the 5WH's (when, what, where, who, what) and 1H (how) of the event clearly and in logical manner.
- **Conclusion** – describes on how the event ended, people's comment, and action taken so far. Contains additional details about the event.

Let's Assess

Activity 11: Newspaper Report Writing

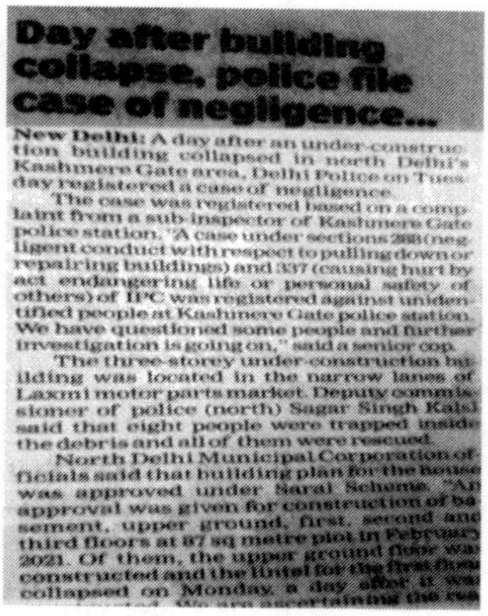

Day after building collapse, police file case of negligence...

New Delhi: A day after an under-construction building collapsed in north Delhi's Kashmere Gate area, Delhi Police on Tuesday registered a case of negligence.

The case was registered based on a complaint from a sub-inspector of Kashmere Gate police station. "A case under sections 288 (negligent conduct with respect to pulling down or repairing buildings) and 337 (causing hurt by act endangering life or personal safety of others) of IPC was registered against unidentified people at Kashmere Gate police station. We have questioned some people and further investigation is going on," said a senior cop.

The three-storey under-construction building was located in the narrow lanes of Laxmi motor parts market. Deputy commissioner of police (north) Sagar Singh Kalsi said that eight people were trapped inside the debris and all of them were rescued.

North Delhi Municipal Corporation officials said that building plan for the house was approved under Saral Scheme. "An approval was given for construction of basement, upper ground, first, second and third floors at 87 sq metre plot in February 2021. Of them, the upper ground floor was constructed and the lintel for the first floor collapsed on Monday, a day after it was

A day after an under construction building collapsed in north Delhi's Kashmere Gate area. Delhi Police on Tuesday registered a case of negligence.

The case was registered based on complaint from a sub-inspector of Kashmere Gate police station. "A case under sections 288 (negligent conduct with respect to pulling down or repairing buildings) and 337 (causing hurt by act endangering life or personal safety of others) of IPC was registered against unidentified people at Kashmere Gate police station. We have questioned some people and further investigation is going on," said a senior cop.

The three-storey under-construction building was located in the narrow lanes of Laxmi motor parts market. Deputy commissioner of police (north) Sagar Singh Kalsi said that eight people were trapped inside the debris and all of them were rescued.

North Delhi Municipal corporation officials said that building plan for the house was approved under Saral Scheme. "An approval was given for construction of basement, upper ground, first, second and third floors at 87 sq metre plot in February 2021. Of them, the upper ground floor was constructed and the lintel for the first floor collapsed on Monday, a day after it was constructed. We are ascertaining the reason for that," said an official.

1. Read the following news report and label the paragraph with the given label A, B, C, D.
   - A - Headline
   - B - Detailed description
   - C - Summary of the event
   - D - Conclusion
2. Read the 1 paragraph of the report and complete the following table.

Who	What	Where	When	Causes of accident	Features of accident	Action taken

3. Read the paragraph 2, 3, and 4 answer the questions.
   - Which kind of case was registered for this accident?

     ....
   - Who filed the complaint for this case?

     ....
   - Where was this building located?

     ....
   - What was the consequence of this accident?

     ....

- What was the further action taken?

....

CONVERSATIONAL SKILL

Let's Do

Activity 12: Role Play

Work in pairs. Do this role play activity. One student asks question that is written below and other student answers with any answer given in second column.

Student A	Student B
Would you like to go the movie?	No, I can't. I'm sorry.
Would you like to have coffee?	Sure, that sounds great!
Would you like to go shopping with me?	Thanks for asking. I'd like that.
Do you want to go dancing tonight?	I'm sorry. I can't. I'm busy.
Do you want to eat lunch together?	Thanks for asking, but I have other plans.
Are you free on Tuesday at 3:00 pm.	Okay. Sounds great.
Are you free next week?	I can't, but may be another time.
Do you want to join us?	Sure, I'd love to.

Unit 5: Workplace

INDEX

Learning Objectives

After reading this Unit, the students will be able to:

- apply the ways discussed in the article that help them in their online interview.
- communicate effectively while appearing in an interview.
- participate in an office meeting.
- compose their CV and covering letter along with it.
- practice to use gerunds and infinitives in their real-life situations for speaking about different topics like talking about their habits, opinions, etc.
- comprehend the meaning of official terms used while interacting at a workplace

READING SKILLS

Let's Do

Read the newspaper article.

How to Communicate Effectively in Online Interviews

Interviews are a test of communication skills and the core principles remain the same even in the virtual mode, writes Vineeta Dwivedi.

How to communicate effectively in online interviews

Due to an extended work-from-home scenario, the future steps in our career would still be taken via online video interviews, bringing new challenges for both parties. The assessors are uncertain about making the best evaluation, while the applicants are worried about the outcome. In this scenario, the fear is to remain limited by the virtual medium and forego the chance to showcase the true power of one's personality.

How then to communicate and captivate? Well, tough times call for a smarter way of preparation. And the core principles of persuasion and influencing remain the same– even virtual interviews are a test of communication and functional skills. Expectations of interviewers are that the candidate is aware, knowledgeable, a good fit and can convince them of it all. It is a tough job for them too.

Here are a few ways you can use to make sure that the impact of your interview is nothing less than phenomenal:

Have an innovative way of describing yourself: There is something unique about each one of us, the timeline of our life events. Tell your own story, in your own way. Write it down, speak it aloud – whenever you falter, alter. Also, do not force orate it and never try and read it from a script. A discerning interviewer would figure out immediately, and you'd be left to pick up pieces of a shattered first impression.

Look people in the eye: Even if it is only the camera, make sure that it is at eye level. Our entire personality is crunched into just our face and some hand movements in the viewfinder of the camera. Smile and greet people as you always do in an in-person interview. Use a good camera, even if you need to attach an external one. You should go where the light is right, and the corner is quiet.

Practice speaking: There is so much meaning attached to how we speak, and the human ear is trained to pick up the small nuances in tone and delivery.

Use a microphone attached to your device so that the volume is always good for the listener and disturbances are cut down. Ensure that you speak slowly and enunciate well. You have their full attention when you take pauses and speak with some thought. Record your mock interviews to develop and hone your style of speaking. Listen to good audiobooks and podcasts to learn more.

Research and read about the institution: You should sound prepared. Interviewers are always looking for honest candidates who know whatever they mention in their application form but have done enough research to show interest in the subjects of their future interest. A virtual interview deprives of the chance to visit the premises and get a feel of the place but does not prevent you from doing a thorough look around on social media. You can read blogs, web pages, testimonials, programme descriptions carefully and mention if needed.

What is your true stand-out quality: Are you innovative, passionate, driven? Your extracurricular interest or hobbies can make you stand out. It can be true love for minecraft, a passionate affair with baking cakes or even being a Potterhead. If you have solved any real-world problems at work, or at home or even at your resident's association/ society, that is worthy of mention, do that. The world needs out-of-the box, creative thinkers who are never shy of taking on a new challenge.

Let's Assess

Activity 1: Comprehension Questions

After reading the above newspaper article, answer the questions below:

1. What are the challenges faced by the assessors and the applicants in the virtual interviews?

   ....

   ....

   ....

2. What are the expectations of the interviewer from the applicant in an interview?

   ....

   ....

   ....

3. What is main concern in this newspaper article?

   ....

   ....

   ....

4. List the 5 ways through which you can make an effective impression on the interviewers during interview.

   ....

   ....

   ....

5. Write, in at least 3-4 sentences about your true stand-out quality.

   ....

   ....

   ....

6. Complete the Word family Exercise Chart.

Verb	Noun	Adjective	Adverb
communicate	....	communicative	....
....	Evaluator	....	....
Mock	....	....	....
....	Passion	....	....
Slow	....	....	Slowly

Let's Understand

WRITING SKILLS

When you know that what kind of a job you would like to do, you can search for that job through several platforms like newspaper, social media (Facebook), ask friends and family, register on a online job portal, search on the internet and read about different companies, or register with an employment agency. Here, given below one of the example of job advertisement published in the newspaper.

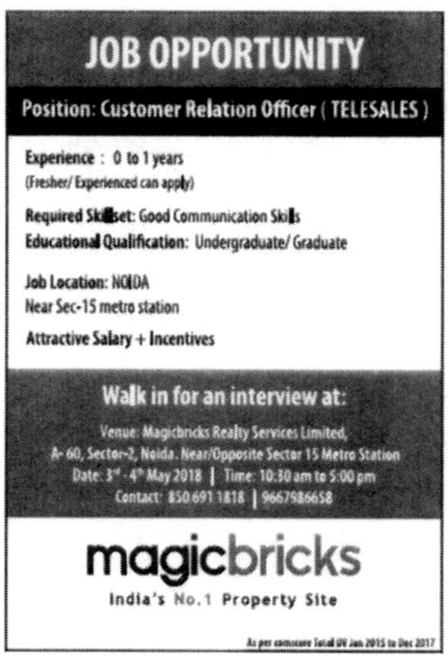

• When you have searched out the desirable job vacancy from any of the platform, next thing is look for company name, job title and its brief description, essential requirement, desirable requirement, working conditions, salary, details of application process.

• Next step is to write your CV; which you have to send to the given email in the advertisement or take along with you in the walk-in-interview. CV stands for Curriculum Vitae, which is a Latin expression. CV is a written record of your work and education history and all the other information that an employer is interested in. One page CV is good but if you have more information to include then two pages of CV are also correct.

Here, one sample of CV is given. Look at its different sections and headings.

‖ HOW TO WRITE A CV ‖

Pragun Miital

Address: 345, SFS Flats, Rohini, Sector 12, New Delhi 110032.

Date of Birth: 10th March, 1997

E-mail: pragunmittal10@gmail.com

Ph. No.: +91-8368552296, 7877931001

Carrer Objective:

Associatecustomerrepresentativewith3+yearsofexperiencedrivingprofitability through strong relation building and quality control.

Able to handle complex situations from a strategic and actical perspective.

Professional Experience:

Customer Representative, Policy Bazaar Pvt. Ltd., Gurgaon. (2019-2020)

- Communicating and helping client with the queries related to Investment products.
- Sound knowledge of Insurance and Investment sector and options
- Active knowledge of Financial market and Stock market

PR Business and Development, New Delhi. (2018-2019)

- Handling, coordinating and leading a team
- Managing product and clients related queries and meetings
- Promoting business and communicating with new clients

Education Qualification:

- Commerce Graduate from Delhi University
- 10th from Maharaja Agarsain Public School
- 12th in Commerce as subjects from CBSE

Skill Set:

- Excellent Communication Skills in written and verbal
- Ability to lead team and build organization towards good performance
- Event Management, Adaptability and Co-ordination
- Analytical thinking and problem solving skills
- MS Office, Internet applications - Web and Mobile
- Hosted various Business Profile Photo shoots for several catalogues.

Interest:

- Reading books
- Watching cricket
- Listening music

References:

1. Mr Anurag Aggarwal

D/O Digital Marketers Pvt. Ltd.

1432/8, Ranu Bagh, Pitampura

Ph: 8762254392

Email Id: anuragagg,sid@gamil.com

At the top of the CV, 'Pragun' name is very clear. That's important.

- And in the top section, he has written his personal information, like his address and how he can be contacted. He could include heading "Personal information" but it is also correct without that.
- Next is 'Employment' – that is, employment history, the places where Pragun worked and what professional experience he has. If you have never had a job, you can still include this and mention, for example, any volunteering work you have one.
- After that you have 'Education' – your academic background. Don't include primary school, write only about secondary and university education and any other courses or training you have done.
- Then 'Skills' – you can write about your skills, especially the skills that are right for this job.
- The next heading is 'Interests' – what kind of hobbies and interests you have. You don't need to go into too much detail.
- Finally 'References' – References are the people like your former managers or college professors – people an employer can contact to know more about you.

So the sections that we have in CV are:

- Personal information
- Employment history
- Education
- Skills
- Interests
- References

Tips for writing CV:

- Start with a short profile to show who you are and what you offer.
- List your emaployment history, starting with the present.
- Explain your gaps, for example time spent traveling or having children.
- Use bullet points for your main responsibilities and experience in each role.
- Then give your educational background. List the relevant qualifications that you have, starting with the most recent. Include the title of your qualification, where you studied and the date you successfully completed it.
- If you don't have a lot of experience yet, write 'Education' above 'Employment'.
- List other experience or interests you may have if they are relevant to the job.
- If you have someone who could support your application, add their contact details in 'References' section.
- When we think about the skills we often talk about hard skills and soft skills. Hard skills are things you can do like typing, good communication skills in English and Hindi, driving, etc. Soft skills are the personal qualities that enable you to interact effectively and harmoniously with other people. Examples are problem solving skills, creative thinking skills, leadership skills, etc.

Let's Assess

Activity 2: Write your CV

Now, it's your turn to write an impressive CV for you.

....
....
....
....
....
....
....
....
....
....
....
....
....
....
....
....
....
....

‖ HOW TO WRITE COVER LETTER ‖

A cover letter is the formal letter that you send with your job application to explain why you think you are the right person. Cover letter should be formal, short, and clear, so use short paragraphs. For writing cover letter, first link directly to the job advertisement, add some extra information like what your strengths are and show your enthusiasm for the job.

Here is a sample of cover letter that Pragun will send along with his CV.

> Phase 2, Ashok Vihar
> New Delhi 110052.
>
> B R Publishing Pvt Ltd.
> Daryaganj, Ansari Road
> New Delhi 10064.
> Date..............
>
> Dear Sir
>
> Sub: Assistant Account Manager Vacancy
>
> I am writing in response to your advertisement published in 'The Times of India' for the position of Assistant Account Manager with B R Publishing.
>
> After graduating from University of Delhi, I have been working as a shop assistant since 2007 in an organization. I have the good required experience.
>
> I also meet the other essential requirements as I have good IT skills and I am fluent in English. I note from the job advertisement that it is desirable for applicants to speak at least two languages and that one of these should be English. I speak very good Hindi too. I believe I have the qualities needed to make me a suitable applicant for the position. I am hard- working, organised and enjoy working as part of a team.
>
> I am sure that I will be a valuable addition to your team and I look forward to having the opportunity to discuss the contributions I can make to your company.
>
> Yours sincerely
> Pragun Mittal

Other useful phrases for job application

(a) Paragraph 1
   (i) I noted with interest your ad for a in today's edition of
   (ii) I would like to apply for the vacancy advertised in .....
   (iii) With reference to your advert in .....
   (iv) As you will see from my CV

(b) Paragraph 2
   (i) Since leaving University, I have
   (ii) Having gained a degree, I
   (iii) While I was working at .....
   (iv) I am currently employed as .....

(c) Paragraph 3
  - (i) This post interests me
  - (ii) I would welcome the chance to gain more experience
  - (iii) I would be grateful for the opportunity to improve my skills
  - (iv) I have extensive experience of .....

(d) Paragraph 4
  - (i) If you consider that my experience and qualifications are suitable.....
  - (ii) I am available for interview any afternoon and would be pleased to discuss the post in person.

Let's Apply

Activity 3: Write a Cover Letter

Write a cover letter that you will send along with your CV. Use another useful phrases given above in your cover letter.

....
....
....
....
....
....
....
....
....
....
....
....
....

LISTENING SKILLS

‖ INTERVIEW ‖

Let's Do

Activity 4: Listen an Interview

Listen an interview of a fresher, Neha over the telephone by clicking on the link below.

https://anchor.fm/payal56/episodes/Interview-of-a-fresher-e1g7qcc

List the questions that have been asked by the interviewer of the company to Neha.

....
....
....
....
....
....
....

Let's Understand

CONVERSATIONAL SKILL

‖ HOW TO PREPARE FOR A JOB INTERVIEW? ‖

- Take care of these things while preparing for Interviews:
- You have to arrive on time for the interview. Try to get there at least 15 minutes before the interview.
- Make a good first impression. You must think carefully what you're going to wear for the interview. You have to dress smartly. You don't have to wear a suit, but you really must not wear jeans. Wear smart trousers and a jacket.
- Practice answering some questions before the interview like, tell me about yourself? You mustn't start talking about your life history and family. Just tell them about job related skills and qualifications you have.
- You must turn off your phone before you go into the interview room.

What kind of questions will the interviewer ask?

Most people get nervous before an interview. The good thing is that most interviews, the interviewer asks similar questions, so you can prepare your answers beforehand. Here are some questions they might ask you at the interview and how you can answer them is also given.

- Tell me about yourself?

Ans. You mustn't talk about your family and life history. You must refer to your job-related skills and qualities.

- What do you know about the type of work we do?

Ans. You must show that you know a lot about the company so it's important to do lots of research before the interview.

- What things do you do well?

Ans. You have to use this opportunity to talk about your skills and show that you're the right person to work for them. While preparing for the interview, write about your soft kills and hard skills.

- What areas do you feel you need to improve?

Ans. You don't have to talk about anything negative in detail. Try to think about areas you're already trying to improve. So, you can end in a positive way like: 'I'm definitely getting better' or 'I'm going to do a course later this month."

- Where do you see yourself in five years' time? (last question in an interview)

Ans. Interviewers like to hear about your goals and they also want to make sure that you are not planning to switch to a different job too quickly. Here are some of the answers that you can give.

– I expect to make valuable contributions to the company's growth.

– I hope to learn more about the efficient communication skills.

– I intend to save as much as to buy a new flat.

– I plan to get married next year.

– I want to get more experience in digital and direct sales.

– I'd like to develop new ideas for the marketing operations here.

When the interviewer asks you to talk about yourself, you'll use adjectives to show your qualities that makes you suitable for the role. Look at the list of positive adjectives-

reliable, efficient, persistent, friendly, hard working, lively, conscientious, optimistic, motivated, cheerful, flexible, creative, calm, patient, so on.

It's not enough to provide the interviewer with the adjectives that describes your personality; you must support these with actual examples. For example,

Candidate: I'm hard working. For example, in my previous job,

I was able to meet the targeted sales as well as earned incentives by over reaching it.

Let's Apply

Activity 5: Adjectives for Yourself

Think of some adjectives about yourself and give examples for it.

- I'm optimistic. For example,

  ....

- I'm a creative person. For example,

  ....

- I'm very patient. For example,

  ....

Let's Reflect

Now, read an interview of Hemant by an interviewer where Hemant answered the questions not in just 'yes' or 'no', he said more that. Look at some of his answers.

Interviewer : Hello, am I speaking with Hemant?

Hemant : Yes, you are, May I know who's on the line?

Interviewer : Hemant, I am calling from WNS. You applied for the associate post through the website 'Jobdekho. com'. So we have reviewed your CV and hence we would like to initiate with the first round of your interview, will it be the good time to proceed?

Hemant : Oh! Yes. I remember and it will surely be a good time. I was even waiting for the reply.

Interviewer : Great! Then let's move ahead with your brief introduction.

Hemant : Ok. My name is Hemant Kumar and I have completed my Secondary schooling from commerce discipline from Delhi Public School. Then I did B.Com (Hons.) from University of Delhi where I also indulged myself in various co-curriculum activities and was majorly involved in theatre group. Then in the final year of my graduation, I got a placement and started working with 'Policybazar' as an associate. I was in their Investment Department and we used to manage NRI clients looking for their secured investment in mutual funds. I used to guide them with the suitable policies. Later on, due to covid, I had to leave the job and just few days back I found your company's profile and felt like I would be the best fit for that same.

Interviewer : That's great, Hemant! Can you tell me that in your former job, how much average sales you were able do as compared to respective targets given?

Hemant : Yes, I would rather say I was able to earn good incentive as I was not only meeting my target but also over reaching it.

Interviewer : That's so wonderful. Can you tell me why you think you are suitable for this job?

Hemant : Yes. First of all, I consider myself a very hard working person. So I'm good at solving problems. That's useful in any business. And also, I think that for this job you need to be patient and work well with the people, which is something I do well.

Interviewer : That's sound perfect! So tell me why you want to join this organization?

Hemant : Oh, interesting! Working for WNS will be something which can be a good scope for me as the company I looking for the google process and it deals in digital marketing sales.

Interviewer : Great! You are quite informed about our company. Hemant, tell me what are your salary expectations?

Hemant : I expect 30-40% hike from my previous salary. Rest, whatsoever company offers that is going to be good.

Interviewer : Okay. So what was the in-hand slaray you were getting in your previous job?

Hemant : I was getting 28K in-hand.

Interviewer : See, Hemant. We have a slab for this profile so the best I can offer you will be 35K in-hand and rest PF deduction and all will be separate. There is one more advantage of earning ample incentive as well.

Hemant : Okay. I am comfortable with it.

Interviewer : Great! So what you need to do is to forward me some of your documents on this given email. Documents will be your class 12 and graduation marksheets, last company's appointment letter and relieving letter with your previous three months salary slips.

Hemant : Okay. I will send you the mail attaching all documents by tomorrow.

Interviewer : Great! Then we will connect back as well.

If you are successful in a job interview, the company offers you **the position** and you accept the offer. Then you will need to talk about the **terms of employment.** You will need to discuss the **working hours** and the **salary**. Before you start your new job, you will need to decide on the **start date**. This will depend on the **notice period** in your current job. This could mean you have to work for a number of weeks after you hand in your notice.

When you have agreed all of this, your new employer will send you **a confirmation letter** and you can sign a **contract** with them.

GRAMMAR SKILLS

Let's Read

Read these sentences and check the highlighted words..

- **I expect to make** valuable contributions to the company's growth.
- **I hope to learn** more about the efficient communication skills.
- **I intend to save** as much as to buy a new flat.
- **I plan to get** married next year.
- **I want to get** more experience in digital and direct sales.
- **I'd like to develop** new ideas for the marketing operations here.

Let's Reflect

Activity 6: Complete the sentences

Now finish the sentences with your own answers using –'to' form:

- I'd like ....
- I plan to ....
- I want ....
- I hope ....

In the above sentences, we have used 'to' form with the verbs like expect, hope, intend, plan, want, would like, etc. These verbs are called infinitives. Infinitives are the verbs which are followed by '-to' form.

Some verbs are followed by the '-ing' form. These kinds of verbs are called gerund. It is not always easy to know if a verb takes '- to' form or the '-ing' form as some verbs can take both!

Verb + infinitive or 'to' form	Verb + gerund or' -ing' form
Would like	Wouldn't mind/don't mind
Want	Enjoy
Prefer	Think of
Plan	Like
Intend	Enjoy
Hope	Hate

Read this comic strip.

In the first dialogue, the verb 'appreciate' is followed by '-ing' form (coming). In the second dialogue, the verb 'hate' is also followed by '-ing' form (being). Some more examples of sentences using gerund:

- I'm not interested in working on this project.
- I am thinking of changing job.
- Riya like playing with her friends.
- I enjoy watching movies in theatre.

Let's Apply

Activity 7: Complete the Sentences with your own answers using '-ing' form'-to' form.

Finish the sentences.

- I'd like ....
- I enjoy ....
- I'd prefer not ....
- I don't mind ....
- I don't want ....

When to use gerund and infinitive

Gerund	In?nitive
We use gerund ('-ing' form): 1. After expressions like can't stand, feel like, don't mind, prefer. For example, • I **feel like having** an ice cream. 2. After some verbs: like, hate, enjoy, love, avoid 3. Gerund can function as the subject of a sentence. • **Swimming** is a good exercise. 4. After a preposition. • Please sit down **without speaking**. • I am interested **in learning** English • I look forward **to hearing** from you.	We use in?nitive ('-to' form): 1. Some adjectivesare followedby in?nitive. • We are **pleased to** receive your letter. • We are **excited to** hear about your wedding. • He is **eager to** know his result. 2. Certain verbs such as want, decide, need, agree, promise are followed by in?nitive. • **I want to quit** thisjob. • I **decided not to sell** my house. • My father **promised me to buy** me a new car.

Activity 8: Complete the Sentences Using Gerund

Complete the sentences using Gerund. Don't change the meaning of the sentence.

1. My sister talks on her mobile phone for hours.
   My sister enjoy ....
2. I do my homework and then I usually play in park.
   After ....
3. I really don't need to watch TV on Sunday.
   I can't stand ....
4. It's not a good idea to spend your money on a new phone.
   It's better to avoid ....
5. Siya didn't want to go to college.
   Siya didn't feel like ....
6. My son uses the pen more often than the pencil.
   My son prefers ....
7. She text me a message. I phoned her.
   Instead of ....

8. Don't let anybody enter into the house before you confirm with me.
   Don't let anybody enter into the house without
   ....

Activity 9: Complete the Sentences Using Gerund and Infinitives

Complete the sentences with the verbs in brackets. Use gerunds and infinitive.

1. I'd like .... (be) an architect.
2. On my day off I only want .... (sleep).
3. I am not .... (interest) in having a desk job.
4. I wouldn't mind .... (play) cricket with my friends in neighbourhood.
5. Would you like .... (have) tea?
6. He is tired of .... (do) work till late night.
7. (watch) TV is one of my favourite hobbies
8. My son has agreed to.. (join) the cricket academy.
9. We are so happy .... (know) from you.
10. It's very easy .... (log) in Twitter.
11. Mohan gave up .... (smoke) last month.
12. She offered me .... (go) with her to the library.

Activity 10: Complete the Conversation Using Gerund and Infinitives

We use gerunds and infinitives to talk about our hobbies and favourite tasks we like to do. Complete the conversation between two friends using gerund or infinitive.

Rahul : Hello, Kriti, how have you been?

Kriti : Hi, Rahul! I have been very well, days without seeing you.

Rahul : You knew that for more than a month, I stopped .... (smoke) because it was affecting my health.

Kriti : Wow, That's impressive! I am very happy .... (know).

Rahul : Hey, what do you think if we go to theatre to watch movie this weekend? Would you like ....(go)?

Kriti : Yes, of course. I enjoy .... (watch) movies on weekends.

Rahul : What do you like .... (do) in your leisure time?

Kriti : I like .... (walk) to walk around the park. I love ....(read) and singing. And is it true that you hate cooking?

Rahul : I don't hate ....(cook). I just don't enjoy .... (do) it. Do you like to work in bookstore?

Kriti : I don't like .... (do work) there, but I definitely like to earn a good salary. I enjoy cooking because I love to eat although I do not enjoy cleaning afterwards.

Rahul : I do not remember .... (have) seen you cooking.

Kriti : Good. I have to go, see you this weekend.

Rahul : Okay. See you and do not forget ....(call) me.

CONVERSATIONAL SKILL

‖ HOW TO INTRODUCE YOURSELF IN OFFICE ‖

- When you are a new joiner in a company, the Manager asks you to introduce yourself to all other seniors and colleagues. You have to mention 3 things in your introduction:
  – Your name
  – Your job title
  – Your responsibilities
- For example, My name is Rashmi Jain, I am the Team Manager working in Sales department. I am responsible for completing sales targets with a team of 15 Telecallers.
- The other English phrases that you can use for introduce yourself.
  – I manage each project from starting to finish.
  – I handle sales and purchase of books.

1. Learn Useful phrases for participating in an office meeting

- Give your opinion or suggest an idea
  – Modal verbs like 'should', 'ought to', 'might want to', 'have to', 'need to' are used to make suggestions or
  ideas in a polite manner'
  – should', 'ought to', 'might want to' – these modals verbs are used to suggest a good idea but it is not a
  obligation. For example,
    - We ought to increase the due limit of paying of this amount.
    - We might want to consider the deadline of this project.
    - I think we should approach other buyers in the market.
  – 'have to', 'need to' – these modals verbs are used when there is a obligation to do that suggested thing.

  For example,
    - We have to work upon the way we deal with our customers.
    - We need to buy new tools to complete the project on time.

2. Response to suggestions – phrase that you can use to give response on a suggestion given by others.

  – I agree with ....
  That sounds good!
  Let's go with this idea

3. If you disagree with the idea, then you can response using these phrases
    - To be honest, I am not sure about this idea.
    - I see your point however.
    - Good suggestion, but I can see a few problems.

  For example,
    - I see your point, however I don't think that advertising in a magazine is good idea. People don't read them as often these days.

- To be honest, I am not sure about this idea. I think improving our website is a high priority right now.

4. Ask a question in a meeting
   – Excuse me, I have a question. Why ....
   – Sorry, does it mean ....
   – Excuse me, how ....
     - For example, Excuse me, how will the launching of new software help us to complete the project on time?
     - Sorry to interrupt, but I have a question.
5. Asking for clarification
   – I didn't understand ....

a. Can you elaborate on this more?
   – Can you clarify ....
     - Excuse me, can you clarify, the third step in the proposal, I didn't get the main idea.

6. Making offers

a. Use 'will', 'can', 'could', 'shall'
   - I can contact the suppliers next week if we need to.
   - Shall I talk to our engineer to get the cost estimate.
   - I'll call the client tomorrow.

7. Refusing Politely
   – I am afraid, I can't ....
   – I am sorry, but I don't think I can ....
   – Unfortunately, I won't be able to ....

Let's learn to use these phrases through reading the discussions happened in an office meeting.

Manager walks on the floor to call everyone in the meeting room and also asked to include new joiners as well. Everybody walks in and greets to the senior director, Mr Mukesh Sahni.

Mr Mukesh : Good Morning everyone! If I ask anyone of you what's so good about this morning other than there's a new joinee between us. So let's start with her introduction. It's better you all get along with her. So Himani, please give a short introduction to all.

Himani : Hello everyone, I am Himani. I completed my graduation in Business Analysis from Amity University. I have joined here as the Business Promotion Analytic. I am here good to be a part of this organisation.

Mr Mukesh : Well, seems great! Now welcome to all on board. Now team, let's come to the point. Our sales have been decresing and it doesn't seem like anybody is keeping track of it, right Vishal.

Vishal : I totally agree with you sir. Numbers as bit less but somewhere we are projecting that by the next quarter we will cover our losses.

Mr Mukesh : Now the question is how that will happen.

Vishal : As we see we have increased our distribution network from three weeks so sales have not driven yet.

But we need to find the good way to increase the sales to especially new distributors.

Mr Mukesh : So, out of everyone who has better idea?

Arti : Sir, I'll go with Vishal. There are good chances that this can happen. I think we should increase our marketing budget and run various new campaign which will increase the demand and so does the sales.

Mr Mukesh : I see your point; however I think that it is another expense you are talking about.

Arti : Sir, in starting it will look like an expense but in the end all will be paid by the sales numbers.

Mr Mukesh : Okay, That sounds good! I was thinking why we don't touch the new belt that we haven't explored yet. What do you think all?

Himani : Excuse me, I didn't understand what it means.

Hemant : It means new distributors in new regions, Himani, Right sir.

Mr Mukesh : Yes, in a different new region.

Hemant : We ought to promote in Rajasthan, we don't have a single distributor there.

Mr Mukesh : Yes, even I was planning for it. So let's do one thing. Prepare a new list of distributors in Rajasthan and Himani, take that list from Vishal and send them an email; keep me in Cc to be in loop of this new chain in Rajasthan with all new distributors.

So will it be done everyone?

All : Yes sir.

Himani : I'll take the list of distributors and mail them by the evening.

Mr Mukesh : Arti, after getting the confirmation mail from all the new distributors, you take this project forward.

Arti : Higly appreciated, Sir.

Mr Mukesh : Thank you all; you can now be on your own respective work stations.

Let's Understand

Activity 11: Role Play.

You can practise these conversations with your friends by doing role plays in different situation. Try to frame your dialogues for the practise sessions.

Appendix - 9

The Distribution of Difficulty Value (dv) and Internal Consistency Discrimination Index (rb) of all the items

Test Items	UG	LG	DV	Interpretation	Disc.Index	Interpre.	decision
1.	6	1	0.155555556	VERY DIFFICULT	0.4166667	VERY GOOD	ACCEPT
2.	6	6	0.266666667	AVERAGE	0	POOR ITEM	REJECT
3.	10	2	0.266666667	AVERAGE	0.6666667	VERY GOOD	RETAIN
4.	5	4	0.2	VERY DIFFICULT	0.0833333	POOR ITEM	REJECT
5.	8	10	0.4	AVERAGE	-0.166667	POOR ITEM	REJECT
6.	9	6	0.333333333	AVERAGE	0.25	MARGINAL ITEM	RETAIN
7.	12	9	0.466666667	AVERAGE	0.25	MARGINAL ITEM	RETAIN
8.	12	7	0.422222222	AVERAGE	0.4166667	VERY GOOD	RETAIN
9.	12	2	0.311111111	AVERAGE	0.8333333	VERY GOOD	RETAIN
10.	10	7	0.377777778	AVERAGE	0.25	MARGINAL ITEM	RETAIN
11.	3	3	0.133333333	VERY DIFFICULT	0	POOR ITEM	REJECT
12.	12	5	0.377777778	AVERAGE	0.5833333	VERY GOOD	RETAIN
13.	2	2	0.088888889	VERY DIFFICULT	0	POOR ITEM	REJECT
14.	11	6	0.377777778	AVERAGE	0.4166667	VERY GOOD	RETAIN
15.	10	7	0.377777778	AVERAGE	0.25	MARGINAL ITEM	RETAIN
16.	12	12	0.533333333	AVERAGE	0	POOR ITEM	REJECT
17.	12	11	0.511111111	AVERAGE	0.0833333	POOR ITEM	REJECT
18.	11	9	0.444444444	AVERAGE	0.1666667	POOR ITEM	REJECT
19.	10	7	0.377777778	AVERAGE	0.25	MARGINAL ITEM	RETAIN
20.	11	6	0.377777778	AVERAGE	0.4166667	VERY GOOD	RETAIN
21.	10	4	0.311111111	AVERAGE	0.5	VERY GOOD	RETAIN
22.	8	6	0.311111111	AVERAGE	0.1666667	POOR ITEM	REJECT

23.	11	3	0.311111111	AVERAGE	0.6666667	VERY GOOD	RETAIN
24.	11	10	0.466666667	AVERAGE	0.0833333	POOR ITEM	REJECT
25.	7	4	0.244444444	VERY DIFFICULT	0.25	MARGINAL ITEM	RETAIN
26.	11	8	0.422222222	AVERAGE	0.25	MARGINAL ITEM	RETAIN
27.	3	2	0.111111111	VERY DIFFICULT	0.0833333	POOR ITEM	REJECT
28.						REASONABLY	
	12	8	0.444444444	AVERAGE	0.3333333	GOOD	RETAIN
29.	12	9	0.466666667	AVERAGE	0.25	MARGINAL ITEM	RETAIN
30.	6	5	0.244444444	VERY DIFFICULT	0.0833333	POOR ITEM	REJECT
31.	31	20	1.133333333	VERY EASY	0.9166667	VERY GOOD	RETAIN
32.	12	5	0.377777778	AVERAGE	0.5833333	VERY GOOD	RETAIN
33.			REASONABLY				
	12	8	0.444444444	AVERAGE	0.3333333	GOOD	RETAIN
34.			REASONABLY				
	6	2	0.177777778	VERY DIFFICULT	0.3333333	GOOD	RETAIN
35.			REASONABLY				
	10	6	0.355555556	AVERAGE	0.3333333	GOOD	RETAIN
36.	12	11	0.511111111	AVERAGE	0.0833333	POOR ITEM	REJECT
37.	12	9	0.466666667	AVERAGE	0.25	MARGINAL ITEM	RETAIN
38.	12	6	0.4	AVERAGE	0.5	VERY GOOD	RETAIN
39.			REASONABLY				
	9	5	0.311111111	AVERAGE	0.3333333	GOOD	RETAIN
40.	9	10	0.422222222	AVERAGE	-0.083333	POOR ITEM	REJECT
41.	36	8	0.977777778	VERY EASY	2.3333333	VERY GOOD	RETAIN
42.	67	17	1.866666667	VERY EASY	4.1666667	VERY GOOD	RETAIN
43.			REASONABLY				
	12	8	0.444444444	AVERAGE	0.3333333	GOOD	RETAIN

44.	9	1	0.222222222	VERY DIFFICULT	0.6666667	VERY GOOD	RETAIN
45.	4	3	0.155555556	VERY DIFFICULT	0.0833333	POOR ITEM	REJECT
46.	3	4	0.155555556	VERY DIFFICULT	-0.083333	POOR ITEM	REJECT
47.	11	4	0.333333333	AVERAGE	0.5833333	VERY GOOD	RETAIN
48.	20	9	0.644444444	AVERAGE	0.9166667	VERY GOOD	RETAIN
49.	12	5	0.377777778	AVERAGE	0.5833333	VERY GOOD	RETAIN
50.	6	4	0.222222222	VERY DIFFICULT	0.1666667	POOR ITEM	REJECT
51.	10	7	0.377777778	AVERAGE	0.25	MARGINAL ITEM	RETAIN
52.	9	3	0.266666667	AVERAGE	0.5	VERY GOOD	RETAIN
53.	8	1	0.2	VERY DIFFICULT	0.5833333	VERY GOOD	RETAIN
54.	10	8	0.4	AVERAGE	0.1666667	POOR ITEM	REJECT
55.	9	4	0.288888889	AVERAGE	0.4166667	VERY GOOD	RETAIN
56.	11	5	0.355555556	AVERAGE	0.5	VERY GOOD	RETAIN
57.	5	8	0.288888889	AVERAGE	-0.25	POOR ITEM	REJECT
58.	52	8	1.333333333	VERY EASY	3.6666667	VERY GOOD	ACCEPT
59.	32	17	1.088888889	VERY EASY	1.25	VERY GOOD	ACCEPT
60.	6	1	0.155555556	VERY DIFFICULT	0.4166667	VERY GOOD	ACCEPT
61.	7	5	0.266666667	AVERAGE	0.1666667	POOR ITEM	REJECT
62.	5	2	0.155555556	VERY DIFFICULT	0.25	MARGINAL ITEM	ACCEPT
63.	23	7	0.666666667	AVERAGE	1.3333333	VERY GOOD	RETAIN
64.	46	22	1.511111111	VERY EASY	2	VERY GOOD	ACCEPT
65.	34	12	1.022222222	VERY EASY	1.8333333	VERY GOOD	ACCEPT
66.	17	0	0.377777778	AVERAGE	1.4166667	VERY GOOD	RETAIN